BEYOND
the
PYRAMIDS

This book is for Grace Carley

BEYOND
the
PYRAMIDS
travels in egypt
DOUGLAS
KENNEDY

UNWIN HYMAN
London   Sydney

First published in Great Britain by Unwin Hyman, an imprint of
Unwin Hyman Limited, 1988.

UNWIN HYMAN
15–17 Broadwick Street
London W1V 1FP

Allen & Unwin (Australia) Ltd
8 Napier Street
North Sydney
NSW 2060
Australia

Allen & Unwin New Zealand Pty Ltd with Port Nicholson Press
60 Cambridge Terrace
Wellington
New Zealand

British Library Cataloguing in Publication Data

Kennedy, Douglas
  Beyond the Pyramids: Travels in Egypt
  1. Egypt - Description and travel
  – 1945 –
  I. Title
  916.2'0455   DT56

ISBN 0 04 910086 6

Printed and bound in Great Britain by Mackays of Chatham Ltd., Kent

Contents

Author's Note

Travel, as many have pointed out, is a moveable confessional box. And, as anyone undertaking a journey quickly discovers, because you're perceived to be *in transit*—somebody who is leaving town on the next bus—the people you meet along the road are far more likely to share personal details of their lives with you than if you were a resident of their own turf. Certainly, this was my experience while travelling in Egypt and, therefore, to preserve the anonymity of many of those who appear in this book, I have frequently changed names, occupations, nationalities, and other such personal details. The whereabouts of certain meetings—and the chronology of certain events—have also been tampered with.

* * * * *

A few 'thank you's:

Several companies were extremely generous in helping me meet the costs of transportation for the journey. They include: B & I Line; Venice Simplon Orient Express Ltd.; Adriatica Line; and Egyptair.

To list all the people who overwhelmed me with hospitality in Egypt would take several pages, but I would like to single out for special mention H.E. the then Irish Ambassador to Egypt, Mr Eamonn Ryan, and the entire staff of the Irish Embassy in Cairo—most notably, its then First Secretary, Alison Kelly. In addition, Tony Walker, Bernard and Amina O'Kane, Patrick Godeau and Carmen Caxiatilla, the sisters of the Carmel de la Sante-Famille Exile, Hassan E. Zakariya, David Farer, Sarwat el Bahr, Pere Xavier Eid and John McFairlane all helped make my passage through Egypt that little bit easier.

Back in Ireland, my parents-in-law, Frank and Irene Carley, lent me their cottage in the West Cork village of Union Hall to get the book started, while Bernard and Mary Loughlin offered me refuge in the Tyrone Guthrie Centre, Newbliss, Co. Monaghan to get the thing finished. In addition, Mark Lambert offered me a room to work in in his London flat whenever I felt the frequent need to flee Dublin. Jean O'Hanlon—an old Egypt hand—patiently provided innumerable answers to innumerable questions, while my parents and brothers—in tandem with many friends—humoured me along as I wrote. And my wife Grace—in the midst of her own professional swirl—provided support above and beyond the call of reasonable sanity and deserves some sort of *croix de guerre* for seeing me through.

Several books proved to be invaluable sources of background information. P. J. Vatikiotis' *The History of Egypt* (Weidenfeld and Nicolson, 1980) and Derek Hopwood's *Egypt: Politics and Society 1945–1984* (Allen and Unwin, 1985) are two superb pieces of scholarship, and provided me with a wealth of historical, political and socio-economic detail. David Hirst's and Irene Beeson's *Sadat* (Faber, 1981) and Mohammed Heikel's *Autumn of Fury* (Random House, 1982) are definitive accounts of the late president's reign, and were extremely useful in their analyses of Egypt's internal tensions. William J. Murnane's *The Penguin Guide to Ancient Egypt* (Penguin, 1983) was an excellent reference source when it came to matters Egyptological. And two venerable guidebooks also came in handy: E.M. Forster's *Alexandria: A History and a Guide* (Michael Haag, 1982), and—my companion for the journey—Karl Baedeker's *Egypt 1929* (David and Charles, 1985).

At Unwin Hyman, I would like to thank Merlin Unwin, Mary Butler and Barbara Fuller for their support and encouragement. Thanks to the Pinpoint Design Company for the map on p. viii, to Richard Kennedy for the chapter illustrations, and to Mark Entwhistle for the jacket illustration. And finally, I would like to acknowledge the fact that I owe Tony Peake—agent extraordinaire and good friend—more than a few drinks.

D.K.

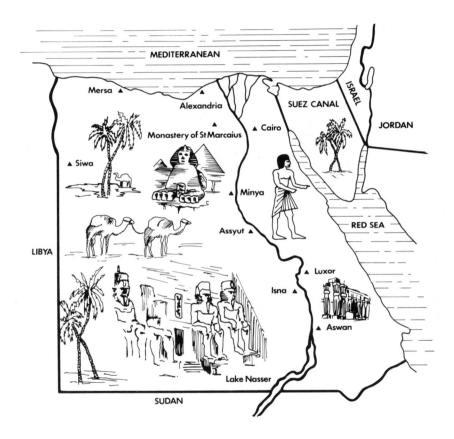

Chapter One
Prologue: South

HIS NAME WAS YUSUF and he sold Toyotas within walking distance of the Sphinx. We met somewhere off the coast of Albania, on the deck of an Italian car ferry that was steaming towards a north-east corner of Africa. Yusuf was a man in his early forties, wearing a carefully sculptured beard and a sharp tan summerweight suit. With his wrap-around sunglasses, he looked as if he was dressed for a night out in Las Vegas. That is, until I caught sight of the dark bruise on his forehead. A bruise that was a tell-tale sign of a pious Muslim who prostrated himself to his God five times a day. Yusuf neither drank nor smoked but, owing to the nature of his business, he did have a thing about cars and told me that his new Mercedes was stored on the vehicle deck below. He'd bought his Mercedes while visting his German wife in Hamburg. She was one of his three wives; the other two being located in separate houses in Cairo. His complex international domestic arrangements tied in neatly with his complex

1

international business arrangements, as he had to visit Hamburg at least six times a year, in between trips to Bombay, Bangkok, Tokyo, Osaka, and New York. Yusuf was a man who evidently got around, but he said that his greatest pleasure in life was escaping to the small farm he'd recently bought on the desert road between Cairo and Alexandria. It wasn't much of a place—a small shack with a large patch of artifically irrigated sand, on which he grew watermelons and guavas—but it still gave him the safety valve he needed. Away from the roar of Cairo, he could divest himself of his city clothes and wear the traditional *galabiya*. He could forget about the pressures of running a Toyota dealership, and of running between his two Egyptian wives, not to mention his *hausfrau* in Hamburg.

'When I am on my farm', he said, 'I do not care about telephones, or paperwork, or dealing with the obstacles that stupid bureaucrats in the government ministries put in my way. I think about nothing but my watermelons, my guavas. I sleep on a mat on the floor of the farm's hut. I eat out of the same pot as the people who work the land for me. I become an Egyptian again.'

'And when you're selling Toyotas, you're not an Egyptian?', I asked.

'When I sell Toyotas, I am a salesman in a suit. I am a man who worries about his business, who works too many hours. I am like an executive in Germany or America.

'That is my problem. I want to be nothing more than a simple Egyptian who lives in his simple hut and grows his simple food. But I want the money of a Toyota dealer at the same time. It is a curious dilemma, yes?'

I acknowledged that few Toyota dealers probably had such problems. Yusuf barked with laughter. 'You are right', he said. 'Only in Egypt would a Toyota dealer want to spend his weekends like a *fellah*—a peasant. Only in Egypt would such confusion exist'.

He gave me a hundred watt smile. 'You like confusion?', he said. 'You like chaos?'

I nodded. 'Then you will like Egypt', he said. 'It is complete chaos'.

* * * * *

Egypt—the stuff of picture postcards:
  The pyramids at Giza backlit by dawn light.
  A felucca coasting through the oily waters of the Nile
  Sunset at the Valley of the Kings.

2

Egypt. A nation which readily lends itself to the figurative language of tourist brochures:

Egypt—a coexistence of water and desert set amidst the ruins of a bygone civilization.

Egypt—land of the Pharaohs!

Was this country to which I was travelling an archaeological theme park sunstruck by its own mythology? Certainly, since the mid-nineteenth century, Egypt had been attracting travellers to its shores in search of the archaic and exotic. To the western mind, it has always been a land apart—*'the cradle of history and human culture'*, as one guidebook put it—filled with the symbolic left-behinds of one of civilization's first big trial runs. And so, to journey to Egypt was to journey into an epic of your own making. For here you could be humbled by the monumentalism of the Pharaonic past, float gently down the river eternal, and meditate on the ebb and flow of time.

Egypt—metaphysical ruminations on five and ten dollars a day. A chance for a little erudite introspection in the shadow of the Sphinx.

But what about the modern state lurking behind this mythic realm? While countless travel chronicles have been written about Egypt the Immortal, few writers have ever undertaken a journey through the contemporary Egyptian condition. And the more I browsed through selected volumes from the vast library of books on Egypt, the more I realized that the country suffered from easy bibliographical classification. The Egyptologist would give you a stone-by-stone account of building the Step Pyramid at Saqqara. The political scientist, historian or journalist would analyse the ramifications of the Suez crisis, of Nasser's attempts to build a socialist state, and of Sadat's fatal flirtation with free-market economics. The travelogues, on the other hand, were generally vivid sketch-books of street scenes in Cairo, village life along the Nile banks and, of course, primal encounters with the Great Temple at Karnak.

And though I found many of these travellers' tales alluring, they generally seemed to be imbued with a turn-of-the-century sensibility; that era when Egyptian travel was the domain of plucky spinsters in tweed skirts, Episcopalian ministers, and members of the gentry in search of an arid winter resort for their tubercular lungs. Even certain contemporary writers fell into this trap when faced with the country. All those elemental images of mankind's ancient evenings—of the *fellahin* at work in the

3

fields—appeared to bring on either an attack of wide-screen technicolour romanticism, or of grand-old-man cantankerousness at the sight of how the modern Egypt was gradually despoiling the Egypt of fable.

But when I visited the country in 1981, it was precisely this counterpoint between the modern and the fabled which so engrossed me. Though my stay was limited to a fortnight in Cairo, I came away rather overwhelmed by the complexities and pressures of a society which appeared to be precariously balanced between a multiplicity of identities. And in the ensuing years that followed this one brief tantalizing glimpse of its capital city, I became an inveterate Egypt watcher, following its current affairs with the avidity of a club supporter. Of course, most of the reports emanating from Egypt painted a bleak portrait of the country's state of affairs. There was talk of impending economic chaos, of an out-of-control population growth, and of a rising tide of Islamic fundamentalism. Sadat had been assassinated and his successor, Hosni Mubarak, had inherited a country which, from all accounts, had reached a critical impasse. But what exactly was this impasse and how had Egypt—traditionally the most progressive and secular of all Arab states—managed to find itself in such a quandary? And, more importantly, what sort of society had evolved in the period since the revolution of 1952?

I knew that a three-month journey through the country would hardly begin to provide any definitive answers to such questions. And anyway, I didn't want my travels to take on such a purposeful demeanour. Rather, my plan of action was a simple one: using Baedeker's *Egypt 1929* as an occasional guide, I would follow the traditional traveller's route through the country—beginning in Alexandria, veering into the outer reaches of the Western Desert, then moving on to Cairo, after which I would gradually work my way south to Aswan. Naturally, this would simply be a rough itinerary and would allow for constant divergences along the way. Moreover, though I'd be following, by and large, a well-worn trail, I would deliberately side-step all the 'must sees' that lined this route. Pyramids, Ptolemaic temples and ancient burial grounds would not figure in my journey. Contemporary Egypt, to my mind, was the far more intriguing attraction, and I would be relying largely on accident and fluke to propel me through its landscape. I had few contacts in the country and didn't want to spend my time there seeking out all the 'right people' to meet. Instead, I would simply drop myself into the whirl of Egypt today and see where it brought me.

And with time on my hands, I decided to begin this modern Egyptian journey in mock Grand Tour fashion—by travelling overland. Which is why I found myself standing on the deck of an Italian car ferry somewhere off the coast of Albania, talking to a Cairene Toyota dealer with three wives.

* * * * *

'What sort of car you drive?', Yusuf asked me.

'A six year old Fiesta with rust', I said.

This disappointed him. 'It is not a good car for travel to Egypt', he said.

'I'm not travelling with it', I said. 'I'm just a foot passenger.'

'Then why do you take the car ferry to Egypt if you don't bring your car? Flying would have been easier.'

He was right, of course. Jet propulsion would have flushed me from Dublin to Cairo in a matter of hours. But having made that air journey once before—and having suffered the sort of cultural stupefaction which comes with beginning the day with livestock reports on Irish radio and ending it with Koranic highlights on Radio Cairo—I foolishly believed that a gentle perambulation from offshore Europe to north-east Africa would not only let me avoid being cannon-balled into Egypt, but would also be in keeping with my idea of following the traditional traveller's route into the country. And in Baedeker's *Egypt 1929*, I discovered that wayfarers of that era generally opted for a sea voyage on a steamer like the P & O Mail, departing every Friday from the Tilbury, Royal Albert, or King George V Dock in London and—after pit-stops in Gibraltar and Marseilles—arriving twelve days later in Port Said. Alternatively, there was a more downmarket variety of steamship leaving Liverpool or Manchester every fortnight, not to mention at least a dozen or so Franco-Italian vessels which pulled out of a string of Mediterranean ports (Marseilles, Genoa, Venice and Trieste) throughout any given week. Those travellers with an aversion to large bodies of water, on the other hand, could follow a seven-day land route to Cairo. Baedeker's description made it sound like the 3.10 to Yuma:

> The 'Simplon Orient Express' (Calais–Paris–Lausanne–Simplon–Venice–Trieste–Belgrade–Sofia–Constantinople) goes on twice weekly (Mon & Fri) through Asia Minor, Syria, and Palestine to Egypt.

From the main station at Constantinople (Sirkedji), by ferry boat over the Bosporus to Haidar Pasha, and by railway via *Eskishehir* (junction for Angora), *Konia,* the *Taurus Tunnel, Adana,* and *Aleppo* to *Tripolis* in Syria. Thence by motor-car of the International Sleeping Car Co. in 8½ hours to *Haifa* or *Jaffa* in Palestine. Finally by railway to *Qantara East,* where we cross the Suez Canal by ferry and proceed to *Cairo* by train.

Had I been interested in conducting a hit-and-run survey of assorted Middle East frontier posts, the old land route to Egypt would have been perfect. Of course, the present-day geo-political complexion of the region mitigated against such an itinerary, especially when it came to stopping off at the town of Tripolis— once part of Syria, now very much a part of the Lebanon. And since crossing the Lebanese/Israeli border these days is a journey usually undertaken in a heavily armoured vehicle—a tank, for instance—I pored through Thomas Cook's International Time-table, trying to see if any of the other old 'approaches to Egypt' mentioned by Baedeker were still operational. And after dis-covering that only one commercial passenger ship still ran between the Continent and Egypt on a regular basis, I was finally able to piece together a series of relatively tight rail and sea connections which, I figured, would at least approximate the original itinerary of an Edwardian Grand Tour. Though I doubted very much if any Grand Tour began where mine began—on a Number 19A bus from Dublin's South Circular Road.

I live in the Arab quarter of Dublin. Here's how to find it. Head up the South Circular Road, proceed past the police club, the Army barracks and the National Boxing Stadium, and just before you reach the cigarette factory, you'll see Ireland's only mosque on the left hand side of the road. If you're lost, ask any of the locals for directions or be on the lookout for a disused synagogue. The synagogue was once the centre of a flourishing Jewish community when this area was known as Dublin's Little Jerusalem. Now, however, most of Dublin's Jews live in the somewhat smarter suburb of Terenure, with the result that the Arabs have moved in and have opened a mosque directly opposite the old synagogue. They have also opened an Islamic Centre next to the mosque, not to mention a few small shops dotted around the area in which you can buy Egyptian newspapers, hummus, tahina, and Islamic approved meat slaughtered under the supervision of a Muslim butcher at the Halal Meat Factory, Ballyhaunis, Co. Mayo.

And it was opposite that mosque on an October evening that I flagged down an oncoming Number 19A.

'Where you going?', the conductor asked, his ticket machine at the ready.

'O'Connell Street', I said. But I was very tempted to reply, 'Alexandria'.

* * * * *

The bus brought me through familiar country: the underwhelming spectacle of Dublin by night. As this was to be my last glimpse of the city for some months, I looked at it carefully, wanting to take it all in. But my eyes inevitably focused on the aluminium hoardings, bricked up windows, and derelict buildings which now form a major part of Dublin's metropolitan landscape. Speculative greed had brought about the destruction of the city's architectural fabric. The urge to show the world that it too could be modern—that it too could easily embrace all the reinforced concrete values of contemporary urban living—had led to the erosion of its Georgian and Victorian finery. And in its place had come the cheap and tawdry. The view up O'Connell Street, where I disembarked, was one of neon palaces built in praise of quarter-pounders and Southern fried chicken; all the most spurious aspects of Americana grafted onto a major European boulevard. Was this a predictable side-effect in most post-colonial societies—this headlong rush into a world bedecked by tinsel? In Ireland, the talk was often of how the country had so easily succumbed to a semi-detached, video recorder-in-the-bog mentality, and in doing so had permanently surrendered a certain part of its individuality. In Egypt—another post colonial society—would the talk also be about a collision of imported and traditional values; the West and Islam meeting head-on?

At Busarus—the city's central bus station—I hopped a coach bound for the port of Dublin. Two dozen German adolescents, fresh from a camping holiday in Killarney, filled the rear of the bus and insisted on singing group renditions of Simon and Garfunkel songs in exceedingly precise, heavily accented English. 'Bridge Over Troubled Water' ricocheted around the coach until an elderly denizen of Dublin stood up and shouted,

'Will yuz give it a fuckin' rest?' The German kids, stunned by this display of local *gemütlichkeit*, sang no more.

When the bus arrived at the Ferryport, I boarded the Liverpool mailboat and was shown to my quarters by a stewardess who had the manner of a pushy novice with her eye on the Mother Superior's job. I dropped my bag in the cabin, a small four-berth cubicle which seemed crowded even with myself as the only occupant, and then, after fetching the wardress to bolt the door behind me, moved off to the bar.

It was a place where drinking was taken seriously and entered into with a spirit of grim resolve. 'Stayin' Alive' blared over the loudspeakers; the lighting was as harsh as the lamps found in a police interrogation cell; and seated on a haphazard collection of plastic chairs were a group of hard men and their broken-down women. It was like being in a lounge bar on the bleakest council estate imaginable; a community of ghettoized emigrants returning home to the grey fringes of urban England. These were Britain's original *gastarbeiters*—the builders of her roads and her houses—and their faces betrayed years of devotion to the gargle and the untipped Woodbines. The floor of this floating saloon was already accumulating its nightly layer of empty crisp bags, fag ends and discarded copies of *The Sun*, and the level at which The Bee Gees was being played made conversation impossible, so the clientele sat without speaking, like figures in a desolate tableau. I found their gloom infectious and retreated back to my cubbyhole.

Six hours later, a stormtrooper-style wake-up call (repeated blows on the door) informed me that we had arrived in Liverpool. The Special Branch were there to greet us. And as we disembarked from the mailboat, we were herded—at around twenty passengers a time—through what appeared to be an aluminium tunnel. The plainclothes officers, dressed in those shiny three-piece suits generally favoured by Mormons, stood at the end of this tunnel and sized us up in a manner similar to cattle appraisers at a Spring Show, pulling over the occasional customer for an impromptu bit of third-degree questioning. If the basic atmosphere on the night boat had been that of an upscale coffin ship, then this early morning greeting by officaldom had a definite 'Paddy, Go Home' flavour to it. And I was relieved to pass inspection quickly, hit the street, and catch a taxi to Lime Street Station.

The taxi driver was full of the joys of autumn, and waxed lyrical about the previous night's riots in Toxteth.

'Had to happen, dinnit?', he said.

'How do you mean?', I said.

'You let the niggers flood into this country, of course you're going to have this kind of trouble.'

This comment put a strangehold on all further conversational possibilities and cost the driver his tip. And as the eight a.m. express to London Euston rattled its way past the urban splendours of Tamsworth and Milton Keynes, I reflected that flying to Egypt might have been simpler.

* * * * *

Some weeks before I set off on this journey, I met a young English filmmaker at a party in Dublin who had just finished shooting a documentary in Ireland. And when I mentioned (during the course of our non-descript cocktail party chat) that I would soon be departing for Egypt, and had managed to wangle free passage on the new Venice Simplon Orient Express, she suddenly blurted out, 'Oh, I've done that.'

'On a freebie?', I said.

'No, we paid full fare', she said.

'But it's a shockingly expensive train ticket.'

'Not really', she said. 'Anyway, my husband is a dentist.'

I remembered that comment while loitering on Platform 8 of Victoria Station, watching the arrival of Gucci and Louis Vuitton luggage, festooned with First Class tags from a variety of airlines. The owners of these designer portmanteaus didn't exactly look like the type of people who had gotten rich on decaying molars or that scourge called dental plaque, but they did, by and large, possess that air of top tax bracket folk who could well afford the £435 tariff being demanded for an one-way journey on the new Venice Simplon Orient Express. One couple in particular caught my attention. She was a diamond-hard blond, of the sort who appears in Harold Robbins-esque novels under the name of January, whereas he was a John DeLorean lookalike: Mr AMEX Gold Card, replete with wavy silver hair; the kind of guy who flashes the Zurich duty-free Rolex Oyster whenever possible and believes that aerobics allow you to devote some *quality time* to your body. Seen together, they reminded me of one of those immaculately groomed couples who always appear in print advertisements for thirty-year-old malt scotch, and their *beau monde* radiance toned in well with the train which awaited us on

9

Platform 8—a remarkably loving reproduction of the original Orient Express.

In name alone, the Orient Express must be the world's most mythic train, conjuring up monochromatic images of oily characters with Viennese accents who trade in illegal penicillin, exiled Albanian countesses, and corrupt Balkan border guards. It is, in short, the Maltese Falcon of international express trains—*the stuff that dreams are made of*—and, as such, an institution that has survived on mystique alone. For, in reality, the true trench-coat-and-trilby heyday of the train ended with the outbreak of the Second World War, and though an 'Orient Express' still leaves Paris daily for Bucharest—thus covering a major portion of the old London-to-Istanbul route—it is nothing more (according to all accounts) than a highly functional, no-frills operation, with about as much glamour as the Victoria-to-Brighton commuter run.

The train I was about to jump on, however, was a romantic Disneyland on wheels; a triumph of rolling stock gentrification which—from the look of the dining car in which a table had been reserved in my name—had made several French polishers exceedingly wealthy. Indeed, it was extravagantly clubby: high-gloss mahogany panelling, overstuffed armchairs comfortable enough to die in, tables covered by starched linen table cloths, a lavish display of silver, crystal and bone china, not to mention ornate brass table lamps. Then again, this is what the customer was paying for—the chance to sit in an art deco setting and pretend to be a member of *the quality* in a supposedly gentler age. And so, when I decided to travel overland to Egypt—to meander gradually towards a purportedly 'fabled' landscape by a purportedly 'fabled' route—hitching a free ride on the new Venice Simplon Orient Express seemed like the obvious way to traverse the fatty midriff of Europe.

'You live in Ireland?', an American woman asked me shortly after the train shunted out of Victoria. 'We rented ourselves a castle there last summer.'

'You rented an entire castle?', I said.

'Not a big castle', she said. 'Just a cute little *mini-castle*.'

Lunch arrived shortly after this exchange, and somewhere between the galatine of duck with new potatoes and the creme caramel in bitter chocolate cases, I learned that this woman and her husband were members of a family who owned half of an east-coast state.

People told you things like that on the Orient Express. At Folkestone—where we were guided into a special lounge on the cross-channel ferry for the crossing to Boulogne—I found myself seated opposite a gent who was built like an articulated lorry and sweated non-stop, to the point where his thatchy hair took on the appearance of a used J-Cloth. He proffered his hand.

'Jake Boyd—BMW dealer for south-western New Jersey.'

Jake, as I quickly discovered, was exceedingly proud of his calling in life. So much so that he failed to introduce the petite woman sitting next to him, who turned out to be his wife.

'Cindy Boyd—I'm doing a masters in Remedial Art.'

Now that I had been made aware of their professional status, Jake dominated the conversation. Shifting his obese form around in the chair, he became imbued with what seemed to be chemically induced bonhomie which manifested itself in an extended monologue about his 40 foot sloop ('I take that baby down to Bermuda for a couple of months, and when I get back I'm ready for anything . . . ain't I, honey?'). But if there was one subject on which he could obtain poetic heights, it was the BMW automobile.

'I mean, the 735i is a nifty little model, and hey, I got a Porsche a couple a years ago, and it's in the shop once a week. But the 735i is something else. Of course, it's a step up from the old 518i which doesn't have the same aerodynamic styling, but you know when it comes to the 320i . . . well, like I say, it's more a car for the little woman. Ain't that right, honey? I mean, a guy driving a 320i just doesn't look right. Know what I mean, Doug?'

An announcement came over the loudspeaker system, informing all passengers that they must clear French passport control while aboard the ferry, and I used this directive as a way of temporarily escaping the company of Jake Boyd—BMW dealer for south-western New Jersey. I ran into him again, however, on the deck of the ship as we slid into Boulogne harbour. He was aiming a Nikon with a sniper-like telephoto lens at an uninspired collection of breezeblock flats strung along the waterfront. His wife Cindy appeared disconcerted by this, her first glimpse of the Continent.

'That's not Europe', she said. 'The urban aesthetics are all wrong.'

I assured her that it was Europe, and silently wondered whether she had picked up the phrase, 'urban aesthetics' in Remedial Art classes.

11

'But that can't be Europe. That looks like goddamn Cleveland.'

At Boulogne, we received the full *noblesse oblige* treatment by being whisked off the ferry without having to queue, and then passing unencumbered through customs and stepping directly onto the continental train that would transport us from 'goddamn Cleveland' to Venice. We didn't even have to worry about carting our baggage, as all our luggage had been taken from us in London and was now being placed in our respective sleeping compartments by the cabin steward in charge of each wagon-lit.

My compartment was a small masterpiece of ingenuity—a sofa with embroidered upholstery that would later be made up as a bed; a writing table with a brass lamp; a small press that opened to reveal a marble sink with copper fittings and two full-length mirrors; and a small brass flap fitted near the door which, when pulled out from the wall, became a reading lamp. Kicking off my shoes and collapsing on the sofa, I decided that I could happily settle here for weeks, and tried to forget that I was being served an eviction notice twenty-four hours from now in Venice.

After spending a half-hour bringing my journal up-to-date, I put my jacket and tie back on (the Orient Express, like a minor public school, has a dress code, and bars anything denim from appearing in the dining cars) and headed off on a brief inspection tour of the train.

There are seventeen carriages of rolling stock on the Venice Simplon Orient Express, the main heart of which is three 'Etoile du Nord' wagon restaurants, and an art nouveau bar car with a baby grand piano and ceiling fans. The pianist played 'The Shadow of Your Smile' and other lie-down-on-the-floor-I-think-I-love-you standards to the accompaniment of a pre-recorded snare drum track, of the type found on home organs. The waiters served champagne at around £40 a bottle. And with the exception of a handful of Britishers, a few groggy Japanese, a quartet of Australian heavies, and two or three French couples, the majority of passengers in this lounge were Americans, who didn't mind letting you know the balance of their chequebooks or the state of their internal plumbing. Like Bob and Babs, a couple from Baton Rouge, who were sitting with Jake and Cindy Boyd.

'Hey fella, join us', Jake said when I entered the bar car. I sat down and was introduced to Bob and Babs. He wore a slick Sunbelt suit and a stillborn moustache, whereas she was a straw-blond southern belle with jet-white teeth and the aura of a faded cheer leader. A bottle of champagne arrived at the table, and then

12

Babs raised her glass and said to Bob, 'Well darlin', I think I should propose a toast to our good news.' And then she told the rest of us: 'We've got one on the way.'

Everyone made all the proper congratulatory noises and I asked when the child was due.

'December first,' Babs said, without hesitation. I looked at her stomach. It showed no signs of a woman about to give birth in two months time. She caught my stare. 'Oh, I'm not having a child on December first,' she said. 'I'm *getting* a child. You see, we can't have kids'. Everyone now made all the proper sympathetic noises. 'And when we discovered I was infertile . . . well, we decided we just had to adopt.'

Bob came in here: 'Yeah, and just about four months ago, I got a call from the hospital when I was at the office—I'm into management consultancy—and they told me, "I think we've got one for you"'.

'And the mother's this Irish girl,' Babs said. 'A real nice convent girl. And we've checked into the father's background as well.'

'Yeah, he's a college grad who majored in economics', Bob said, 'which made me feel a whole lot better.'

The conversation drifted into matters of infertility: the merits of artifical insemination; the difficulty in finding a sperm bank you could trust; and even a new miracle cure involving urine from a nun.

'I kid you not', Jake Boyd said, 'I know this woman who couldn't have a kid, and she tried everything until somebody told her about this clinic down in Mexico where—and I'm not shitting you—they've got this new treatment in which they inject an extract made up of nun's urine. She got knocked up within two months.'

While I made a mental note to ask my wife's aunt—Sister Margaret Therese of the Carmelite convent in Cairo—whether she'd heard about this remarkable new form of Christian aid, we were called to dinner. And over the salmon with caviar, the medium rare tournedos, and the light vanilla mousse, Bob and Babs and Jake and Cindy discussed Bob's recent root transplant to counteract the effects of his receding hairline, and the escalating price of South Florida condos, and mutual bond options, and, of course, the BMW 735i. Theirs was a world in which your standing depended upon how you rated in a free-market economy, and where a journey on the new Orient Express was

considered to be a status investment. And when I thought back
to the previous night's scene on the Dublin-to-Liverpool mail
boat, I was tempted to dismiss the Orient Express as some sort of
phantom form of travel; a make-believe soireé for the con-
spicuous consumer. But there was, in fact, absolutely nothing
make-believe about this hyper-luxury train, for what it sold its
customers was prefabricated class. Within its confines, you could
assert your position as a higher roller, and one who, naturally,
has an appreciation for that which is posh. And it struck me as
ironic that overland travel today is either the domain of those
who cannot afford the airfare, or those members of the moneyed
classes who will gladly pay big bucks for a bit of *olde world*
atmosphere. Indeed, the new Orient Express was a shrewdly
marketed piece of nostalgia which pampered you into believing
that this is what *haute travel* is all about. And the passengers,
dolled up in their evening finery—'Dinner provides you with a
marvellous opportunity to recreate the style and glamour of a
bygone age'— joined in this conspiracy of elegant illusion.
They'd paid for the myth and were determined to get their
money's worth. And when I thought of my ultimate destination, I
began to feel like an interloper who had gate-crashed one myth
and was about to gate-crash another.

After dinner, Jake ordered a tumbler of the Armagnac which
probably dated back to the time of the French revolution since it
cost something like £18 a shot. He downed it in one go and
pronounced it, 'Kinda rough for that kinda cash.' I got back to my
compartment sometime after midnight and, six hours later, was
jolted awake when we slid into the outskirts of Zurich. The
steward brought a breakfast tray laden with freshly squeezed
orange juice, hot croissants, a pot of fresh coffee, and a folded copy
of the International Herald Tribune, and left me to breakfast with
my hangover. By lunch, we had arrived in Innsbruck, and as we
roared through that Alpine spectacle known as the Brenner Pass,
Jake pointed to the window and said, 'Look at that environment!'

I had a razor-sharp connection to make in Venice, and spent
the next four days aboard the *Expresso Egitto*. It was a floating
cappuccino maker of a ship, manned by a crew who acted as if
they were a commune of insomniacs assigned to this passage as a
punishment for crimes against humanity. On my first night
aboard, I stood on deck and watched the Piazza San Marco fall
away as the ferry headed out into open seas. On my second night
aboard, I stood on deck with Yusuf the Toyota dealer, who told

me about his three wives and said that his greatest ambition in life was to live alone. On my third night aboard, I stood on deck while, down below in the passenger lounge, a video of an Egyptian soap opera was screened. And on my fourth and last night aboard, I stood on deck while a corner of the passenger lounge was turned into a impromptu mosque for prayer.

Egypt was near.

Chapter Two

On the Waterfront

I WOKE AT SIX. A few moments later, a steward banged on the door of my cabin and shouted 'Alessandrio'. We had evidently arrived. I showered and shaved and dressed quickly, then went out on deck. The sun had just risen and Montazah Palace could be seen from the starboard side of the ship. Yusuf joined me at the railings.

'Every time I make this voyage, I always get up early on the final morning to see us approach the coast of Egypt. You like the palace? It was the home of King Farouk. And then, *King* Sadat.' He smiled thinly. 'We have had many kings in Egypt. Too many kings.'

We went below to the ship's cafeteria. Two large tables had been set up, behind which sat a group of officers in white naval shirts with epaulettes. The tools of their trade were laid out in front of them—stacks of official forms, rubber stamps, ink pads. They announced they were open for business, and a surge of people rushed forward. One of the officers began to yell in Arabic, the other in a language that resembled English, telling the passengers to form two separate queues. The passengers attempted to follow these instructions, but were met with further cries from officialdom, as it was explained that the first queue would be for Egyptian nationals, the second for all foreigners. Immigration formalities had begun.

I joined the queue for non-nationals and waited twenty minutes until I edged my way to the desk. An officer studied my passport and said, 'You must first change money in the bank. After you change money, you come back here.' As it turned out, he had been telling everybody in the queue the same thing.

The bank was a small baize-covered table, suitable for a two-handed game of gin rummy. An elderly man with half-moon spectacles was hunched over a calculator and a thick, dusty ledger. Around him were Egyptian bank notes of the old variety; faded and decayed, and about the size of a picture postcard. The bank clerk had a bad case of the shakes and his fingers trembled every time he counted out a wad of notes. This would cause him to lose his concentration, and he would have to begin again. The queue swelled, children began to cry and the bank clerk continued to lose his concentration. I wanted to break ranks and leave, but there was no way around this formality. The bank clerk was there to enforce a law. A law which states that every non-resident foreigner must change the equivalent of one hundred and fifty dollars upon entering the country. Yusuf explained this regulation to me by saying, 'Egypt likes hard currency.' But he was at a loss for words when, five minutes later, the bank clerk stood up and announced that he had run out of Egyptian currency. This meant waiting another forty-five minutes while he was taken back to the port in a small launch, collected a fresh batch of bank notes, and returned to the ship to continue the business at hand. Another hour passed before I found myself in front of the card table, collected my wad of Egyptian pounds, and then rejoined the queue for passport control.

The immigration officer had a cigarette locked between his teeth. Ash fell on my passport as he slowly worked his way through every page, taking down details of all my previous visas and studying my photograph with evident concern. After a moment, he looked up at me and, pointing to the passport photograph, said, 'You are certain you are him?' I assured him that I was, and shrugging his shoulders, his stamp did its work.

Freed from this set of official hurdles, I collected my bags and began to walk towards the main exit of the ship. I didn't get very far, as one of the Italian crewmen blocked my path.

'Where you think you go?', he asked. I explained that, having completed landing formalities, I was planning to disembark.

'Can you walk on water?', he said, pointing to a port hole. I looked out and saw that we were still hovering out in the middle of the harbour and had yet to pull into our berth. 'We wait until everbody has their passport stamped, then we dock, then we let you off the ship. Egyptian rules.'

I returned to the cafeteria, which was now beginning to look like the Fall of Saigon. The entire contingent of passengers had been herded into this area, their belongings strewn around them, making movement virtually impossible. Having claimed my own personal patch of floorspace, I was now anchored to that spot, unable to budge until the immigration officers had cleared the last of the passengers. I turned around and saw that Yusuf was standing next to me.

'Is it always like this?'

'It is all the fault of the Libyans', he said. 'The Libyans, they come into our country and make trouble, so we must be very careful that we do not let in the wrong people. This is why we must wait until all the passports have been examined. Be patient —this is for the good of Egypt.'

With that, the ship's engines began to hum again, and there was a full-scale scramble towards the exits. As everyone quickly discovered, however, the *Espresso Egitto* only had one main passanger exit. And, within minutes, this passageway had become a varicose vein threatening to bring on an embolism as all the foot passengers tried to bulldoze their way into the small space provided. The ship docked, and there was increased jostling for position as expectations grew that our release from incarceration was imminent. But then, things neatly turned ugly. A pair of Egyptians, returning home with a small washing machine, proceeded to hoist it into the passageway. Two Greek gentlemen took exception to this attempt at queue jumping, especially as one Egyptian lost his grip on the packing case and just managed to avoid fracturing a pair of Greek feet. Strong words were spoken, there were threats of grievous bodily harm, but before a scuffle could break out, we were all pushed forward. And I suddenly found myself on the gangplank, blinking into the Egyptian morning.

* * * * *

Arrive in a new country by plane, and your first glimpse of territory outside the terminal building will be that predictable strip of petrol stations, grim suburbs, and industrial parks which are the standard features of airport roads the world over.

Arrive in a new country by ship, however, and there is no time for adjustment: no outlying boroughs or gasoline alleys to act as a prelude before you hit town. The city stands beyond the harbour gates, waiting to suck you into the business of its day.

And in Alexandria, you leave the walls of the port in the safety of a taxi, and plunge impetuously into the centre of a vortex.

It was the car horns I heard first as we pulled away from the harbour gates. They honked and tooted and whistled, making the city sound like it has been taken over by a deranged marching band. And then the taxi fought its way down a congested side street and entered the eye of the storm—the souk in full midday swing. The streets were packed with tradesmen lining the pavements, and fruit merchants negotiating their donkey carts through the maze of traffic. Shops spilled out into the gutter, and the stench of rotting vegetables made the air a thick and glutinous substance which adhered itself to my clothes, my face, my hair. Women in black were performing remarkable balancing acts with groceries piled high upon their heads, and a beggar, his left eye socket covered by a thin membrane of skin, approached the taxi, only to be hooted out of the way by the driver.

Above me, housewives stood on the balconies of their tenement flats, yelling down to their children below, and up ahead, a traffic cop was trying to make order out of chaos, but failing fast. The roar of the car horns hit a delirious pitch, the heat became absurd, and I quickly realized that, in Egypt, *the street* is not simply a thoroughfare for commerce and dwelling, but an extremist form of theatre in which all must participate. The groundlings have taken over the stage and are running the show.

We fought our way out of the souk, and emerged on to a spacious wide boulevard. Back-street Egypt had suddenly been transformed into a shabby *fin de siècle* stage set, with crumbling ornate mansions lining our route. From this angle, Alexandria could have been an Eastern European city—that same landscape of architectural dereliction which one sees in Bucharest or Prague, where the remnants of an imperial past stand in forlorn contradiction to the ideology of the regime. In front of us, however, was the main commercial district of the city, and the sight of shops packed with the spoils of the West broke this image of Warsaw Pact bleakness, and yanked me right back into the gaudy mercantile world of Egypt today.

The taxi driver was also doing his best to yank me towards my hotel, but his vehicle—a Lada, way past retirement age—was refusing to co-operate. It wheezed and rattled like a chain smoker's lungs, it suffered from arthritis, and was prone to the occasional seizure, stalling twice in the souk. But just when it was about to suffer the final coronary of its career, we turned a corner and pulled in front of the Hotel Cecil on the Place Saad Zaghlul.

In Alexandrian lore, the Hotel Cecil holds a special place—a dark, murky international rendezvous, peopled by shadowy men and women with a past; an illicit casbah where the sweet aroma of corruption always lingers in the air. Or, at least, that's the narcotic atmosphere described by Lawrence Durrell in *Justine*—a 'moribund hotel', where 'the palms splinter and refract their motionless fronds in the gilt-edged mirrors', and Syrian businessmen puff hashish over coffee.

Today, however, the Cecil is about as byzantine as a hotel for commercial travellers in the Irish midlands. From the front, it still has that imposing colonial veneer of a Governor General's mansion. Once inside, it's all Edwardian gloom: heavy wood panelling, overstuffed armchairs with pockmarked upholstery, grill-room smells of grease and burnt chops, and cavernous bedrooms furnished with only the most utilitarian of essentials. The gilt-edged mirror in the main foyer still survives, though, as does a splendidly antiquated cage of a lift. And after four nights in my cell aboard the *Espresso Egitto*, the sight of a proper bed and a bathtub cancelled out any reservations I may have had about the high cost of staying in this faded pleasure palace.

I sat in a hot bath for an hour, and then flopped on the bed and switched on my radio. On the BBC World Service, Bernard Levin was telling the eastern Mediterranean about his new book on Hannibal. Further down the dial, the Voice of America was broadcasting an English language lesson.

'What are you going to do in Miami?', one voice said, giving emphasis to every syllable.

'I'll call my cousin as soon as I arrive', a second voice said. 'I'll stay with him while I'm there. We're going to spend a lot of time together on the beach. I'll see all my old friends.'

'It sounds like a wonderful vacation', the first voice said. 'Have a good time.'

'Thanks, *Ahmed*. I'll drop you a postcard as soon as I arrive.'

I left Ahmed waiting for his postcard and turned on the room's colour television. A sheikh filled the screen, giving the afternoon reading of the Koran. I napped to the sound of his voice, and woke several hours later to discover that he had been replaced by Martina Navratilova, wiping her opponent off the court in some distant land. Befuddled by this collision of worlds, I decided that it was time for a walk.

Like any port city, Alexandria is a hybrid; a mutation of cultures. The Greeks came first, led by Alexander the Great in 331 BC. The founded the city, and also brought with them the architect Deinocrates to turn this strip of beachfront property into a flashy Mediterranean seaport. When Alexander died, his second-in-command, Ptolemy I Soter, established a dynasty which transformed Alexandria into an important centre for commerce and the favourite watering hole of the Greek *cognoscenti*. The mathematician Euclid spent some time on the beach, and also founded a school of mathematics that survived for 700 years. Later on, the orator Demetrius Phalereus, a disciple of Aristotle, was dispatched from Athens to create antiquity's most renowned library. And by the time Caesar and the Romans showed up in 48 BC, no city in the known world could touch Alexandria when it came to trade or erudition.

Antony and Cleopatra went to seed here, and St Mark was said to have visited the city in 45 AD, ushering in an era when Alexandria became a focal point for Christianity in the Mediterranean basin. The Persians stopped by briefly to capture the city in 619, but it was the arrival of the Arabian forces of the Caliph Omar in 642 that was to change the face of Egypt forever. Islam had arrived in the country, and with it came the gradual, but steady conversion of the populace to the world of Allah. The power of 'Christian' Alexandria diminished, and when a new capital—Cairo—was established on the Nile banks in 969, the fabled city went into an eight hundred year decline.

It was Napoleon who wanted to put Alexandria back on the map. Though only a backwater of 5,000 inhabitants when he arrived with an expeditionary force in 1798, he quickly decided that it would become the seat of his eastern domain. Admiral Nelson put a stop to such plans, and it was left to Muhammed Ali to restore the city to its former prominence. Ali was an Albanian born in Macedonia, and a shrewd political operator who managed to convince the Sultan of Turkey to name him Viceroy of Egypt in 1805. From there, he went on to found a political clan that would rule the country until the revolution of 1952, and would also drag Egypt into the modern age. Alexandria figured significantly in his plans, as Ali set out to re-establish the port as a major nautical centre. A French architect was commissioned to redevelop the harbour; Italians and Greeks found employment in the shipyards; and Ali—now controlling every hectare of arable land in the country—sought out European representatives to sell Egypt's commodities overseas. Expatriate ghettos began to develop, the city prospered and expanded, and within a short time, Alexandria re-emerged after centuries of decay to become the cosmopolitan centre of north-east Africa.

This cosmopolitanism survived the bombardment of the city by British forces in 1882, as well as the subsequent British occupation of the country. As late as 1929, Baedeker's guide to Egypt reported that Europeans made up to 20 per cent of Alexandria's population. And these foreign communities even managed to stay intact during the years of the Second World War, when Rommel and Montgomery were shooting it out down the road in El Alamein.

But they did not survive the coming of Gamal Abdel Nasser. In 1957, following the Suez crisis, Nasser ordered the last of the French and British communities out of the country, and Alexandria—host to a parade of outside invaders—now suffered an invasion from within. Nasser's own brand of Arab socialism rid the port of its worldly, libertine flavour, and that pungent Mediterranean town was no more.

From all recent accounts I had read, present-day Alexandria sounded like a bleak place indeed. But perhaps that's the fate of cities with a storybook past. The modern equivalent never lives up to the dazzling image which literature and history have implanted in our minds, and we come away feeling cheated because the city lured us in with a promise of bygone romance and then failed to deliver. What we tend to forget, however, is that cities rarely stand still, and are constantly being modified by the political and economic realities of a given time. The history of Alexandria is a testament to that principle: it has known greatness and insignificance, and has seen its identity ceaselessly altered to meet the requirements of a specific regime. And as I left the Hotel Cecil for my first proper look at the city, I wondered how it was faring in the uncertain climate of Egypt today.

It was the billboards that hit me. There seemed to be dozens of them, turning Ramleh Square—the city's main tram station—into a miniature 42nd Street. There were revolving neon signs for Canada Dry Sport Cola and a big display for Orange Crush, but what really caught my attention were the massive film posters, heralding the arrival of a new box-office sensation from the Egyptian cinema. They had all been executed by someone who had been trained in the video nasty school of commercial art, and had a strong flair for cheap melodrama. In one, a distraught father was shaking his fist at his jail-bait daughter, while his wife pleaded for clemency. Nearby, a woman engulfed in flames was understandably screaming her head off, much to the amusement of a demonic looking gent in a three-piece suit.

It wasn't just the film companies who were advertising their wares. The sides of the ageing buildings surrounding the square were a mosaic of placards, publicizing the services of Dr Samir Fayez Youakin (Ex-surgeon, Eastman Dental Hospital, London), not to mention solicitors, accountants, and a doctor who specialized in venereal and mouth diseases. Down below, on the street, the commercialism was no less blatant. It was 7 pm—the hour when Egyptian cities wake up from their afternoon nap—and Ramleh Square was thick with vendors, hawking anything from shaving cream and cigarettes to copies of the Koran and hand-tinted photographs of President Hosni Mubarak. I stopped by one stall where a portrait of Nasser was for sale.

'Do people still buy Nasser's picture?', I asked the salesman.

'Nasser still very popular', he said 'Good for business.'

'How about Sadat? Do you sell many of him?'

The salesman laughed. 'Nobody wants that man in their house.'

'And Mubarak?'

'I sell a few. He makes a bit of money for me.'

'Then your best seller is still Nasser?'

'No', he said. 'My best seller is Michael Jackson.'

'Michael Jackson?'

'Very popular in Egypt', he said. 'You like one? I give you Michael Jackson at good price.'

'No thanks,' I said. Moving off, I remembered that when I was in Cairo in 1981, it would have been considered offensive to the regime to sell a portrait of Nasser on the street, let alone photographs of an American pop star. Only posters of Sadat were on display, and they dogged me from the moment of my arrival. Leaving the airport at the time, I saw Sadat standing in the middle of a traffic island, greeting me with outstretched arms, like a benevolent father ushering you into the house of his children. He was lit by two powerful floodlights, and above his head was a sign that said '*I Welcome You To Egypt . . . Land of Peace.*' Half a mile down the road, I had another chance encounter with President Sadat, only this time he was looking stern and unforgiving: an Old Testament figure dressed up in the sort of uniform usually worn by Argentinian generals. And by the time I had reached the centre of Cairo, I had counted no less than a dozen billboards depicting the many moods and humours of Anwar el Sadat. Meant to convey the stability and popularity of his rule, they immediately sounded the sort of Third World warning bells that always begin to peal when an autocrat loses control over the hearts and minds of his people.

Now, however, it was the very absence of large-scale propaganda for the new president that was intriguing. Certainly, there were a few posters of Hosni Mubarak dotted around Alexandria's main square, but the approach was low-key. No sense that the Pharaoh of the moment was staring down at you. No need to promote Mubarak's greatness on every street corner. No fears about having his portrait displayed alongside those of his predecessors. Of course, Mubarak was still being advertised as the man in charge, but the cult of personality which Sadat so relentlessly pursued—and failed to achieve—was dead. It's Michael Jackson who's the cult figure now.

I turned away from Ramleh Square, and attempted to cross the street. This can be a nervy adventure in Egypt, where the rules of the road go something like this: ignore all traffic lights, stop signs, or pedestrian crossings. Drive at maximum speed, even in the most congested streets. Never indicate that you are changing lanes (use your car horn instead). Always cut across an oncoming vehicle's path. Consider any pedestrian a suitable target for liquidation.

I made the mistake of thinking that a green light in my favour actually meant that I could cross the street in relative safety. This turned out to be a bad deduction, for half-way across the road, I turned and saw a batallion of cars bearing down on me. It was like being an alien craft in a game of Space Invaders, and I drove for the pavement, just missing the wrath of a Fiat. An elderly man dressed in a *galabiya* helped me up after I had landed, dusted me off, and seizing me by the arm, led me back into the fray.

'This time I think we make it, *Inshallah*', he said.

Inshallah means 'Allah willing', and the principle of divine intervention seems to be at work every time you encounter a motor vehicle in Egypt. There is a grim fatalism about Egyptian driving habits—a belief that you can be wildly dangerous behind the wheel because Allah is the only traffic cop worth listening to, and He alone will decide whether or not you'll make it around the next hairpin curve. The passion for chaos on Egypt's road is an indication of the degree to which accepted western notions of order are given low priority in this society. And it leaves you wondering: is everybody in Egypt living on his nerves?

Safely reaching the other side of the street, I thanked the gentleman who had come to my assistance. 'No problem', he said. 'You are most welcome in Egypt. But do learn how to cross our roads.' And with that, he bid me goodbye and disappeared into the crowd.

I followed him several minutes later, rejoining the flow of pedestrians drifting up to Saad Zaghlul Street. Saad Zaghlul may have been a much-revered Egyptian patriot in the early decades of this century but today his name adorns the street in Alexandria where, among other things, you can buy just about every brand of men's after-shave on the market. Every second shop window I passed was piled high with the stuff, and groups of Egyptian men would gather in front, arguing over the merits of Paco Rabanne and Chanel Pour Homme. Then, they would move on to a shop specializing in watches, and size up the Omegas and Seikos on display.

Further down the street, video recorders were attracting large crowds in front of one store window, while nearby it was German food processors and portable cassette recorders that were the talking point among this floating community of night-time shoppers. In the midst of all these hi-tech luxuries were smaller merchants dealing in coffee, fabrics, and spices, and it was intriguing to see how people were matter-of-fact when they shopped for their basic household requirements, but then became almost reverential when faced with a new Sony colour television. When I later learned that the majority of the population earned around the equivalent of £30 per month, I began to understand why so many people looked at such western goods as if they were the great unattainable beyond. It was not just a plate glass that seperated them from these luxuries—it was the economic reality of Egypt today. And yet, the sight of all that electronic wizardry fuelled aspirations for 'the good life' which the state didn't have the means to fulfil. It made Saad Zaghlul Street a potential danger zone, for in the new consumer society which Sadat had originally created, only a select few were able to afford its pleasures, while the rest had to look on in silent frustration. And perhaps it was only a matter of time before that frustration found expression in the sort of political unrest that can make a government think about taking the next plane out of town.

Cutting down a side street, I walked along a lane where the only source of light was a pile of rubbish on fire, and soon found myself entangled in a Chinese puzzle of back alleys and dead-end streets. I was on the point of turning back and trying to retrace my steps when I heard a curious noise in the distance. A noise one doesn't usually associate with the backstreets of Alexandria: Neil Diamond singing *Love on the Rocks*. Intrigued, I started walking in the direction of Mr Diamond's sob story, turned a corner and stumbled upon a small establishment with a large warplane painted over its entrance: The Spitfire Bar.

I stepped inside and left Egypt behind me, as the interior of the Spitfire had been done up to resemble a college bar in smalltown America. There were the predictable cheap beauty boards on walls, gingham table cloths, old pin-up calendars, neon beer signs, and a sound system which switched from Neil Diamond to the Rolling Stones. There were even a pair of blond, well-scrubbed American kids sitting at a table with three Egyptian friends who were striving for the Middle Eastern preppie look— Italian trousers, Chemise Lacoste shirts, Adidas sneakers. None of them could have been more than sixteen.

I sat down at a table and ordered a beer. 'Hey', the American guy said, poking me in the shoulder, 'Where you from?'

'Originally from New York, but I now live in Ireland.'

'Hey, that's kinda neat. 'Cause my name's Brendan, which makes me kinda Irish as well. Mind if I take a cigarette?' Not waiting for me to reply, he reached over and grabbed the packet of Marlboros on my table.

'What exactly are you doing in Alexandria?', I said.

'Kinda going to school. This here's my sister Suzy, and these guys are friends of ours from Schultz's American School in Alex.

My dad's over here working on the new sewage system that's being put in for the city. Kinda interesting, huh?'

'Kinda', I said.

Sewage was also a topic of conversation at a nearby table, where four beefy English gents were sitting, with at least three dozen cans stacked in front of them. Their faces were cherry red from the sun, and their bellies had all gone beyond the point of no return.

'So I told that fucking Gyppo', one of them said, 'Don't pour the fucking concrete over the fucking pipes. But does he listen? Of course he doesn't. Pours the fucking concrete over the pipes, and right over me.'

Back at the children's table, Brendan was pouring out a tale of post-pubescent woe to one of his Egyptian classmates.

'I mean, I told Ruthie I kinda love her, but then I see her making eyes at Hosni in class, and you know, it kinda breaks me up being treated like that.'

'What's your home, mate?', one of the English gents asked me.

'Dublin.'

'Here that, lads? Paddy here's from Dublin. No fucking Guinness in this pub, mate.'

'You working out here?', I asked.

'The W.W.C.G.', he said. 'That's the West Water Consultant Group. Sewage pipes, mate. We specialize in Egyptian shit.'

I called for the bill. The sewage pipe specialists did the same.

'Hey Abdullah', one of them yelled to the quiet man who tended bar. 'Add all this up like a good lad.'

'He'll have some fucking job', another chimed in.

Abdullah came over and began to count the empty beer cans. This took some time, as there were 44 of them, making a total bill of 135 Egyptian pounds.

'You can pay the fucking rent this month, Abdullah.'

I decided to leave.

Back in my room in the Hotel Cecil, I turned on the television. Robert Redford, subtitled in Arabic, was playing a candidate for the United States Senate. I dozed, and woke briefly to catch the final programme of the day: the closedown reading of Koran. The sheikh on the screen sang of the glories of Allah, then the picture went black, and I slept.

* * * * *

I changed hotels the next morning, moving my bags across the street from the Cecil to a small pension called The New Capri. It was located eight floors up in an office building which seemed to be on the verge of collapse. Entering the building, I had to wade through a foyer strewn with loose bricks, burst bags of cement, and an old bathtub which lay idle in the centre of the floor. Then there was the matter of the lift—a creeping timber box with a large gash in its ceiling, which had the habit of landing with an ominous thud. It made reaching the New Capri an unsettling experience, but the pension was clean and cheap, and my room afforded me an excellent view of the rooftops of the city.

I unpacked, and then hit the streets again, walking down to the seafront. A bus halted briefly and I hopped aboard, deciding to see where it would take me.

The seafront of Alexandria is a property developer's dream. It stretches for some twenty-five kilometers, making it one of the longest corniches in the world—a thin strip of prime Mediterranean coastline, in the process of being high-rised and air-conditioned. Old photographs of the Corniche show a sweeping crescent of baroque palaces fronting the sea, but as the bus limped eastwards along the beach-front, I thought I was on an inspection tour of an endless building site. The palaces have gone, and it is now steel girders, cranes, and deep cavities in the earth which define the landscape. The Sheratons have built a circular tower of concrete and glass across from Montazah Palace, and Ramada have constructed one of their 'Renaissance' hotels in the aesthetically pleasing style of a muncipal car park. Kentucky Fried Chicken and Wimpys have also claimed their corner of the seafront, and every streetcorner is being gradually colonized by condominiums and purpose-built flats.

Traditionally, Alexandria has always been a summer resort; 'the lungs of Egypt' during the months of July and August when those who can afford it flee the microwave heat of Cairo to seek cooler comfort on the beaches of the Corniche. But the sight of all those tower blocks let it be known that a different sort of tourist is now being courted, as Egyptian developers team up with the big American hotel chains to provide antiseptic lodgings for the package holiday brigade. In the process, the Corniche has begun to take on the appearance of an architectural fire sale, as part of the big push to turn Alexandria into an Arabian Costa de Sol.

At Montazah Gardens, I got off the bus and grabbed a taxi heading back towards the city. Halfway there, the driver told me that he had to pick up a fare at the British Council, so I was dumped out on Rue des Ptolemees, a narrow street fronted by large turn-of-the-century mansions.

As it turned out, Rue des Ptolemees was a shopping precinct specializing in foreign languages. It was a buyer's market, in which you could pick up BBC English at the British Council, sample Deutsch at the Goethe Institute and, during the Nasserite years, learn how to say *dasvidaniya* without tears at the Soviet Cultural Centre. The Russians had been closed down since 1972, when Sadat evicted all Soviet advisers from the country, but the other centres were open for business, so I wandered into the Goethe Institute and asked to meet its director.

Mr Dieter Vollsprecht was a greying gentleman in his mid-fifties; a pleasant, low-key cultural diplomat. He greeted me cordially, and when I explained in my barely functional German that I had spent two months in Rothenburg ob der Tauber several years back on a Goethe Institute fellowship, and was friendly with Dietrich Kreplin (his counterpart at the Dublin Goethe Institute), he ushered me into his office and offered coffee.

We sat in a 'conversation area'—the same Scandinavian-style three-piece suite that can be found in the offices of Goethe Institute directors throughout the world. After exchanging a few pleasantries, we were joined by Dr Michael de la Fontaine, the head of the institute's language programme. Blond, steel-blue eyes, with more than a whiff of aristocratic after-shave, he was one of those people who live in a state of perpetual intensity and live and speak in articulate rapid-fire bursts. 'So, you are a writer?' he said after we were introduced. 'I dabble a bit myself. Poetry and lyrics for music. But I cannot make a living out of writing poetry and songs, so I teach German. What do you think of Alexandria? I always tell visitors that they must remember it is not our own culture. It is like outer space to us.'

He was about to launch into a long discourse on the subject when Sarwat el Bahr came into the room and was introduced to me as 'one of Egypt's leading painters.' Sarwat cast his eyes heaven-ward upon hearing such extravagant praise, and lit the first in a long chain of cigarettes. It was a self-mocking character-istic that I came to recognize in him – a disregard for his public image as 'an artist' which masked the intensity with which he applied himself to his work. Large and imposing—he looked like a matinee idol who'd given in to middle-age spread—he im-mediately struck me as someone comfortable in his milieu, yet very aware of its limitations.

We shook hands, a servant brought cups of thick Turkish coffee, and after Mr Vollsprecht excused himself to attend a meeting, Dr de la Fontaine—steel-blue eyes as intense as ever—launched back into his discourse.

'I was just saying that is seems to me there are many masks to the Egyptian character. At home, in Egypt, they have one sort of mask: authoritarian, Muslim, rigid towards their women. But when they come to Europe, they wear *our* clothes, adopt *our* lifestyle and—if you'll excuse me for saying so—fuck *our* women. They cannot reconcile one mask with the other.

'And there is no way the young people can channel their vitality. Have you seen an Egyptian school? I was walking by one the other day, and stood watching a group of boys playing in the schoolyard. It was like watching the military being trained, the way those children were ordered around with a whistle and a stick.'

Sarwat came in here. 'You must understand that there are many types of Islam in the Arab world. There is petroleum Islam, which the Saudis use to control money, and which keeps a woman in a cage. Then there is practical Islam, which is about praying and family life. But all Islamic religion comes from the desert, where everything is poor. You must have a dream in the desert—the dream of Allah—because there is nothing else. But if you take away the dream, if people lose the dream, they become very confused.

'In Egypt, Nasser gave people a dream—a dream to be something in the world. But when he made the revolution, most other countries like ours were still occupied by England or France. Now they are only occupied by *the dollar*'. He paused and smiled at me. 'The West is very clever.

'But do you know why America does not understand Egypt? Because they do not understand the meaning of the word *Maaleesh*. In English, *Maaleesh* means 'doesn't matter', and it is the one word you need to understand Egypt. In America, everything is *now, now, now*—make the money now, make the career now. But in Egypt, everybody believes in life after death, so everything in life is *Maaleesh*.'

I asked Sarwat if he felt that America was not only occupying Egypt with its dollar, but with its mass culture as well.

'You should see the Sporting Club here in Alex', he said 'It is for high society. In the Sporting Club, the rich young girls make themselves up like film stars and sit in cars. They are *flat*—totally empty. They know the songs of this Michael Jackson, but about Egypt they know absolutely nothing.

'When I say "Egypt", I speak of my home. But to many young people, it is just a house they live in. And that saddens me.'

Dr de la Fontaine had to go off to attend to administrative matters, and Sarwat invited me to see his studio. We left the Goethe Institute and walked for several minutes down a side street until we reached a palazzo in a state of total disrepair. A gold sign said 'L'Atelier' on the front gate.

'This was the Alexandrian Arts League', Sarwat said. 'Once there were a thousand members. Now we are 150, and we cannot afford to have the building look better.'

The main foyer of the Arts League was lit by a lone light bulb, and covered in a thick film of plaster dust. Beneath the dust, I could make out the occasional glimpse of inlaid wood panelling, ornate plaster work, and a curious wall mural depicting a pastoral country house scene. It was like entering an archeological dig, in which the remnants of an elegant past could only be discovered by burrowing through the debris.

Sarwat's studio was on the first floor, and I took to it immediately. There was a broken-down leather couch, shelves of paint, piles of half-finished canvases, stacks of art books, postcards, photographs, and cryptic messages pasted to the peeling walls, empty Scotch bottles, a collection of brimming ashtrays, and a few sad dying plants. It struck me as the best sort of hideaway— unapologetically cluttered and cut off from the city's roar outside.

Sarwat disappeared for a moment with an empty Ballantine's Scotch bottle, returned with it filled with water, and proceeded to drown the parched greenery. Then, digging around a few dusty boxes, he managed to excavate two cans of Beck's beer. We cracked them open, lit cigarettes, and drank.

I pointed to one of his paintings—a pyramid enclosed in a square. 'You know that the square originally comes from ancient Greece', he said. 'The triangle is Oriental. So here, in this painting, I am showing the vitality of the East locked in by the logic of the West.'

He then drew a circle, a triangle, and a square on a piece of paper, and asked me to put all three inside each other without thinking too much about it. Picking up his pen, I drew a square, placed the circle inside it, and then finished off with the triangle inside the circle.

'Now', he said, 'the square is logic, the circle emotion, the triangle vitality. You see the world logically, then with feeling, and then you place your vitality inside that. Most of my friends here in Alex, they start with the triangle—the vitality—and end up with the logic. This is the difference between someone from the West and someone from Egypt. Logic means everything to you, and little to us.'

'Does Coca-Cola mean much to you?', I asked, pointing to a postcard of another recent canvas which showed a mummified figure embracing a Coke bottle. Sarwat laughed. 'In Pharaonic times', he explained, 'they would bury the Pharaoh with an apple or bread, so he would have something to eat if he got hungry in the afterlife. In Egypt today, they would bury him with Coca-Cola.'

Two more cans of Beck's beer were excavated and cracked opened, and Sarwat invited me to drop by the Goethe Institute the next morning to meet a group of young artists who worked out of a studio space which he had set up in the Institute's basement.

'These painters, they like working in the Goethe Institute because they see it as a place where they can breathe different air.'

'Are you saying that, if you want to function as an artist in Egypt, you have to seek shelter in a western environment?'

'I tell you a story', he said. 'My wife works in the German consulate here. Every day, she must have around 100 people coming in, looking for a visa. And many of the young people who come to ask about a visa, they speak to her in German. But their German is so bad that she answers them back in Arabic. Just the other day, she asked one man, "Why do you speak to me in such bad German?" And he said, "I try to forget my Arabic". You see, for many there is a freedom in speaking a language that is not associated with Egypt. It is the same thing for an artist. There is a freedom in foreign ideas.'

'Might you ever leave Egypt to work elsewhere?', I asked.

'You know the circuit', Sarwat said. 'For a painter, it is London, Paris, Amsterdam, Rome, Munich, Berlin, New York, and no-where else. And in these places, you become a marionette. And maybe one day someone decides you are the marionette to play with that month. I think it is better to be an artist here than in the West, because here you can make what you want.'

He paused for a moment, took a deep drag off his cigarette, and stared out the window. 'The only problem is that, in Egypt, you make what you want inside a cage.'

* * * * *

Sarwat gave me a lift back to the city centre. After agreeing to meet again the following morning, I made my way through a series of side streets until I reached a large square called Midan el Tahrir. My intention had been to seek out a restaurant for lunch, but instead I found myself standing in front of an architectural curiosity: a Victorian church which seemed to have been transported intact from the Home Counties and then abandoned on a street corner in Alex. A sign in the courtyard informed me that this was *St Mark's — The Anglican Church in Egypt* (Chaplain and Parish Priest — The Rev. H. Levett, A.K.C.). And, as the gates were open, I wandered inside, entering what could have been the local house of worship in Maidstone or St. Albans. Notices in the vestibule emphasized this feeling of being in a small town parish, with 'Getting-To-Know-You' receptions for newly arrived Anglicans, and church bazaars in aid of Ethiopian famine relief. But a potted history of the church hanging next to the noticeboard told a different story. St Mark's was a left-over from the colonial past. Founded by the British community in Alexandria, the church was consecrated in 1855 by the Bishop of Jerusalem, having been completed with donations from such luminaries as Queen Victoria, the Viceroy of Egypt, and the Archbishop of Canterbury. And when the British Navy shelled the city during the Orabi uprising of 1882 — a revolt by Egyptian military officers which led to the British occupation of the country — the admiral in charge ordered all guns to be trained away from the area around St Mark's. Alexandria was almost completely levelled during the attack, but this symbol of British Christian enlightenment survived unscathed.

As I was reading the history of St Mark's, an elderly Egyptian gentleman came out from the body of the chapel. He introduced himself as the church manager and asked me my business. I said that I would like to meet the Rev. H. Levett A.K.C. if he were available, and he was about to lead me to his office when a young African entered the vestibule.

'May I help you?', the church manager asked with more than a touch of coolness in his voice.

'I need to see the priest', the African said.

The church manager shot me a quick glance. 'The priest is not here', he said, motioning for me to retreat to a side room. I entered a small library and loitered near the door to hear the young African explain to the church manager that he was from Tanzania, and had been travelling in Greece before coming to Egypt. However, while he was in Cairo, a taxi driver robbed him of all his funds, and now he was in Alexandria trying to raise the finance to get himself back to Athens.

'So you would like to see the priest to ask for money?', the church manager said.

'I have no one else to turn to for help', the Tanzanian said.

'Let me ask you something', the church manager said. 'If you got robbed in Cairo, why are you in Alex? Why didn't you go to your embassy?'

'I want to see the priest', the Tanzanian said, getting adamant.

'I tell you—he is not here.'

'But I must see him. I am a Roman Catholic.'

'Idiot!', the church manager said. 'This is an Anglican church.' He led the Tanzanian somewhat forcibly to the door and pointed into the distance. 'If you are a Roman Catholic, you go to the cathedral over there. Maybe they listen to your story.'

After seeing the Tanzanian off, the church manager returned to me and smiled.

'You must excuse my harshness', he said. 'But we get people like that coming here every day. Liars, thinking because we are a church, we hand out charity to anyone. I am a retired bank official, so I can always tell when somebody comes here to ask for money. Believe me, I have an eye for these things.'

I was led through the chapel to a small office crammed with account books and stacks of hymnals. While waiting for the Rev. H. Levett A.K.C. to finish a phone call, I was introduced to the church bursar, a retired Commodore in the Egyptian Navy. I asked him if he too was a follower of the Church of England.

'No, I am not an Anglican', the bursar said. 'I am a Presbyterian.'

It was an absurdly quaint set-up—two genteel pensioners from a predominantly Muslim country serving the cause of Anglicanism in the evening of their lives. And as they offered me a cup of tea and spoke about church affairs ('You must read our newsletter, *The Alexandrian Anglican*. Very informative'), I began to develop an identikit photograph of the Rev. H. Levett A.K.C. in my mind. He would have to be a stock vicar; the sort of once-patrician, now down-at-heel Oxbridge gent who ends his days tending to a handful of the faithful in a humid outpost of a moribund Empire. On the surface, he would be exceedingly jolly, enthusing on about his busy life in the parish and his plans to raise money for a new organ loft. But the frayed cuffs on his worsted suit and his wounded eyes would expose him as a profoundly disappointed man. Passed over for higher position in the church back home, he was probably dispatched to this obsolete parish as a way of sending him out to pasture. Disillusioned and embittered, he would also have to be a secret tippler, with a bottle of gin stashed away in the wardrobe where he kept his clerical robes. And, late at night, he would lock himself away in his study, tune in the World Service on his wireless, gaze wistfully at the prints of Devon and Cornwall on his walls, and have a good old fashioned spiritual crisis while tucking into the last of his duty-free Beefeater's.

I was embellishing this scenario in my mind when the Rev. Howard Levett emerged from his study and shattered all my preconceptions. A man in his late thirties, wearing a starched white shirt, gold-framed spectacles, and a wispy beard, he greeted me with a quiet, almost formal courteousness and ushered me into his office. It was a bookish, wood panelled room, and as he motioned for me to sit in a leather armchair opposite his desk, I could sense that he was carefully appraising me, in the same manner in which a university lecturer might size up a new student on the first day of tutorials. There was nothing stock about this vicar. Precise and articulate, Howard Levett evidently took his calling seriously, but he did not display his piety for all to see. If anything, he seemed quietly devout; a man who had confronted all the difficult questions regarding his faith and his role as an Anglican priest. And even if he found many of these questions insoluble, he accepted that the struggle between belief and doubt was part of the spiritual territory he had chosen to occupy. Like the church he now served in Alexandria, the Rev. H. Levett was obviously a survivor.

'So what brought you to St. Mark's?', he asked. I explained that I was walking along Midan el Tahrir, saw the church, and curiosity drew me in.

'I see', he said in a confessional box tone of voice which suggested that he wasn't buying my story and it might be best to come clean with him. So I dropped my front as a casual visitor and explained why I was travelling in Egypt.

'Ah, then you're a writer', he said, and I quickly found myself owning up to the name of my publishers, the plays I had written, the magazines and newspapers I free-lanced for. He didn't cross-examine me, but I sensed that he was subtly telling me that, before he talked about his work and his parish, I would first have to speak about myself. Just so we would be on equal footing. This Anglican was nobody's fool.

'So, you were surprised to discover an Anglican church in Alex?', he said.

'A bit intrigued', I said. 'Is your parish quite small?'

'My parish is all of North Africa', he said with a slight smile. 'I'm the Anglican Archdeacon for the entire region, as well as for Ethiopia and Somalia. My bishop is an Egyptian in Cairo. Here, in Alex, we have a parish of approximately 150. Some expats—English and American mostly—but a high percentage of Egyptians as well. I preach here, and on Fridays at All Saint's—that's the second Anglican church in the city, over by Stanley Bay. So, between my work here and all my travels in the North African diocese, I find myself with little free time.'

He'd been in Alexandria for five years, and when I asked him how much longer he planned to stay, he said, 'That's up to several factors—God, the trustees of this church, my superiors back in England, and myself.' As he was speaking, I noticed that he was fingering a postcard on his desk—a postcard which depicted a classically English thatched cottage surrounded by classically English rolling fields. It seemed very far away.

'Out here, you don't get the ordinary satisfactions of life in a small parish—that sense of being part of a community.' He fingered the postcard again. 'The rewards in Egypt are different.'

'Different from your last post?'

'My last post was as an inner-city London priest, working at Elephant and Castle. Quite an irony, isn't it? Trading Elephant and Castle for camels and pyramids.'

* * * * *

That evening, as I sat nursing a beer in a Greek cafe on Ramleh Square, I thought again about my encounter with The Venerable Howard Levett, and how I had been guilty of the sin of prejudgement. Because I had stumbled across an Anglican church in an Egyptian port city, I had immediately assumed that the vicar in charge would have to be the archetypal whisky priest—after all, aren't all expatriate men of God in sweaty climates supposed to be seedy and tumbledown? I had entered St Mark's convinced that I would meet such a character, and had instead found myself coming face-to-face with a thoroughly modern Anglican who defied such a stereotype. And I realized that Alexandria was the sort of city that encouraged you to write such fictions in your head. The souk was one fiction—it enticed you in with its whiff of byzantine perfume, but then showed you a Sony video recorder. The Corniche was another fiction—it promised rococo splendour, and then hit you with Kentucky Fried Chicken. Even here, in this ornate cafe, you could see the confrontation between romantic myth and contemporary reality. The Athineos—with its high vaulted ceiling, suspended brass lamps, marble floors, mahogany tables, and Grecian columns topped with gold leaf— was a film set cafe; the perfect place for an assignation with Ingrid Bergman. And yet, from the moment the tuxedoed head waiter approached your table, you found yourself caught up in a bureacratic burlesque. The head waiter took your order, and then passed it on to a waitress. She, in turn, handed it over to an elderly bushboy. After a few minutes, the bushboy returned with a tray and presented it to the waitress. Her job now was to set the bottle of beer and the empty glass in front of you, whereupon the head waiter showed up to open the bottle and pour your drink.

Three people to serve a beer! It made me forget about the heady atmosphere of the Athineos, and forced me to take a closer look at the curious social hierarchy that exists in Egypt today. No wonder so many casual visitors hated Alexandria. Every time they were on the verge of recapturing some of its nostalgia, contemporary Egypt burst in to spoil the party. But, perhaps, this was a cunning game that the city played with a newcomer. It tricked you into succumbing to its mythic charms, and then destroyed your illusions by making you confront its present-day reality. In doing so, it also made you realize that you had arrived in a land brimming with incongruities. And if you were going to come to grips with the country beyond here, you would have to abandon your preconceptions and stop being seduced by the atmosphere of the past.

Don't be fooled by archetypal images, Alexandria seemed to be telling me. Nothing is what it appears to be in this country anymore. Everything is in a state of change and up for grabs.

I left the Athineos and walked down to the seafront. It was late and the Corniche was nearly deserted. A low night fog hung over the Mediterranean, and except for the occasional pool of street-lamp light, the city was veiled in shadow. Having just vowed not to be deceived by its romantic veneer, I now found myself succumbing to Alexandria's ghosts once again. But then, a voice from the present-day spoke from the shadows and broke the illusion.

'My friend, my friend', the voice whispered. I turned around and saw a man wearing a shabby Army greatcoat over a pair of striped pyjamas. He held up a bundle wrapped in old newspapers.

'You want this?', he said, opening the bundle. Inside was a litre of Vat 69 Scotch. It looked like it had been kept in storage for over a decade, and when he shook it, I could hear the liquid hissing inside the bottle.

'Fifteen pound', he said.

I walked on.

'Ten pound', he shouted, but I didn't turn back.

'Five pound', I heard him yell as I crossed the road and was swallowed up by the darkness of the Place Saad Zaghlul.

* * * * *

Over breakfast the next morning at the New Capri, a business-man sitting opposite me pointed to the front page of his news-paper and said, 'America very stupid'. I looked up from my coffee and bread rolls, and asked him how he had come to that conclusion.

'You mean, you no hear about the ship?', he said.

'What ship?'.

'Achille Lauro. Italian cruise ship. Hijacked by Palestinians after it left Alexandria two days ago. You no hear about this hijacking?'

'I haven't seen a newspaper for days', I said.

'You miss big story. The Palestinians, they hijack the ship, say they will kill all the passengers. They shoot one American, throw him over the side. America and Italy, they ask Egypt for help. Egypt talks to the men, tells them, "If you stop this hijacking, we fly you out of the country". The men agree, there is no more killing, and Egypt puts them on a plane to Tunis. But then, after the plane takes off, this cowboy Reagan, he sends his airforce to intercept the plane.'

'He *what*?', I said.

'He sends in jet fighters and makes the Egyptair plane land in Sicily, so the hijackers can be arrested.'

'That's a ridiculous story.'

'Of course it is ridiculous story', the businessman said. 'But Reagan is ridiculous man. Now he has Egypt very angry. Like I say, America very stupid.'

I excused myself and returned to my room. It was five to nine, and after roaming through several wave bands on my radio, I managed to pick up the hourly news bulletin on the BBC World Service. The Achille Lauro incident was the first item and the whole story came tumbling out largely as the businessman had described it to me. Reagan had decided to avenge the death of Mr Leon Klinghoffer (the American murdered aboard the ship) and show terrorists the world over that they could run, but not hide from the United States. But, in ordering the interception of the civilian Egyptian aircraft transporting the gunmen to Tunis, he had obviously cared precious little about the offence this might cause to Egypt. It was yet another example of his 'Shoot from the hip and stand tall' foreign policy, and one that was bound to have repercussions for the government of Hosni Mubarak. After all, Egypt was America's closest ally in the Arab world, and a voice of moderation in an increasingly immoderate region. It had signed the Camp David accord with Israel and, in doing so, had forfeited its traditional leadership role within the Arab family. And even though Mubarak was trying to reintegrate Egypt back into that family, the peace pact with Jerusalem still held firm, and Egypt remained solidly in the American camp.

But now, through one extraordinary action, Reagan had gambled with Egypt's fragile stability. And it made me wonder if the Americans had learned anything from the assassination of Sadat four years ago? Had they forgotten that he was murdered by Muslim extremists within the Egyptian Army because of his treaty with Israel and his pro-American policies? Didn't Washington realize that, since that time, Islamic fundamentalism had become a growth industry in Egypt, and was now looked upon as a potential future threat to the Mubarak regime? Weren't they aware of Egyptian reaction to Israel's adventures in the Lebanon and to their recent bombing of the PLO headquarters in Tunis—events which had made many Egyptians think twice about Camp David? And didn't they know that, by forcing the Egyptair jet to land in Sicily, they would not only be wounding a friend's pride and undermining its role as a peacemaker in the region, but would also be giving the Fundamentalists a propaganda victory?

No doubt, Reagan's advisers had considered such possibilities. No doubt, they also knew that middle America would cheer their President for heading off a bunch of Palestinian gunmen at the pass. And they probably reasoned that if, in the aftermath of the event, Mubarak screamed and shouted for a few days, he'd soon see sense. Especially since his country was dependent on the $2.8 billion it received annually in American aid. That's the problem with being a client state—you can't bite the hand of the super-power that feeds you.

So Reagan had gone ahead with his public relations stunt, and Egypt had suffered a humiliation in the process. Would a wave of anti-Americanism now sweep the country? Would Egypt stand up to its *padrone* and demand an apology? And if Mubarak didn't take a strong line with Washington, would his compatriots interpret this as a sign of weakness? As I listened to the BBC reports coming in, all these questions raced through my mind. One thing was very clear to me, however: I had picked an interesting time to be Egypt.

* * * * *

In the basement of the Goethe Institute the talk was not of hijacked ships or intercepted planes, but of Sarwat's recent exhibition in Cairo. A group of young painters and general enthusiasts had gathered for what appeared to be their weekly salon, and it was in this crowd that I met Moustafa Mehrez. He was decked out in a check cowboy shirt and purple braces, making him look like an ageing country-and-western singer. But it wasn't his curious wardrobe that first caught my attention; rather, his manic eyes and eccentric laughter, which immediately singled him out as a crank worth meeting. Our conversation got off to a poor start, as I mentioned just hearing about the Achille Lauro affair.

'You know what I think of this entire business?', Moustafa said. 'I think it is idiocy. American idiocy. Egyptian idiocy. Politics is a game for fools.'

Obviously, I wasn't going to draw Moustafa out on the subject of current affairs, so I tried a different tack—I asked him about the sort of cultural life that existed in Alexandria. This too turned out to be a mistake.

'You ask me about Egyptian culture? I say to you—*what* culture? There is no culture in Egypt. Only the belly dancer and stupid popular music. That is not culture. That is garbage.'

Sarwat—who had been listening to this exchange with malicious delight—pulled me aside for a moment and whispered, 'You must not take him too seriously. He likes to go way over the top. But ask him about classical music and he will become a saint.'

I returned to Moustafa and said two words: 'Gustav Mahler.' His reaction was volcanic.

'You like Mahler! You are a Mahlerian!' And with that, he began to boom out the closing bars of the Resurrection Symphony. 'I have given 100 lectures at the Goethe Institute on music. But when I lecture on Mahler, I don't talk about just another composer. I talk about God!'

Moustafa's adoration of Mahler led me to assume that he must be a musicologist by profession. As it turned out, he was an accountant working as a consultant to a foreign company. Classical music was his drug, however. And listening to him compare Bernard Haitink's recording of Mahler's Fifth with that of Bruno Walter, it became clear that his orientation was totally European, to the point where he admitted to feeling culturally disenfranchised in his own country.

'Under Sadat, the illiterates flourished', he said. 'They all made a lot of money and became millionaires, even though most of them could barely read. Egypt today is like a reverse pyramid. There is no pinnacle—everything is flattened.'

'Then Mahler is something of a minority taste in Egypt?', I said.

'Of course he is. Why should they care about great music when they can have the belly dancer?'

'But isn't there a symphony orchestra in Cairo?'

'Have you heard them?'

'Not yet.'

'If you do hear them', Moustafa said, 'you will quickly understand why they are *not* a symphony orchestra. They are unbelievably terrible. But what can you expect? They have a conservatory to train them in Cairo, but they only make £40 a week in the orchestra, so after performing Rachmaninov, they have to go to the nightclubs on the Pyramids Road and play music for belly dancers. Rachmaninov and belly dancers, they do not mix, you know.'

Moustafa looked at his watch and said that he had to pick up a friend who was just finishing a German class upstairs. They were planning to have lunch in Montazah Gardens, and would I care to join them? Saying goodbye to Sarwat, we went up to the main foyer of the Institute where a crowd of students were filtering out of classrooms. A pretty young woman in her twenties, her clothes and hairstyle defiantly western, waved to Moustafa from across the foyer. Her name was Nadia, but after Moustafa introduced us, she said, 'Please call me Nelly'.

We set off in Moustafa's Peugeot. As we headed towards the Corniche, he chose a cassette from a box on the dashboard, and plugged it in. A flute concerto by Vivaldi filled the car.

En route to Montazah, Nelly told me that she used to live in London. She'd gone there to perfect her English, and had managed to land a job as a secretary with a firm owned by a distant Lebanese relative. Her life seemed to be on course. She had digs in Acton Town, moving later to Putney. And even though she didn't think much of English landladies, she was nonetheless delighted with her job, her British working permit, and the freedom of being away from Egypt.

But then, Egypt intervened. She had gone to London accompanied by her two brothers, but when they returned to Alexandria and she stayed behind, her mother began to make noises. Noises about a single Egyptian girl being on her own. In London. A big foreign city. Exposed to potentially harmful outside influences. So pressure was brought to bear on her, family commitments more than mentioned, and Nelly came home.

'I was just looking at the map of the London Underground today', she said. 'I wonder if I will ever see London again.'

'Egyptian families', Moustafa said with a snort.

'Is there no chance of you going back to England?', I asked.

'I would like to,' she said, 'but my mother is now worried that I am not married. She keeps asking me when I will find someone, but I meet few Egyptian men I like.'

Moustafa later told me that Nelly could have been married several times over by now, but dreaded the straightjacket of Islamic married life. Living with someone, however, was absolutely out of the question. And I could sense her fear that, if she didn't soon meet someone who could cope with her non-traditional attitudes, the net would close in very fast.

We drove into Montazah—a lovely wooded parkland commissioned by the Khedive Abbas in 1892 as a summer resort for the Egyptian royal family. Today, one of the Khedive's palaces has been turned into a casino, and you have to pay a small admission fee to enter the gardens.

'This is still one part of Alexandria which they haven't ruined,' Nelly said.

'They ruin everything in Egypt', Moustafa said as we plunged deeper into the park.

'Are you hungry?', Nelly asked. 'Could you eat a hamburger?'

'A hamburger?'

Ahead of us, in the centre of a circular car park, was a Wimpy Bar. Nearby, a party of schoolchildren were picnicking on cheeseburgers and Cokes in the scorched grass, and playing the Egyptian Top Twenty on a ghetto blaster. Nelly went off to get our take-away lunch and Moustafa rolled up the windows of the car, using Vivaldi to drown out the number one hit from Cairo.

'These hamburgers, they do nothing for me', he said. 'But Nelly likes them. They remind her of London.'

Nelly returned to the car, and we ate our hamburgers and listened to the final moments of the flute concerto. Then we drove to an outdoor cafe fronting the sea, where we drank foamy guava juice and watched the breakers roll in. Moustafa hummed a few bars from the opening movement of Mahler's Fourth and said, 'You must come to my house. I play you Tennstedt conducting Mahler. Or Solti. Or Bernstein. And I have my cassettes of BBC music programmes. You don't know how hard it is to meet someone in Egypt who is interested in classical music.'

'You have no friends who share your interest?', I said.

'There was one man—a doctor. I had gone to him for a check-up, and what did I see in his office? A recording by the London Symphony Orchestra. So naturally, I went crazy when I saw this record, and he was so happy to meet another music fanatic that he ordered his nurse to close his surgery for the afternoon so we could listen to Shostakovich.' Moustafa laughed at the memory of this, but then shook his head. 'Last year, the doctor emigrated to France.'

Nelly said that, through Moustafa, she had begun to develop an appreciation of classical music, though Mahler was still a bit much for her to take. They had become friends while attending German classes together at the Goethe Institute, and I could see that she looked upon him as a doting uncle—a fellow outsider in their society, and someone who also identified with a world that was not Egyptian.

We finished our guava juice and headed back into the city. After saying goodbye to Nelly in front of her parents' house, we drove off and quickly found ourselves stuck in traffic. Moustafa put on a cassette of a Bach cantata and fell silent, staring out at the endless vista of cars.

'Do you know the expression, "the futility of life"?', he finally asked. 'There is Nelly—a wonderful girl, everything I look for—and I meet her thirty years too late. And everybody in Alexandria talks behind our back, says we are having an affair. They cannot understand that we can be friends without anything going on between us.'

He then told me a story of woe. It seems that Nelly was once engaged to a Swedish engineer working in Alexandria. From all accounts, they were madly in love, and he had even agreed to convert to Islam in order to marry her (though, according to Moustafa, 'religion means nothing to her'). So preparations were made, 'her dress and shoes bought', but then the engineer decided to take a little pre-nuptial holiday by himself in India. And upon arriving in Simla, he followed the time-honoured tradition of going mystic. Strange letters began to filter back to Nelly—letters which spoke about the senselessness of middle-class life and his fear of bourgeois commitments. She wrote back, but the responses she received from this transcendental Swede became infrequent and even more cryptic. Eventually, the correspondence dwindled away to nothing. Silence from Simla and a crushed Nelly in Alexandria.

'When I first met her, she was a broken person', Moustafa said. 'Crying all the time, unable to think about anything else. Now she is better, and she has all these bridegrooms knocking at her door, though she wants none of them. But I worry for her. There is this one Egyptian engineer who she thinks is okay, but nothing special. He works in Saudi Arabia, and wants her to marry him and go there. And she's thinking about it because her mother keeps telling her she must get married, and Nelly feels this pressure and thinks that this may be a way to keep her mother happy. But I tell her, if she marries this man and goes to Saudi, it will mean wearing the veil and acting like the good little Arab wife. It will be like a prison for her.'

'It sounds like a rather grim option', I said.

'Of course it is grim', Moustafa said. 'But what can a woman in Egypt do?'

* * * * *

'Don't do that', Ted Wallace said.

Don't do what?', I said.

44

'Don't cross your legs like that.'

'Why not?'

'Because', he whispered, pointing to a woman in black sitting opposite us, 'when you cross your legs like that, the sole of your shoe is pointing at that lady over there.'

'Big deal', I said.

'It's gonna be a big deal when she sees the sole of your shoe. Don't you known it's a helluva insult in Egypt to point the sole of your shoe at someone?'

'Who told you that?'

'My company. They gave us a training course in stuff like that before we came out here.'

'What else did they warn you not to do?'

'Avoid giving people the evil eye', he said. 'That's real bad news in these parts.'

'I'll keep that in mind.'

'Yeah, and while you're at it, how about uncrossing your legs before you get us into trouble.'

Ted Wallace was like that. A play-it-by-the-book man. Methodical and cautious in his approach to Egypt. Determined to get through his stint out here without pointing the sole of his shoe at anyone.

He was a Canadian from Vancouver; a systems analyst with a giant computer corporation who had been living in Egypt for just over a year. We'd met the previous afternoon in Ramleh Square. I was buying a packet of cigarettes in a kiosk when he approached me and said, 'Do you speak English?' We got chatting after that, and eventually adjourned to a nearby cafe. Over coffee, he explained that he wasn't in the habit of approaching strangers and asking them if they spoke English, but his company had just transferred him from Cairo to Alexandria, and he and his Scottish wife had few friends in the city. By the time the bill arrived, I had an invitation to dinner at his flat the following night.

And so, here we were, sitting together on a tram, heading out to the residential district where he lived. To get Ted off the subject of the soles of my shoes, I asked him how a chap from Vancouver had come to marry a woman from Scotland. His answer sounded like an instruction manual in courtship.

'Well, I was studying computer science at the University of British Columbia, and I was sharing this apartment with this guy, and one night he said, "You want to go to a party?" And I said, "Sure". And then he said, "You mind if I bring this girl along?" And I said, "Okay by me". And then he said, "This girl's got a friend—an exchange student from Scotland. Mind if I bring her along too?" And I said, "Sounds good". And that girl—the exchange student from Scotland—was Angela. So we went to the party, and we danced and talked. And at the end of the night, I said, "Can I see you again?" And she said, "Yes". So we saw each other again, and again after that, and pretty soon it became a love relationship, and about a year after that, we got married.'

Not exactly romance at its most passionate. Then again, passion was not one of Ted's strong points. He was the new breed of expatriate who lived in Egypt—the technological emissary from the West. Unlike the past generation of foreigners who had come to Alexandria in search of sensual pleasures, the city held little attraction for him. His was the world of microchips and solid-state circuitry, and listening to him speak about his home-life and his two-year contract in Egypt, I got the impression that he saw his life as a complex software system he was determined to master.

From the moment we entered his flat, however, it became apparent that Ted wasn't interfacing too successfully on the marital front. Angela was twenty-three, from Morningside in Edinburgh; a one-time Scottish rose, now thin and brittle, with a ferocious cigarette habit. She gave Ted a perfunctory peck on the check, and then reached for a packet of Benson and Hedges.

'Whatcha up to, honey?', he asked her after introducing us.

'Making carrot juice', she said flatly.

'Hey Doug, come on into the kitchen. Got to show you this nifty little gadget I just bought.'

On the kitchen counter sat a high-speed juice extractor that looked like it ran on nuclear fuel, and basically atomized any fruit or vegetable you subjected to it.

'Bought this to beat the high price of fruit juice in Egypt', Ted said. 'I mean, they're asking four bucks for a quart of fresh O.J. in the local grocery store, so I figured there's gotta be a better way of getting my daily dose of Vitamin C. Which is why I bought this baby. Best juice extractor on the market. Only problem is, you got to be real careful about washing the fruit, since everything that's grown out here is fertilized with human shit. Which means you first gotta wash the fruit in potassium concentrate, then soak it in fresh water. Isn't that right, honey?'

'Tell me about it', Angela said. 'I've just spent two hours treating these carrots.'

'Yeah, and you're using the wrong carrots as well.'

'What?', Angela said.

'You're using *small* carrots', Ted said, and then turned to me. 'I keep telling her, don't use small carrots—use large ones. But *she* never listens.'

Angela smiled thinly and lit a fresh cigarette.

'How 'bout getting Doug a drink?', Ted said. We adjourned to the sitting room, and Angela brought out a tray of salads and hors d'oeuvres, as well as a bottle of vodka, a bottle of Scotch, and a pitcher of carrot juice. She poured a large Scotch for me, and then mixed herself a vodka and carrot juice. Ted restricted himself to water.

'If you need anything else, Doug, just ask and she'll get it for you.'

Ted had this habit of referring to his wife as *she*. When Angela mentioned that they used to live in an outlying suburb of Cairo called Heliopolis he said, 'Yeah, but *she* didn't like it out there.'

'That's not true', Angela said. 'What I didn't like was the women's club you suggested I go to.'

'But it was something for you to do.'

'Sitting around with a group of unhappy women from Britain and America, talking about how they hate Egypt, telling stories about their maids, planning to raise money for some silly charity . . .'

'Hey', Ted interrupted, 'what's wrong with raising money for charity?'

'It is boring.'

'Well, you're one to talk. I mean, what do you think your work is? Nothing but paid charity.'

I winced. Angela stared at her husband coolly and stubbed out her cigarette. 'I know you don't think giving grinds in English is much of a job', she said. 'And I also know that you think the pay is nothing. But, at least, it is a job—a job which *I* found myself. A job which I happen to enjoy.'

Ted quickly backpedalled. 'Look honey', he said, trying to sound conciliatory, 'I know how hard you worked to find that job, and I mean, I think, even though it's just a part-time job, it's terrific. Just terrific. But all I was saying is that you shouldn't knock those women in Heliopolis, I mean, if you had your way, you could just as easily be sitting at home, doing nothing.'

'But I don't sit at home', Angela said, the anger now showing.

'I'm not saying you sit at home. What I'm trying to say is that those women in Heliopolis aren't sitting around either. They're doing something.'

'You call their amateur drama group "doing something"?'

'I see nothing wrong with amateur dramatics in Egypt', Ted said.

Angela poured herself another vodka and carrot juice and reached again for the packet of Benson and Hedges. I tried to shift the conversation by asking if they'd got to know any of the foreign community in Alexandria.

'I've basically met teachers', Angela said, 'and the usual foreign engineers, though I can't say I take much to them. They're usually out here without wives or girlfriends, so they're always on the make. And they're also known to every prostitute in Alex. And if they don't go to prostitutes, they chase any expat women they see. The other night I was at this party and I asked this English engineer where I could learn Arabic. And he said, "I'll give you my room number"'.

Ted suddenly sat up. 'Hey, thanks for telling me. I mean, this is the first time I heard about it.'

I excused myself and went to the loo. When I returned a few minutes later, I overheard Angela saying, 'Don't tell me you're jealous again?'

More drinks were poured, and Ted kept talking about 'the guys who chase my wife'.

'There was this Egyptian photographer who worked for this sleazy society magazine in Cairo. He took a real shine to Angela and started plaguing her. Kept coming over to our flat. Bought her this negligee which he asked her to model for him. Even started calling me up at the office, asking me where my wife was.'

'He was just a child, Ted.'

'We finally shook him by moving. Twice.'

'All Egyptian men are children when it comes to foreign women', Angela said.

Around eleven, Ted looked at his watch and said that it was his bedtime. 'I get up to work every morning at 5.30, so I'm not too big on late nights', he explained. 'But don't let me break up the party. And if you want to spend the night, we've got a spare bedroom. *She'll* give you sheets and stuff.'

He went off without saying goodnight to Angela. When he closed the bedroom door behind him, she exhaled loudly.

'He's so bloody protective', she said. 'And now he's all worried about anti-American reaction after what Reagan did.'

'Why should he worry about that?', I said. 'He's Canadian.'

'He thinks he'll be mistaken for an American.'

Another large vodka and carrot juice was poured. Another cigarette lit.

'I keep thinking, maybe I should move out, find my own place here. I've decided I don't really believe in marriage anymore.'

'You must have believed in it at one time.'

'I was twenty then. In Vancouver on this student exchange programme. And Ted was the first person I met who ever took a relationship with me seriously. So when my year was up, and I had to go back to Edinburgh, marriage seemed like a practical decision. Ted could work in Britain, we could travel together a lot easier . . . But then, after six months, he got this job out here, so he went off to Egypt and I stayed behind to finish my degree.'

'How long were you apart?'

'A year. I only joined him here ten weeks ago.'

She drained her glass and lifted the vodka bottle. It was dead, so she switched to Scotch. And said that three weeks after Ted left for Cairo, she began to feel lonely. So lonely, in fact, that she sought out company. But when Ted paid her a surprise visit in Edinburgh three months later, and she gave him a run down on her extracurricular activities, he became volatile. 'I told him about the other men because I don't believe in hiding things. But it got very destructive between us after that.'

However, they did manage to patch things up before he returned to Egypt. But then, four months later, 'I met this man in Bucharest Airport.'

'You met a Romanian?', I said.

'He was English. I was coming out to Egypt to meet Ted, and had gotten this cheap flight on Romanian Airlines, which meant I had a stop over in Bucharest. And that's where I got talking to the English chap who was waiting for the same flight to Cairo. So we sat together on the plane, and before we landed, he asked me for my phone number. When I got back to England, he called me up, said he was coming to Edinburgh on business, asked if we could meet for a drink.' She took a large gulp of Scotch. 'It happened after that.'

It was like getting drunk with an expatriate Madame Bovary. And when she began to talk about a marriage counselling session that Ted had dragged her to in Cairo, I pleaded exhaustion and asked to be shown the spare bedroom.

'You're tired?', she said, the words slurring.

'Dead tired', I said.

'Not as tired as me', she said bleakly. 'You can't be as bloody tired as me.'

I slept badly that night, and woke vowing never to touch Scotch again. Ted and Angela had already gone off to work, but left me a note telling me where I could find the instant coffee. I made myself a cup of weak Nescafé, turned on their radio, and tuned into the BBC World Service. As I listened to the news headlines, I peered through the window and saw a market in full swing outside. And I thought: expatriate life in Egypt is like this. London crackling on a wireless inside a luxury flat; two men beheading a chicken in the street below. Downing my coffee, I scribbled a thank you note and headed out, rejoining Alexandria as it went about the business of its day.

* * * * *

'Do you know what the perfect Egyptian short story is?', Said Salem said. 'It is only eight words long, and it goes like this: "Oh my God. I'm pregnant. Who's the father?"' Said grinned at me. 'Do you understand its meaning?'

'Not exactly', I said.

'Okay, I explain it to you. "Oh my God"—*religion.* "I'm pregnant"—*sex.* "Who's the father?"—*the unknown.* You see— the perfect Egyptian short story. It has everything.'

We were sitting in Moustafa's flat, drinking tea. Said was a friend of Moustafa's; a short story writer and novelist, considered by many to be one of the better practitioners of his craft in Egypt today.

'Do you know what they tell me in Cairo?', Said said. 'They say, "Said, you are one of our best young writers; a promising talent." I am 49 years old, and have written seven novels and five short story collections, and in Cairo they still call me a young writer. And do you know why? Because I live in Alexandria. If you want to be a big writer in Egypt, you have to live in the capital. If you live in Alexandria, you are considered provincial.'

It was a familiar sounding lament, and one which I had frequently heard among writers in Dublin—that same frustra-tion which comes from being an established man of letters in a parochial city, and a mere fledging in the literary jungle of the Big Smoke. Alexandria was Said's home and he didn't want to leave it, but he knew that Cairo was the place where you made your reputation as a writer in the Middle East. Or, at least, it used to be a place where writers were taken seriously. Nowadays, however, Said often wondered whether people even read books in Egypt any more.

'There are three major problems facing a writer in this country now', he said. 'The first is that 70 per cent of the population is illiterate. That leaves 30 per cent, of which only 10 per cent would think about sitting down with a book. This means we are writing for a very small segment of the population. So our audience is terribly limited.

'The second problem is the television invasion. The people who may have read in the past now sit at home and watch the pictures on the television. I listen to young people on the tram — they talk about pop songs and football matches, but you never see anyone on the tram with a book. We have become a nation of non-readers.

'The third problem is publishing. There is a state publishing house in Cairo and a few private ones, but all they are interested in is money. So it is very hard to find a publisher who will take a chance on a writer, especially if he is young. This means an Egyptian writer cannot only work as a writer. I work as a chemical engineer. Yusuf Idriss — our best short story writer — is a journalist. Naguib Mahfouz — our greatest novelist — was a civil servant. Even the best writers in Egypt cannot live without a job.'

Moustafa interrupted Said, and suggested that we move on to a restaurant near the souk. But before we left he made a point of showing me his book collection — a curious assortment of old American, French, and British editions, most of which he bought cheaply after Nasser ordered the foreign community out of Alexandria in 1956, and the city's second hand bookstores suddenly did bonanza business. Then, opening a small cabinet, he pulled out four thick bundles of paper and handed them to me with great ceremony.

'My life's work', Moustafa said.

'A novel?', I said.

'A dictionary. The first dictionary of classical music ever written in Arabic. I have spent years working on this encyclopaedia, and I die a happy man if it is published.'

The manuscript already ran to 700 pages and had been hand-written in beautiful calligraphy. Every subject was listed in English, with a follow-up description of the composer's life and works written in flowing Arabic script. Moustafa had evidently set out to create his own version of Grove's *Dictionary of Music and Musicians* for the Arab world, and looking at that vast stack of paper, I didn't know whether to be overwhelmed by the monumental research that had gone into assembling such a volume, or to shake my head at the sheer folly of the enterprise. Moustafa also seemed to be riddled with doubt about his achievement.

'It has taken me six years to write this', he said. 'But sometimes I say to myself, "You are crazy to be doing this. Nobody in Egypt, nobody in the Middle East wants to know about classical music. No publisher in Cairo will ever be interested."'

'*Inshallah*, you will find a publisher', Said said.

'Allah is not interested in Gustav Mahler', Moustafa said.

Moustafa chose Mahler's Second Symphony as the background music for our drive to the restaurant. Half-way there, Said handed me a photocopy of a recent story of his that had been published in *October Magazine*, Egypt's most prestigious current affairs and literary journal. He had translated it himself, and though the English used was often flat and ungrammatical, the implications of the story were unmistakably clear.

Emigrant to Sky is a fantasy, in which an astonishing creature named Clod—part human, part extra-worldly phenomenon—appears 'in an unknown spot in our spherical land', manifesting many of 'the human characteristics that were prevalent before the beginning of this century'. His first port-of-call is a factory, where the workers are surprised to discover this huge giant playing with the buttons of their machines. A foreman approaches Clod and says, 'What are you doing here, you idiot? Who are you?' Clod responds by pushing the foreman right into the heart of the rotating machine. The workers look on with open mouths, but nobody tries to save the foreman, and instead make excuses for their lack of action. Clod stares at the men 'with a despairing ironical look, full of scorn' and stops the machine. The foreman tumbles out unscathed and the workers congratulate him on his narrow escape from death.

'Poor men', Clod says and leaves.

Clod appears next at a church, where he disturbs a priest during his sermon.

'What are you doing?', Clod asks.

'Preaching to people', the priest says.

'Look at them carefully. Most of them are sleeping, and the rest are chattering.'

'They have been doing that, sir, for tens of years.'

'Then why are you talking to yourself?'

'Doing my duty, fulfilling my job.'

'You are blowing into the air', Clod says.

'Have you any alternative?', the priest asks.

That same day, Clod stops by a mosque where he confronts a sheikh with similar questions about his congregation's lack of interest, but the sheikh is also at a loss for answers. Then, he moves on to visit a district governor who is about to seduce a woman in his extravagant palace. Clod breaks into the bedroom and the governor, outraged, threatens to arrest him. But before he can call the police, Clod vanishes. News of this event spreads throughout the community, as people whisper about the scandalous behaviour of the governor. Yet, when he appears shortly thereafter at a public ceremony, his people mob him, shouting, 'Long live our great governor!'

Clod, however, didn't simply vanish from the governor's palace—he actually flew away. And the police investigating this incident find a coat he left behind, in which there is a note that reads, 'Everything here in this country restricts you, Clod. Why don't you fly?'

Eventually, Clod drops back to earth and, returning to the palace, he talks his way into the bed of the governor's wife. But her hysterical cries at the moment of climax draws a crowd to the palace, and they set upon Clod, brutally beating him. He manages to break away, and turning back to the crowd, he shouts, 'People . . . do not wait for new prophets!' Then, he disappears.

A few days later, a corpse of a giant is found, and though a team of doctors confirm that it is Clod's body, other members of the community report seeing him hovering in the sky above. A new man is appointed governor of the district, and his first action is to pass a law prohibiting the citizens from talking about Clod—a law that is punishable by death. And nothing is heard of Clod again.

Though veiled in fantasy, it was not difficult to see the contemporary significance of Said's story. A mythic figure, embodying the values of Egypt's recent past, journeys through the hypocrisy of the nation today; a country where religion is a sham, politicians are unscrupulous, and the vast majority of people are complacent and ineffectual. Said's Egypt was morally bankrupt: 'Don't wait for new prophets!', Clod shouts back to the mob that is trying to kill him. Look around you. See the hollowness of your faith. See the venality of your leaders. See the way you sit back and allow a corrupt system to perpetuate itself. See the ethical wasteland of your country.

Said seemed pleased with my reaction to the story. 'Yes, I agree with you', he said. 'It is a bleak picture I show of Egypt.'

'But a true picture,' Moustafa said. 'This country is a catastrophe.'

Said smiled indulgently at his friend. 'Would you live any-where else?', he asked.

Moustafa fell silent for a moment and then reluctantly said, 'I suppose not.'

'You see', Said said. 'We all fear for Egypt. We all fear for the future. And yet we would not live anywhere else. It is a crazy relationship to have with your country.'

'And you'll always stay in Alexandria?', I said.

'I think about leaving sometimes', Said said. 'And Yusuf Idriss—the short story writer—he keeps saying, "Come to Cairo, work for a newspaper, and then you will become a famous writer." But I cannot take Cairo. The crowds, the noise, it is too much. Of course, Alexandria is getting just as bad. Once we were a nice small city. Now we are three million and becoming a madhouse. Still, it is home to me, so I stay.'

'What would you miss most about Alex if you ever moved away?', I asked.

'The sea. And the stories. Alexandria is a city of stories. Have you heard many stories while you've been here?'

'Too many stories. It will be hard to leave.'

'Then don't go', Said said. 'Stay for a while.'

It was an inviting proposition. Alexandria—that sepia photo-graph of a city—had its attractions. There was something com-fortable about its seediness, and once you saw through its bogus myths, it encouraged you to linger for a while and discover your own capacity for idleness. I could have easily set up residence in the New Capri, squandered mornings in the Athineos cafe, listened to Mahler in Moustafa's flat, dropped in on Sarwat's weekly salon, and happily surrendered to sloth. That was the hidden danger of Alexandria: its languid temperament thwarted ambition or the desire to move on. It was a metropolis still suffering from the effects of a massive historical hangover and, like someone facing up to the morning after a binge, it often tried to convince itself it wasn't the person it was the night before. It called itself an Egyptian city and yet its entire cityscape turned its back on the rest of the nation and looked only towards the sea. To stay here would be to hanker after a world north of here; a world which Alexandria deemed itself to be a part of, but secretly knew it had been banished from. And having just arrived from that world, I needed to turn my gaze away from it and look to the desert.

So I told Said that I would be leaving Alexandria the next day.

'You will be back', he said. 'And Alexandria will still be here. It is always here. And do you know why it is always here? Because it has stories. As long as Alexandria has stories, it lives.'

Chapter Three
Militarized Zones

THE BUS CONDUCTOR had an interesting command of English. He spoke the language in a rapid series of exclamation marks.

'You want to go Mersa Matruth! No problem! Four hours with bus, no more! You go to Siwa tomorrow! No problem! Five hours with bus, no more!'

His colleague, the driver, was young and dangerous. He had a thing about oil tankers. Every time he saw one ahead of him on the road, he would put his foot to the floor, and send the bus hurtling towards it. Then, with only seconds to spare before a major accident, he would screech to a halt and gently kiss the tanker's rear bumper. This was not a sign of affection; this was a signal for the tanker to get out of our way.

I had been assigned a front seat on the bus and therefore had a clear, unimpeded view of the driver in action. I also had a clear, unimpeded view of the windscreen, and quickly noticed that there was nothing to stop me flying into that wide expanse of plate glass should the driver fail to brake the next time we met an oil tanker. Grabbing the armrest of my seat, I held on, watching my knuckles turn white.

We slipped through the outskirts of Alexandria and entered an industrial landscape dotted with petroleum refineries. After our first encounter with an oil tanker, the driver put on a cassette of inspiring selections from the Koran. 'In the name of Allah . . .' sang the sheikh on the recording. Up ahead of us was a fork in the road, but as we began to pass it by, the driver suddenly changed direction and veered to the right so sharply that the wheels on the left side of the bus lifted off the tarmac for a few dreadful seconds. 'In the name of Allah, the Compassionate, the Merciful', the sheikh sang on.

The refineries disappeared, and after shooting across a plain of scrubby vegetation, the desert began to envelop us. The sea—a constant point of reference on the right side of the road—faded from view and soon there was nothing but buff-coloured sand everywhere.

Another oil tanker was gently kissed on the bumper as the driver cranked up the engine to 130 km per hour. He kept this speed up for the remainder of the journey, slowing down only once to inspect the scene of a recent accident, in which a bus and a tractor had greeted each other head-on. It was not a pretty sight.

'That happen yesterday!' the bus conductor shouted over to me. 'Three people dead!' My knuckles turned whiter.

The sun bled away, and as night crept in, the driver gave us a further demonstration of his mettle behind the wheel by failing to turn on his headlights. It was a curious sensation, barrelling down a desert highway without illumination; a bit like flying blind. Fortunately, the road was free of traffic for a while, but then I saw two beacons of light approaching us. At this point, the driver turned pathological. Rather than flick on his lights and warn the other vehicle that we were on a direct collision course, he kept speeding towards it in the dark. The oncoming car began to blast its horn in panic, but our driver took no notice of this and continued to pump the accelerator. I was about to duck under my seat when, suddenly, there was a white-hot flash of light as the high-beams of the bus blinded the other driver. He swerved madly to avoid us and skidded straight into an embankment of sand. The bus driver was delighted with himself. He grinned wildly in triumph and, turning off his headlights, continued the journey in the dark.

My fellow passengers took this incident in their stride. For them, it was just another trip to Mersa Matruth, and there was nothing unusual in having a kamikaze pilot as a driver. But I found little comfort in their stoicism, and was greatly relieved when we passed through a military checkpoint and saw the promising glow of street lights in the distance.

At first sight, Mersa Matruth was a large village of reinforced concrete and dusty streets; a market town with one main drag and little else. At second sight, it still looked like a market town with one main street and little else. And yet, after the cosmopolitan veneer of Alexandria, there was something refreshingly no-nonsense about Mersa Matruth. It was a backwater and made no apologies for it; a sleepy community of dry-goods shops vegetable stalls, and sandy streets, positioned on the edge of the Western Desert.

In summer, Matruth is a seaside resort; a down-market alternative to Alexandria's Corniche. Historically, it began life as a port during the time of Alexander the Great, but later became known as a holiday spot after Cleopatra dragged Caesar here for a few dirty weekends. More recently, Nasser used Matruth as a place to unwind from the pressures of building a socialist Egypt, and his photograph still hangs in many shops and cafes along the main street. But perhaps Matruth's best known visitor was Field Marshall Erwin Rommel. During the Desert War, Rommel rented a cave on the eastern edge of town in which he mapped out the battle of Tobruk. Today, his cave is a museum and the local citizenry have honoured his memory by naming a cheap hotel after him.

I took a room in the Rommel House Hotel. Ten Egyptian pounds bought me a clean bed and a loo that stank of blocked sewage. Dropping off my bag, I wandered back outside and watched as a convoy of Army jeeps bumped along the unpaved road. Two soldiers were on guard duty near the hotel, and as I walked towards the main street, I noticed the radar dishes and hi-tech antennae that loomed above the town's anthill skyline. It was a reminder that Libya was near. So near, in fact, that Matruth was now almost a garrison; a major military command post guarding Egypt's western front. Drive three hours along the coast and you end up at the border; a border that has been closed for years. Around Mersa Matruth, security was tight. You couldn't get in or out of town without passing through an elaborate system of checkpoints, and much of the surrounding region was off-limits to non-military personnel. Even walking on certain sensitive areas of the beach could get you into trouble because Col. Qaddafi was just 220km down the road and the Egyptian Army was taking no chances. To them, Mersa Matruth was their Fort Apache—a frontier outpost on the fringes of Injun country.

Along Alexandria Street, however, the threat from Tripoli seemed far away. It was the off-season, and Matruth was shuttered and enjoying its autumnal dissipation. A few cafes were open for business, the occasional Beduoin pushed a donkey cart along the road, and all the shopowners had their televisions tuned to the latest instalment of an Egyptian soap opera. Even Theo didn't seem to mind the lack of business. When I poked my head inside his Greek taverna and asked if he was serving dinner, he shrugged his shoulders and said, 'Okay, I find something for you.'

Theo was a Greco-Egyptian; a squat man dressed in a Nasserite safari suit and permanently perched on top of a high stool in front of a Victorian writing table. It made him look like a Dickensian character stranded on the Mediterranean.

'What you want? Fish? That's what I have, so that's what you eat. Okay?'

As Theo was giving me the run-down on his menu, another man entered the taverna and greeted him amiably.

'*As salam alaikoom* ya sonofabitch. How ya doin', Theo baby?'

American. I looked over at him. 'Well don't just stare at me, fella', he said. 'Come over here and join me in a brew.'

I sat down at his table and he proffered his hand. 'Jack Bradshaw. Listen, ya gotta excuse me if I sound a bit outta it, but I've been drinkin' all fuckin' day.'

Another American entered the taverna. He wore coke-bottle glasses and appeared to have had a football implanted in his stomach.

'Hank man, what is this shit about you ridin' a donkey?', Jack said.

'I tole you, boy, I's gonna take a donkey for a ride before I go', Hank said.

'Hank on a fuckin' donkey. Too fuckin' much. You watch your ass on that mule, ya got me?'

Hank staggered out to look for his donkey. 'That guy', Jack said, 'he works for an oil company in Houston-goddamn-Texas. Out here doin' some surveyin' for them, and tomorrow he's goin' back to Cairo, so tonight he's gotta ride a donkey. Un-fuckin'-believable, huh?' Two bottles of Stella Artois arrived at the table. 'Whatcha say your name was, kid?'

Jack was a civil engineer working in Mersa Matruth on a project for a company based in Colorado. He was an old overseas hand, and had done time in Iran, Vietnam, Malaysia, Saudi Arabia, and the Sudan. Backwaters were his speciality, and he always volunteered for assignments in obscure and exacting places.

'I spent a couple of months workin' on a project in the asshole of the Sudan. Lived with the fuzzy-wuzzy in the goddamn bush. No running water. No place to take a shit. Nothing. Best time of my life. Fantastic people, the Sudanese. Really the best goddamn people you'll meet anywhere. But Christ, that place is so screwed up now with all that Islamic stuff. It's a goddamn tragedy.'

Mersa Matruth appealed to him. 'Quiet kind of a place, which is okay by me. But listen, after all those months with the fuzzy-wuzzy in the Sudan, this is the modern goddamn world, baby.' He lowered his voice. 'But lemme tell you something—don't trust Egyptians. Arrogant goddamn people. You hire a guy off the street, two weeks later he's tellin' you how to do your job. I mean, my company's thinkin' about investin' in this town, but the people here, they act as if they're doin' you a favour.'

Jack polished off his beer and called for two more. 'You gotta wife, kid?', he asked me.

'Yes, I'm married.'

'How many times you've been married?'

'Just the once.'

'Only married once? Shit, kid, you're a fuckin' juvenile. You wanna put somethin' in that notebook of yours', he said, tapping my journal which was now being used as a beer mat. 'I've been married six times. First wife was an American. Then a French lady. After that an Iranian. Followed that one up with a Vietnamese . . .' He paused for a moment, looking confused. 'Have I got this right? Sorry, the Vietnamese came before the Iranian. Then, after the Iranian, there was another Vietnamese. And now I'm hitched up to a Malay—that's what you call a broad who's from Malaysia.'

He took out his wallet and showed me a photograph of his wife and newborn son. 'My first kid.' he said.

'Only your first? I'm surprised.'

'You weren't the only one who was surprised. Doctors told me for years I was sterile. Then I met this Malay, and after a couple of months of marriage, bam! At forty-nine fuckin' years of age, I finally got a kid.' He smiled into his bottle of Stella.

'Where are they now?', I asked.

'Kuala Lumpur. They're joinin' me here next month. She's a great lady, my wife. Don't got much education, but she's a fantastic mother.'

For the next three hours, I was treated to the world according to Jack Bradshaw. It was a disjointed, but frequently entertaining travelogue. He began in the States with a story about breaking his back while on a practice parachute jump with the Green Berets. Next, we were in Vietnam where he was working in satellite communications and managed to photograph the Tet Offensive from the top of a telecommunications mast. After that, it was off to Tehran for a dissertation on the suicidal tendencies of Iranian bus conductors. Then we jump cut to Saudi Arabia and heard a few yarns about the dangers of drunken driving in Jeddah. This was followed with a play-by-play account of flying through a sandstorm on Sudan Airlines, and then it was back to Saudi for the following story:

'I was sittin' in a coffee shop in Riyadh with this English engineer. And d'you know what that fuckhead told me? He said, "Jack, I once sat on the walls of Mecca". And d'you know what I said? "Well, pal, if you *did* sit on the walls of Mecca, then I'd like to see the bullet holes in your ass".'

It was a Cook's tour through that segment of the world where Third World professionals drift from one underdeveloped landscape to the next. Jack had been on this tropical road for twenty years, and though defiantly American, he was also stateless. America was no longer home for him ('I'll never go back—it's too goddamn dull for me'), so he now dwelled in a permanent transit lounge of malarial dorps and sunstruck hamlets, adding a bit more footage to the travelogue of his life, venturing that bit further towards the geographic end of the line.

Theo finally kicked us out at midnight. We staggered into Alexandria Street, full of beer. Jack looked at the empty dirt road that snaked its way into the desert beyond.

'You know somethin', kid?', he said. 'It ain't a bad life.'

We parted. And as I watched him walk off, I thought: in every arid town like this one on the fringes of nowhere, there will always be a Jack Bradshaw.

* * * * *

Look at a map of Egypt and force your eye away from the vertebrae of the Nile. Let it wander westwards into a region with few place-names. Towards the centre of this blank canvas, you'll discover a small constellation of dots stretching south and joined together by a thin red line. The dots are the oases of Bahariya, Farafra, Dakhla, and Kharga; the line, the tertiary road that links them back to the river. At first sight, they are the only signs of habitation in an immense sandbox of land. But if you keep moving west, you'll eventually find one more dot within that void; a dot that lies only centimetres away from the Libyan frontier. The dot stands out because of its isolation. There's nothing else around it. It floats alone in an arid wilderness, cut off from the rest of the country. It grabs your attention because it seems impossible that some form of social order could exist somewhere so solitary, so forbidding, so extreme. Can there actually be life in this place called Siwa?

I asked myself that question months earlier when I first discovered Siwa on a map of Egypt. Prior to that time, I hadn't been aware of its existence. But from the moment I saw that tiny speck of habitable land on the edge of the Western Desert, its seclusion gripped me. This was the back of beyond—a geographic dead-end—and I pored through standard texts on Egypt trying to find some information on this remote outpost in the sand.

What I initially discovered was precious little. Siwa merited a few paragraphs in most guidebooks on the country and hardly figured at all in any historical studies of Egypt. From Baedeker's *Egypt 1929* I picked up a few sketchy facts. The oasis of Siwa was once the seat of the oracle of Jupiter Ammon—one of the most famous oracles in the ancient Mediterranean world—and had been visited by Alexander the Great in 331 BC. After that, no European set foot in the oasis until 1792, and the only other information I could glean from Baedeker's was that its inhabitants were chiefly Berbers who spoke a language of their own.

I searched other books for a more detailed background to the oasis, but inevitably found myself re-reading the same potted history of Siwa. It wasn't until I reached Alexandria that I finally came across a volume which dealt entirely with Siwan society and culture. Dr Ahmed Fakhry was an Egyptian academic who wrote a three volume study of the oases of Egypt, the first of which is a treasure-trove of unorthodox information about Siwa. Reading Dr Fakhry's book was like delving into a serious historical survey which also contained the sort of lurid 'vice scandal' stories which one usually finds in the pages of a tabloid newspaper. And though the author tried to play down the more baroque aspects of Siwan morality, it was quite clear that, until very recently, Siwa was known as an oasis with *a reputation*.

Though eminent in antiquity for its famous oracle, modern Siwa came into being at the beginning of the thirteenth century. Its main settlement was a walled fortress, behind which two tribes lived in less than fraternal harmony. Perhaps the names of these two opposing fractions had something to do with their contentious relationship, as they were known as the Easterners and the Westerners. Considered now, it strikes one as ironic that East co-existed with West behind a set of walls, rather than being separated by them, as is today's geo-political practice in Europe. And even though Siwan history records a non-stop series of internal feuds between the two sides that went on until the nineteenth century, the Easterners and the Westerners did close ranks whenever their citadel came under attack by outside forces. And they shared one common characteristic: a deep-rooted suspicion of the world beyond their battlements.

This desert xenophobia, combined with the oasis's extreme seclusion, allowed the Siwans to rewrite the rule book of conventional morality. Dr Fakhry quotes a British District Commissioner of the early twentieth century who visited Siwa frequently, and had this to say about the population's code of sexual conduct: 'They are not immoral, they simply have no morals . . . they seem to consider that every vice and indulgence is lawful.' What the District Commissioner was referring to was a common practice whereby men could marry each other. King Fu'ad put a stop to the state of affairs during his visit to the oasis in 1923 (when, one imagines, he told the male Siwans, 'Boys, the party's over'), but before this time a marriage contract between two men was not considered to be an unusual legal document. The fact that the servant class of the oasis—the *Zaggalah*—were forbidden to enter into wedlock with a woman before the age of forty probably had something to do with the popularity of homosexual marriages, and gave Siwa the reputation of being the San Francisco of the Western Desert.

This libertine atmosphere, Dr Fahkry assured his readers, no longer existed today. But it wasn't just Siwa's past notoriety as an 'anything goes' playground that made me want to venture across a formidable desert to reach it. It was also the mystique of its locale. Desert outposts always have a certain romantic appeal and I was curious to find out whether this one had yet been touched by the modern state which lay beyond its sandy frontiers.

As I soon discovered, however, visiting Siwa is not an easy business. Its proximity to Libya has turned the oasis into a militarized zone, and a special travel pass must first be issued by the governate of Mersa Matruth before you are allowed to depart. However, even procuring this pass can be tricky, and I had heard a variety of conflicting reports about how long it took to obtain security clearance. Jack Bradshaw told me that he had a friend who received his permit after a six hour wait; another engineer had to cool his heels in Matruth for three days before receiving the green light. It all depended on how the bureaucracy was functioning on the day you applied for the pass, and whether current events were on your side. If Col. Qaddafi was behaving badly, if Egyptian-Libyan relations had hit a new low, you could forget about going to Siwa, as the oasis was immediately sealed off from the outside world.

The governate of Mersa Matruth is a desert Wormwood Scrubs —a Victorian bastille with stone ramparts and castelled look-out towers. A small platoon of soldiers guard its entrance, and as I approached the front gate, one of the recruits trained his rifle on me, encouraging me to walk no further.

'Permission to go to Siwa?', I said, noticing that the soldier was having difficulty finding the trigger on his gun. He didn't seem to understand what I was saying, so I repeated the question but he kept the barrel of his rifle pointed in the direction of my head. We both stood motionless, like figures in a tableau, until a young officer came out and ordered the soldier back into the compound.

'I am sorry', the officer said, approaching me, 'He is new and enthusiastic. You are here for a permit to Siwa?'

I nodded.

'Have you permission from us?', he asked.

'No—that's what I'm here to get.'

'You must obtain permission first to obtain permission from us', he said.

'But where do I get permission first to get permission from you?'

'At the place where you get permission.'

There was an awkward silence as I stared blankly at him, wondering how I always managed to get into conversations like this one.

'You do not know where to get permission first?', he finally said, the penny dropping.

'I'm new in town.'

He took out a small pad of paper, scribbled a note, and handed it to me. 'You go there to get the first permission. Then you go to the photography studio and they make a picture of your passport. And then you come back here and we give you the final permission. See—it is very simple.'

I trooped off up the road, past a rubbish tip festering in the sun. A pair of baby goats were in competition with a swarm of flies for possession of a chicken carcass and the flies seemed to be winning. Up ahead, two soldiers sat sleeping in front of a military command centre. I stepped over them and entered a small courtyard where two foreigners were loitering with intent under a palm tree.

'Siwa?', I said.

'If we ever bloody get there', one of them said in a definitive Australian accent. His name was Geoff, and he looked like a bassist in a heavy metal band; his mate, Ian, was English, shy and retiring. They both taught in a language school in Cairo and were hoping to head off to Siwa on their motorbikes that afternoon. We sat chatting in the courtyard for almost half an hour before the official in charge made an appearance. Ian, in his excellent Arabic, explained that we all wanted to go to Siwa, and the official collected our passports and disappeared. Fifteen minutes passed before the official returned with a copious set of forms that had to be filled out. This process took another half-hour, and then he disappeared again and we were brought into a small concrete bunker to continue the wait. Geoff and I both began to suffer from an attack of impatience, but Ian seemed to take this delay in his stride. Patience, as someone had told me, is a religion in Egypt, and Ian was obviously a convert.

It took a further twenty minutes for the official to return with the authorized forms. Freed from this first set of hurdles, we were now directed to a small photographer's studio which contained the only photocopying machine in Mersa Matruth. Here we each had a photocopy made of the front page of our passports, and then it was off back to the governate. This time the soldier didn't train his gun on me, but instead ushered us into a gate lodge. It was decorated with posters warning the recruits not to speak about military business in public, as sinister characters in trench coats were lurking behind every sand dune, working for Egypt's enemies. Forty more minutes elapsed while another fuctionary filled out an additional set of forms and took down details of every foreign visa in our passports. Finally, three small slips of paper were handed over, giving each of us permission to reside in the oasis of Siwa for four days. I looked at my watch. It had taken just three hours to negotiate this bureaucratic obstacle course, but I wasn't complaining. Compared to the other stories I had heard about the nightmares of obtaining a Siwan travel permit, we had been afforded express service.

Outside the governate, I wished Ian and Geoff a safe journey. Geoff gunned the motor on his bike and said, 'If you get there first, book us a room in the Hilton', and then they both bounced off down the dirt road. I returned to the Rommel House and collected my bag and walked the mile to the bus depot. It was a fenced-in breeze-block hut which looked out over an open latrine. Plastic chairs were bolted to its floor, and its only occupants were a handful of soldiers waiting for the afternoon express to the oasis.

'Where you go?', one of them asked me.

'Siwa', I said.

'You have a travel permit?', the soldier said. I showed him the slip of paper, and he seemed relieved. 'Without travel permit, they throw you off the bus in middle of desert. Desert no good. Siwa no good. Why you go to such a crazy place?'

I didn't have time to answer him as the bus pulled up in front of the depot. It was a vehicle from another era; the sort of jalopy that transported migrant farm workers through the dust-bowl during the American depression. The bus was packed with soldiers, most of whom were raw recruits heading off to do their nine month stint in the desert and not exactly looking pleased about it. All the seats were occupied, so I stood among the conscripts until an officer, dressed in an exceedingly sharp khaki uniform, ordered a private out of his seat. 'You sit here', the officer said to me. I tried to protest, but the order came again— 'You sit here.' Embarrased by this preferential treatment, I shrugged sympathetically at the soldier who had been evicted and took his place. And with a rickety jump, the bus hit the road.

We lurched through a market, dodging stray donkeys and suicidal sheep, and then came to a military checkpoint, where a soldier boarded the bus, and checked my passport and travel pass. Next to the checkpoint there was a small sign on a pitched stake which said *Siwa 285km*. In front of us, a narrow expanse of tarmac stretched into the desert—the caravan trail that Alexander the Great had once travelled. Up until the visit of King Fu'ad in 1928, it had remained a sand track and you needed at least three days to cover the distance between Matruth and the oasis. The king had promised the Siwans a proper road, but after around half of it was finished, Cairo lost interest. Decades passed, but then Col. Qaddafi set up shop in Tripoli, and within a matter of years the road to Siwa was fully paved.

The bus began to pick up speed as we pulled away from the checkpoint. Then, there was nothing. Nothing but sand. A plain of sand that travelled straight into the horizon. Its monotony was hypnotic. An empty quarter without scenic definition. No vegetation, no dunes or ridges to break up the flat landscape. Only sand and road; a jet black strip of tarmacadam that sucked us further into this limitless vacuum. We had entered outer space— the visual equivalent of infinity.

For the first hundred kilometres, we had the road to ourselves. No other vehicles, no signs of life within this chilling wasteland. Two figures suddenly appeared in the distance: a Bedouin woman and her little daughter. They stared at us as if we were emissaries from a world beyond their comprehension, and then turned away and kept walking into the void.

Halfway to Siwa, we came across the only house that stands along this ancient thoroughfare. It was a small bunker that had been turned into a squalid roadside cafe, serving tea, plates of *ful*, and dusty bottles of fizzy orange. Everyone trooped off the bus and went out into the desert to pee in the direction of Libya. After relieving myself, I was called over by the officer who had arranged for me to have a seat on the bus.

'I saw your Irish passport', he said. 'You from Belfast?'

'Dublin', I said.

'Ah, then you are not used to being in the company of soldiers, unlike someone from Belfast.'

This officer evidently knew a thing or two about Irish affairs. We introduced ourselves. Lt Col Hakim was from Alexandria; a career soldier in the Army, finishing off a three-year stint in Siwa. He had gone to university and, under his country's conscription laws, had received an immediate commission as an officer upon obtaining his degree. It was one of the disadvantages of being a graduate in Egypt. National Service was mandatory, but for anyone without third-level education, the tour of duty was considerably shorter. Officers, however, had to serve a minimum of three years, and many university students tried to have themselves down-graded to the rank of an ordinary conscript to avoid the lengthy commitment. Lt Col Hakim, on the other hand, had extended his commission after his initial three years of service and then decided upon the Army as a career. He seemed happy in his work and didn't even mind being posted in Siwa. Its isolation never ceased to fascinate him, and his years there had taught him how to do without the vicarious pleasures of urban life.

The owner of the cafe came out and presented us with a pot of mint tea and two small shot glasses. Light was beginning to recede and the tea took the edge off the desert chill. I looked out into that ceaseless sandbox and feared for anyone who would dare to hike into such emptiness. Lt Col Hakim also had similar fears. Pointing to the western horizon he said, 'You walk in that direction for 100 km, you say hello to our friend, Mr Qaddafi.'

The bus driver honked his horn and we all reboarded. The engine spluttered into something approaching life and soon we were rolling down the road for the final three hour push to Siwa. It had been an overcast day, but the sun was now putting on quite a finale. Breaking through the clouds, it managed to throw four pencil-thin beams of light on to the sand. Accompanying this heavenly floorshow was a thin wisp of cloud, scrawled across the sky like a piece of Arabic calligraphy. The soldier sitting next to me pointed up to it and said 'Beautiful yes?'

'Very beautiful', I said.

'The work of Allah.'

When night arrived, the driver broke with tradition and turned on his headlamps. None of the lights inside the bus worked, so there was nothing to do but sit there in the dark and watch the interplay of high-beams and tarmac. After two hours, I noticed the vague, lustreless outline of a distant village. A military jeep approached us, flashing its lights. The bus jerked to a halt and Lt Col Hakim got off and waved goodbye to me as he climbed into the jeep. We were now only ten kilometres outside of Siwa, but as the bus lurched closer to its destination, the light from the oasis still remained faint and imperceptible, as if hidden behind muslin. I nodded off for a few minutes, waking with a start when the driver blasted his horn and pulled up in front of a petrol pump.

I peered out of the window, but could see nothing except a purpose-built structure and a few Army vehicles. The soldiers collected their gear and disembarked, but when I tried to leave, the driver shouted, 'You sit down.' He then disappeared, and disobeying his instructions, I walked out into the road and spent quite a bit of time looking at the petrol pump and the pre-fabricated building, and wondering if this was Siwa. After twenty minutes, the driver returned, but when I asked him about finding a hotel, he ordered me back into the bus and said, 'You sit down.'

We took off again, passing through a deserted village square. The street light grew dimmer as the dirt track narrowed and the bus pushed its way through a meagre laneway. Once again, I asked the driver about the possibilities of finding a hotel, but the only response I got was, 'You sit down.'

'Where are you taking me?', I asked.

The driver said nothing. A quarter of a mile later, he braked in front of a concrete box of a building and grunted, 'You get off here.'

'But where am I?'

'Get off', he repeated, and as I stepped down from the bus, he slammed the door and drove away.

I looked around. There was a sign on the concrete box of a building that said 'Intelligence Centre', but the place was shut-tered and black. Nearby, I could see a few angular blocks of flats, but they too were without light. A soft wind began to blow, and soon my bag and my clothes were covered by a grainy cloak of sand. I stood there in the darkness, shielding my eyes against the billowing sand, and realized that I had nowhere to go. This was Siwa—the end of the road.

A hand touched my shoulder and I jumped.

'I am sorry to have scared you', a voice said in flawless English. 'Do you have your passport and travel permit for Siwa?'

I dug out the documents and handed them over.

'I do not need to see them', the voice said, 'I was just asking.'

'You mean, you're not with the military?'

'You obviously do not respect my intelligence if you think I am with the military.'

The voice stepped closer and in the moonlight I could make out the figure of a young man in his mid-twenties with a thin gold watch strapped to his wrist. Though unshaven and haggard, his accent remained clipped and up-market.

'What are you doing in such an eccentric place at this time of night?', he said.

'I've just arrived off the bus to spend a few days in Siwa', I
said. 'I *am* in Siwa, aren't I?'

'I am afraid so. May I ask you a question? Do you often do
foolish things like come to an absurd oasis in the middle of
nowhere?'

'I'm travelling around.'

'Do yourself a favour—leave on the first bus tomorrow morning. There is nothing here.'

'If there's nothing here', I said, 'then why are you here?'

'I am not here by choice, my friend.' He pointed to a landrover
parked several yards away. It had racing rally stickers pasted to
its side doors. 'I am Dr Sabry from Cairo', he said, 'and I am
taking part in the Rothman's 6,000 km motor rally through the
oases of Egypt. The man who is asleep on the ground next to the
vehicle is the driver. Our chassis broke down four days ago in the
middle of the desert, and it has taken all that time for us to reach
Siwa. We were very lucky to have made it out of the desert alive.'

Dr Sabry went on to tell me that he was a resident paediatrician
in an university hospital in Cairo ('The largest hospital in
Africa—very advanced'). He also let me know that he had little
sympathy with my desire to find a hotel.

'You will not be allowed to go into a hotel until you are first
interviewed and registered by the Intelligence Officer.' he said.

'But where is the Intelligence Officer?'

'A group of soldiers have gone off looking for him. We've been
waiting an hour so far. The electricity in this part of the oasis has
also failed, which is why we are standing in the dark and there is
no power in the Intelligence Centre.'

'Terrific', I said.

'Do you now see why coming to Siwa was not the most
intelligent decision you ever made?'. He pulled out a Cartier
lighter and a packet of Cleopatras. 'Would you like a cigarette? I
am afraid they do not sell anything but this Egyptian rubbish in
such an outpost, so I cannot offer you a Dunhill, my usual brand.'

Egyptian rubbish. The phrase stuck in my mind. To Dr Sabry,
just about everything in his homeland was rubbish. It was a
primitive 'outpost' in which he had been condemned to dwell.
He saw himself as a member of the quality who, through an
unfortunate accident of birth, had ended up a citizen of the Third
World. And to compensate for the stigma of being an Egyptian,
he had adopted what he considered to be the smart accoutre-
ments of Europe—Cartier lighters, Dunhill cigarettes ('my usual

brand'), and a classy Swiss time-piece to adorn his wrist. It was the sort of false western identity that could be purchased easily in any duty-free shop; a conscious display of posh brand names that advertised the fact that Dr Sabry was no common *fellah*, but a man of position who could hold his own in the developed world. Someone who could afford to take part in an international motor rally through the oases of Egypt. A playboy doctor now beached on the sands of Siwa, and cursing its lack of a decent hotel or a proper cigarette kiosk. And listening to him speak in his carefully polished public school voice, I realized that he was just as much a foreigner in Egypt as I was.

After finishing our inferior cigarettes, a soldier showed up and escorted me into the Intelligence Centre. We stumbled up a flight of dark stairs and entered a room lit by a kerosene lamp. Behind a desk sat a middle-aged civil servant. He was screaming into a field telephone, giving whoever was on the other end of the line a bad time. He screamed steadily for two minutes before slamming down the receiver. Then, he rifled through some papers on his desk and started screaming again. A soldier standing outside the door came barrelling into the office, and the civil servant pointed at me and screamed some more. I gather he was shouting, 'You bring this guy in here at 10 pm on a Sunday night!', but I couldn't exactly follow his machine-gun bursts of abuse. The soldier, a kid, stared at his feet, and I turned away and saw a photograph of Hosni Mubarak peering down at me. He didn't look amused.

Eventually, the screaming stopped and, with great weariness, the civil servant stood up and motioned for me to follow him. We entered an adjacent office, and soon there was more screaming as the young soldier had forgotten to bring in the kerosene lamp and we were sitting in total darkness. The lamp arrived, and the civil servant snapped his fingers and said, 'Pass'. I handed him my passport and travel documents which he scrutinized with great care. He then opened the sort of massive ledger that Bob Cratchit probably slaved over in Scrooge's office and entered in all my particulars.

'You stay four days', he said.

'No', I said, 'I'm only planning to be in Siwa for three days.'

'Pass is four days. You stay four days.'

'But I don't want to stay for four days—only three days.'

'You must stay four days.'

'The pass allows me to stay *up to* four days', I said, 'but that

71

doesn't mean I have to stay four days.'

'You stay four days', he repeated.

I tried a new line of argument. 'All right—can I stay *five* days?'

'No! Four days only.'

The kerosene lamp suddenly died and we were sitting in the dark again. Another series of screams brought back the unfortunate soldier who ransacked a shelf and managed to find a small stub of a candle. He lit it and the interview continued.

'Let me ask you something', I said. 'I have a one-month visa for Egypt. And if, say, I decided to only spend two weeks in the country, would they turn me back at Cairo Airport and insist that I stay a month?'

The civil servant thought about this for a moment and said, 'Four days'.

He picked up my passport and tossed it into a desk drawer. 'I keep', he said.

'May I go to a hotel now, please?'

'You wait.' And with that the candle died.

More abuse was hurled in the direction of the soldier, but when he couldn't get the stub lit again, the civil servant led me back into the other office. A chubby fellow now sat behind the desk. He was dressed in a starched white officer's uniform and clutched a set of worry beads in one hand. The civil servant pointed to him and said, 'Intelligence Officer'. The officer smiled and offered tea. I smiled back and explained that the civil servant and I had differing views on the length of my stay in Siwa. The civil servant went into a tirade, gesturing wildly at me, slapping his hand against his forehead, and popping a few blood vessels in the process. When he subsided, the officer twirled his worry beads and smiled at me again.

'Four days', he said.

The tea arrived and the officer insisted that I join him in a cigarette. Despite the fact that my passport had been seized and I was being temporarily detained by the military, it was nonetheless essential that I be treated as a welcomed guest. Every bureaucratic encounter in Egypt was like this—you found yourself thrown into an absurd labyrinth of rules and regulations that defied logic, and then discovered that your captors had a humane face. They didn't understand the rules of the game they were playing any more than you did, and therefore looked upon their business as an elaborate piece of theatre not to be taken seriously. Patience, as I kept learning, was the key to understanding the world of Egyptian bureacracy. Stamp your feet and scream at the *petit fonctionnaire*, and you would get nowhere. Join him in a cup of tea and a cigarette, and you might just convince him to let you leave Siwa after three days.

So I drank my glass of tea and smoked my Cleopatra and decided that it was pointless to carry on the argument any further.

'Okay', the intelligence officer said after we all finished our tea, 'you can go to hotel. I send this soldier with you, and you must come back here tomorrow at 10am to meet your guide.'

'But I don't really want a guide', I said.

'You have no choice. All foreigners in Siwa must have a guide. That is the rule.' He then shook my hand and continued playing with his worry beads. I turned to say goodbye to the civil servant, but he was already back at work, screaming into the field telephone.

The soldier escorted me down the road to the Siwa Hotel. It was the best accommodation on offer in the oasis; a flop house with two rooms, each lit by a single naked lightbulb that was used as a conference centre by mosquitoes. The rooms had bare concrete floors and were crammed with beds, most of which looked like relics from a sadistic Victorian hospital. The mattresses on the beds were stuffed with straw and covered with a soiled yellow sheet and a pestilent blanket. The washing facilities in the hotel consisted of a muddy stall with a tap and a tin bucket, and a hole in the floor that served as a loo. At one Egyptian pound a night, the Siwa Hotel was expensive.

I was thrown into a room already occupied by two French journalists: Jean-Claude Aunos and Patrick Godeau. They were both free-lancers based in Cairo, and had been resident in Siwa for a few weeks working on a story about oasis life. Jean-Claude—a photo-journalist, dressed for Beirut in war correspondent fatigues and a field vest—was heading back to Alexandria in the morning, while Patrick was hanging on until the end of October, finishing research for his feature. Together, we shared cigarettes, bottled water, and stories about the Siwan bureaucracy at work. They both knew the screaming civil servant in the Intelligence Centre—*un imbecile*, according to Jean-Claude— and advised me not to mention that I was a writer when speaking to anyone in the military, as foreign journalists weren't allowed to visit the oasis without obtaining special permission from the International Press Centre in Cairo. I dreaded to think how the civil servant might react if he discovered that I was in Siwa under false pretences.

The light bulb in the room began to dim, and Patrick mentioned that power failures were a standard feature of the Siwan day. In fact, the oasis had so few generators that it did without electricity until after sunset. This lack of daytime power created a few problems, especially when a football match was being broadcast on television. Just last week, an emergency generator had to be hooked up to a television set in the town square so the locals wouldn't miss an afternoon game broadcast live from Cairo.

'You mean, they actually have television in Siwa?', I said.

'Television has only been here for six months', Patrick said. 'There are, perhaps, three sets in all of Siwa.'

Television on the edge of nowhere. In an oasis where the electricity only functioned for ten hours a day, and intelligence officers worked by kerosene lamps. Nothing made sense in Siwa. Here, in Egypt's last frontier, the eccentric was commonplace. Beduoin watched football matches and civil servants insisted that you serve out the entire sentence of your travel pass. Where was the logic to the place?

'Logic in Siwa?', Jean-Claude said. '*Pas possible*. Siwa defies logic.'

With that, the light bulb faded away into blackness. Siwa had shut down for the night.

* * * * *

I didn't sleep that night. The blanket on my bed was a playground for bugs, and the smoke from Patrick's mosquito coil failed to stop the insects from launching an air raid on my body. Around 6am, Jean-Claude went off to catch the dawn express to Alexandria, and I lay fully clothed in bed listening to a muezzin chanting the daybreak prayers atop the minaret of a nearby mosque. An hour went by. Then, I decided to brave the shower.

The shower was a concrete chamber with a tap and a corroded tin bucket. Adjoining this cell was the hole-in-the-floor loo, and the only way to cope with the breathtaking aroma of human faeces was by puffing madly on a cigarette while washing. I stripped off quickly, lit a Cleopatra and enveloped my head with smoke as I waited for the bucket to fill. Then, balancing the cigarette on a nearby ledge, I dumped the ice-cold water over me, put the cigarette back into my mouth, and continued to smoke feverishly while soaping up. I repeated this process to get through the agony of rinsing off, and dashed back to the room dripping wet. Patrick was awake and gave me a deadpan smile.

'Did you enjoy the shower?', he said.

After dressing, we set off on his motorcycle in search of breakfast. The town of Siwa is actually two towns: a market area spread across two medinas, and the ruins of an ancient city, built in the style of a demented folly. The main square of the market contained a few dry goods shops, a butcher's, two cafes, and a hole-in-the-wall from which a barber conducted business. At this hour, the square was deserted and the village had a look of an impermanent film set—something a production company threw up in a hurry and then left behind them when it moved on to the next location.

We parked in front of a cafe, and breakfasted on *ful* and mint tea at makeshift tables. Halfway through the meal, a young tough approached us. His face was pockmarked and dour, and he spoke to Patrick in rapid-fire Arabic.

'He says his name is Abu', Patrick said, 'and has been sent from the Intelligence Centre to give you the tour of Siwa.' Abu stared at me sullenly, and I realized that I had seen his face before in countless French gangster films. He was the minor hood in every Belmondo movie; the guy who ran errands for The Boss and beat up prostitutes on the quays in Marseilles. Patrick had a similar opinion of Abu. As we stood up to settle the bill, he whispered to me, 'He is not a guide. He is really with the secret police, so be careful what you say to him.'

Patrick left us, and Abu informed me of our itinerary for the morning. 'First we go to the old city. Then the mountain. Then the temple. Then Cleopatra's pool. This is the tour.' His enthusiasm was overwhelming.

We strolled over to the old city. This was the medieval fortress founded in 1203 by the local families of the oasis to ward off hostile Bedouin from the wrong side of the desert. The elder Siwan leaders—*the agwad*—decreed that all new houses had to be built within the walls of the town, and forbade women to leave its ramparts. This siege mentality posed a few town planning problems. When the population of Siwa began to expand, the accommodation situation within the garrison became critical. Naturally, the obvious solution was to build beyond the walls of the town, but the *agwad* were dead-set against the development of any outlying suburbs. So, to meet the demand for new housing, they hit upon a novel idea for 1203 AD: high-rise architecture. Like the city planners in Manhattan and Hong Kong centuries later, they realized that, given their small geographic confines, there was nowhere to go but up. And an order went out to every Siwan family to add an additional floor to their houses as the need arose. If, therefore, your son got married and brought his wife to live with you, it was time to call in the builders. Similarly, if your daughter in-law had twins, that meant raising the roof a little higher.

By all accounts, it was a successful venture in tower block living; that is, as long as it didn't rain. Rain was bad news in medieval Siwa because it had the tendency to melt down the entire city. This was due to a suspect building material called *karshif*—a form of mud derived from soil that had been heavily saturated with salt. Once dried, it became the medieval version of concrete. If subjected to prolonged rainfall, however, the salt in the *karshif* would melt with the result that much of the town became one big mudslide. Of course, the Siwans gambled on the fact that it wasn't supposed to rain in the middle of a desert, yet history recorded several occasions when a freak downpour eroded the skyline within a matter of hours.

The Siwans lived behind their walls for over six hundred years. Then, in 1820, the troops of Muhammed Ali conquered the oasis and offered the *agwad* a deal—you bow to Cairo rule, we'll offer you protection against the marauding Bedouin. Six years and several battles later, the Bedouin threat was finally eliminated, and the *agwad* began to allow their people the right to live outside the fortress. Gradually, a new town developed, and a few sporadic showers over the next hundred or so years turned the one-time garrison into a crumbling Tower of Babel that had outserved its usefulness.

Abu and I scrambled up a slag-heap of broken stone and dry powdery rock to reach the summit of this mud castle. From the top, the entire sweep of the oasis could be seen: lush palmy vegetation, a great salt lake, patches of shimmering spring water, and then the bare gritty carpet of the desert beyond. Keeping up my front as a tourist, I aimed my camera at a low-lying ridge of granite hills dotted with telecommunications masts. Abu immediately put his hand in front of the lens and said, 'Please not that mountain. It is against regulations.'

Abu took his job seriously. Siwa was a sensitive area. There were things to be kept from public view. No visitor could be trusted. They had to be guided around and watched carefully. Perhaps it wasn't just fear of Libya that made the military so conscious of security. Perhaps they too were affected by the secretive nature of the oasis itself. Standing atop this derelict mud castle gave one an interesting perspective on Siwa's traditional sensitivity to the outside world. Encircled by an inhospitable landscape, threatened by nomadic tribes, the medieval Siwans created an island within their island, and locked themselves behind their fortifications. Seclusion breeds insularity, and Siwa shut itself off from conventional morality and created its own social order. Even when they finally had to accede to rule from without, they still shrouded themselves behind a clandestine veil. Now the Army and the intelligence services had arrived to shield the Siwans from another external threat. With them had come telecommunications and the sophisticated hardware of war. The island was an armed camp once again, suspicious and distrustful of any stranger who knocked on the gates of its fortress. It was as if the military was repeating Siwan history and creating their own bulwark against a hostile world. Perhaps Siwa had that effect on anyone who came to dwell here—its isolation turned you inward and made you fear what lurked outside its borders in that boundless plateau of sand.

Abu only seemed to fear one thing—the direction in which my camera was pointed. As we descended through the rubble of the castle, we came across a few families who still lived in mud houses at the foot of the city. I raised my camera to snap a young Siwan girl milking a goat, but before I even peered through the viewfinder Abu ordered me to stop. 'I am sorry, but this is not allowed', he said. 'Military regulations forbid this.'

'Why would the military worry about me taking a picture of a girl milking a goat?', I said.

'That is the rules, my friend.' I put the camera away, and decided not to turn myself into a security risk by photographing any more milkmaids.

We crossed through the main square of the town, and passed by a school where the students were lined up in military formation. A master stood in the middle of the yard, barking orders. The students came to attention and, on command, began to stamp their feet, shouting *Misr!, Misr!,* ('Egypt, Egypt'). Then, they executed a crisp right-face and marched back into their classrooms. Even at the age of eight, the Siwan elders of tomorrow were being trained to defend the realm.

A car was supposed to be available at the local ministry to take us to the Temple of the Oracle but after wandering through a maze of offices where desert bureaucrats sat behind desks piled with dusty paperwork, Abu couldn't find the driver. So, we went back to the market and after haggling with a young boy—barefooted, dressed in a *galabiya,* and a shrewd operator when it came to agreeing on a price—we engaged his donkey cart to bring us deeper into the oasis. Abu insisting on taking control of the reins, and immediately failed his donkey driving test by running us right into a wall. After giving the ass a stern lecture, he got him moving again and we set off down a dirt path.

The path was shaded by thick palm trees, verdant and tropical. It was designed for two-way donkey traffic, yet we still had to veer on to the hard shoulder of the path when another cart was approaching us. It was commandeered by a grizzled man in his sixties, his face a cracked bas-relief. His young wife was ceremoniously seated in the rear of the cart. As we passed by, she pulled her veil tightly around her face and turned away. Further on, a group of young girls came running out into the path. They shouted, 'Hello! Hello!' and blew kisses at the young owner of our donkey. And I couldn't help thinking that one day they too would end up seated in the back of a cart, tightening their veils at the sight of other men.

At the Temple of the Oracle, we parked the donkey and scrambled up a footpath, entering another walled ghost town. Here, Alexander had a private meeting with the oracle Amun, yet refused to divulge the details of their consultation to his friends. More secrets, more enigmas. Everywhere you turned in Siwa, you found evidence of a cryptic past. The oasis, renowned in ancient times for its supernatural oracle, still believed its own mysteries. This temple was yet another wing of an immense ghost mansion. In ancient times, you came here to consult a god who could gaze into the future. Today, you arrived escorted by a secret policeman who made certain that you weren't gazing into the militarized future of Siwa through the viewfinder of your camera.

After leaving the temple, we stopped by a natural spring pool where Cleopatra was once rumoured to have bathed, and then crawled back into the village. I paid off the young boy for the use of his donkey cart, and then Abu and I sat in the shade of a grocer's shop, drinking Cokes. Our conservation during the course of the morning had been virtually non-existent, as Abu remained taciturn and distant, doing his job and not liking it. But now, as I was about to be released from his custody, he opened up a bit, telling me he was from Alexandria.

'I want to go back to the city, but the military say I must work here first. Siwa is bad. No cinemas, no nightclubs, nothing. I go crazy here.'

I could sympathize with Abu's situation. Three years as an intelligence goon in Siwa seemed like excessive punishment. But it was difficult to warm to the man. His pitted baby-face gave him the look of a minor-league torturer, and he delighted in scenes of cruelty like the one being enacted in the market at the moment. The owner of the grocer's was chasing a baby kid around the square. He finally cornered the animal and, seizing him by all four legs, bound them together with twine. Abu began to giggle as the kid howled with fear. The grocer deposited the kid in front of us and then picked up a large rusted machete. Abu was now prodding the kid with his foot, enjoying its terror. I stood up and walked away . 'You no watch?' Abu said, shouting after me. I didn't answer him. The kid's howls hit a crescendo, echoing through the square. Then, there was a loud thump, followed by silence.

The official tour of Siwa had ended.

* * * * *

By two in the afternoon, the sun over Siwa was incandescent and merciless. The market emptied and I retreated to my hotel room, napping for an hour until Patrick came in and woke me. He said that two foreigners on motorcycles were outside the hotel inquiring for me. Ian and Geoff had finally arrived.

'Bloody points on my bike packed up yesterday when we were only 10 kilometres outside of Matruth', Geoff said. 'Had to turn back for the night. Only got here two hours ago.'

'And we've been in the Intelligence Centre since then', Ian said.

'Dealing with some fuckwit who kept screaming into a field telephone', Geoff said. 'Know the guy?'

Another young hoodlum from the secret police showed up to lead Ian and Geoff to their hotel—our two-room flop house being fully booked up—and I returned to my bunk bed and my notebook. In the little shop adjoining the hotel, someone was blaring Michael Jackson's *Thriller* on a ghetto blaster, and to baffle out the sound I asked Patrick for a loan of his Walkman. He only had one musical cassette with him—Sir Colin Davis's recording of *The Messiah*—so I wrote to the accompaniment of Handel ringing through my head. At one point, I looked up from my notebook to watch an Army convoy rolling past our window. And as they drove by, the baritone on the recording began to sing:

Make straight in the desert,
A highway for our God.

Patrick interrupted the baritone just as he was about to give me good tidings from Zion. 'Come on', Patrick said. 'I show you oasis nightlife.'

Nightlife in Siwa was television. That new highway in the desert hadn't just brought the military to this outpost; it had also brought images from the external world. The first television set had arrived in the oasis six months ago, and its effect had been immediate and profound. Patrick brought me to a small restaurant off the main village square which contained one of the few sets in Siwa. The place was packed; a standing-room-only crowd of Siwan men and Bedouin sitting in orderly rows of chairs and gazed at the new Sony suspended from the ceiling. On the screen, a group of blond California girls sang of the pleasures of Dentyne Chewing Gum. They wore running shorts and singlets, and smacked their lips in syncopation. After this, there was an ad for a Cairo furniture showroom which specialized in imitation Louis Farouk love seats, followed by a commercial featuring a team of singing butchers and close-ups of cold cuts.

The Siwans stared silently at the Dentyne girls and the singing butchers. It was a glimpse of a world that had little bearing on their lives, yet they were gripped by what they saw. For many, it was their first taste of the synthetic glamour of urban Egypt, and one could only speculate on how they interpreted the gaudy commercialism radiating from that Japanese picture tube. One thing was certain, however: television had already changed certain social patterns in Siwa life. The cafe in Siwa is, by and large, an all-male preserve; a Boy's Night Out club and a forum for conversation. But in any cafe equipped with television, talk was almost forbidden, as that only distracted everyone's attention from the box with the vivid pictures. After centuries of warding off outsiders, the Siwans had now lowered their defences to welcome a new invader who, given time, would alter

80

their world-view and their perception of their own lives. Unlike all past foreign intruders, television had managed to penetrate the fortress mentality of Siwa without a fight.

Patrick and I left the restaurant just as everyone was settling down to watch the latest episode of a new Egyptian costume drama. We walked back into the market square, stopping at a small comfortable broken-down cafe without television, where a group of men passed the time with dominoes and chat. The proprietor greeted Patrick warmly and then told him that the Head of Military Intelligence for Siwa had requested that we join him for tea at another cafe across the square. Patrick said that we would first drink a cup of tea here before joining him, and then complimented the proprietor, noting that he made the best tea in the oasis.

'You must do such things here', Patrick said to me. 'There is rivalry between the two cafes, and you must always be careful not to injure someone's pride. Pride means everything in Siwa.'

Pride meant everything to the Head of Military Intelligence as well. Mr Badawi was in his early thirties and a snappy dresser. He wore a custom-made safari suit in camouflage colours and smoked Marlboros from an ivory cigarette holder. His face was surprisingly boyish and soft, yet his cold steel eyes gave him away as the sort of chap who wouldn't think twice about applying electrodes to certain delicate parts of your body if it was a matter of getting you to talk. Surrounded by underlings, being ushered into his presence was like attending the court of a Sicilian Don.

'Ah yes, you are the gentleman from Ireland', Mr Badawi said. 'I saw your passport this afternoon.' He gave me a knowing smile that was designed to make me feel uncomfortable. 'And you are a tourist in Egypt?'

'That's right', I said.

'And what is your business in Ireland?'

'I write plays for radio and the theatre.'

'And you write journalism as well?'

I lied. 'No, only plays.' My answer seemed to satisfy him, as he then became expansive.

'A beautiful country, Ireland.'

'You know it?'

'I have been in Cork and Rosslare. And I have lived in London for a year.' He pulled out his wallet and, with almost childish delight, showed me two prized souvenirs: an old pass from the

London Underground, and an official identity card from the British Foreign and Commonwealth Office. This last document was particularly interesting, as it stated that Mr Badawi was employed as a *driver* by the Embassy of the Arab Republic of Egypt, London. The identity card was dated February 1984, and I wondered how someone who was a mere Embassy driver in 1984 ended up as the Intelligence chief of Siwa in the autumn of 1985. Either Mr Badawi's rise in the Intelligence services had been meteoric, or he must have been doing some pretty interesting driving for the Egyptian embassy in London. It was yet another Siwan secret, and as I discovered, one best left unexplored.

'Did you enjoy driving in London?', I said handing the card back to him.

Mr Badawi smiled, showing shark-like teeth. And I dropped the subject.

* * * * *

The lights were still out in the Intelligence Centre, and the civil servant was still screaming into the field telephone. He slammed down the receiver, and then turned to me.

'What you want?', he said.

'My passport, please. I'm leaving Siwa tomorrow.'

'Pass', he said. I handed him my travel permit. He studied it. 'Four days', he said.

* * * * *

At five in the morning, the oasis was mine. No Army convoys, no secret policemen, no crazed civil servants. Just silence and darkness. I crept out of the Siwa Hotel and stood in the middle of the road, enjoying the stillness and the night sky. For the first time in days, I was not being watched, followed, or restricted in my movements. I had Siwa to myself.

Night, I decided, was not a mystery in Siwa. Night here was like the desert—empty and infinite. It blacked out all secrets, hid everything from view. Night was the intelligible time of the Siwan day. First light, however, brought all the enigmas back into view.

A sandstorm forced me to start walking. I passed the Intelligence Centre for the last time and boarded a bus parked outside a block of flats. The bus filled up with soldiers and a handful of Siwans, the driver revved the engine into action, and we began the ten hour journey back to Alexandria.

On the fringes of Siwa, night crossed into day. The black ribbon of tarmac came into view, pointing the way north. I looked back as we picked up speed, but saw nothing. Nothing but a cloud of sand.

Siwa had gone into hiding again.

Chapter Four

The Big Smoke

BUD WAS WORRIED about riots. Anti-American riots. He'd heard on the radio that students at a university in Cairo had taken to the street to protest against Reagan's interception of the Egyptair jet. I hadn't heard anything—I'd been out of town for five days. Bud said the demonstration had turned ugly and the cops had to be called in. 'Egypt's real pissed off with us', Bud said. Mubarak hadn't gotten the apology he demanded from Washington, and now the Americans were sending an envoy to Cairo to try and patch things over. 'Ain't gonna do much good, 'cause Egypt's real pissed off with us', Bud said. Bud also said that if I wanted to catch a lift with him from Alex to Cairo, that was no sweat, as long as I didn't mind hitting the road around eight in the morning. 'If we get up early enough, we might just avoid the riots.' Bud was real worried about riots.

Bud drove a Thunderbird. A real honest-to-god Detroit Ford. It came with the job. A job as a quality control supervisor with an

American conglomerate. A few years ago, when his company was looking for personnel to staff their new Cairo office, Bud volunteered. He'd just caught his wife cheating on him for a second time, and after the divorce came through, Iowa City just didn't look the same to him. He needed a change of scene. So Bud came to Egypt. He liked it here. Sure, the place was crazy, but the perks of the job were fantastic: the car, the housing allowance, the tax break. You wouldn't get this sort of deal working in Iowa City. And the cost of living here was cheap. Real cheap. Bud played the black market. He knew a shop in the suburb where he lived which nearly gave him 50 per cent above the official exchange rate for his American dollars. That meant cut-price living in Cairo, and a nice chunk of change to deposit in the bank back home. The way Bud figured it, if he could stick Cairo for another couple of years, he'd have enough cash to retire at fifty and buy that boat he always wanted. It was a prospect that made Egypt quite an attractive place. That is, as long as there weren't riots. Bud got kind of jumpy at the thoughts of riots.

I met Bud in Alexandria while resting up for two days after coming in from Siwa. He was in town doing a little business for his company, and he was heading back down to Cairo on Friday; the day I was also planning to travel to the capital. So I bummed a lift with him, and we set off early. Friday is the Muslim Sabbath day, which meant that the streets were empty. Bud wanted to get to Cairo before noon. Noon was the time when everybody would be going to the mosque, listening to the sheikhs denouncing infidel America. Noon was the time the riots might just start.

The desert road from Alexandria to Cairo is an industrial eyesore: a scrubby expanse of sand punctuated by petroleum works, parched vegetation, and billboards featuring the Marlboro cowboy and the Michelin man. Bud and I were spared looking at much of this landscape as we drove straight into a sandstorm around fifty kilometres outside of Alexandria. The Thunderbird was enveloped by a mushroom cloud of sand, forcing us to roll up the windows and reduce speed. It was like driving through a blizzard; a near white-out which made visibility impossible and blanketed the highway with a thick crust of grit. The storm dogged us all the way to Cairo, and lifted only briefly to give us a fleeting glimpse of the Pyramids at Giza in the distance.

The desert ended; the city began. Sand was taken over by pavement, and a strip of petrol stations and hotels running parallel to the pyramids. As we cruised along this Pharaonic gasoline alley, Bud said, 'Hey, I got a real bad case of the hungries, so how about stopping off at the Holiday Inn for a bite to eat before we hit the Big C?'

'Raindrops Keep Falling On My Head' was the featured selection on the muzak system at the Holiday Inn Sphinx. There was a display of photographs on one wall of the foyer, showing the hotel's manager presenting Employee of the Month awards to a pair of smiling desk clerks. The waitresses in the coffee shop wore name tags and used expressions like, 'Have a nice day'. Bud ordered an Egypto-American lunch for us: *hummus* and *tahina*, followed by chili burgers and percolated coffee. 'Funny', Bud said, 'but this place always reminds me of Florida.' He had a point.

The last stretch of road into the city centre brought us through a shabby suburban strip. We passed by a mosque where the amplified voice of a sheikh ricocheted off the walls of high-rise flats. His sermon sounded bad-tempered and belligerent.

'He's probably telling the people to go out and kick American ass', Bud said.

The citizens of Cairo didn't seem to be following his advice, as the city was unnaturally still and deserted. Had I never been in the Egyptian capital before, I would have questioned all the reports one hears about Cairo being a metropolis on the brink of a nervous breakdown. But I knew this sabbath day calm was only temporary. For the next few hours, Cairo would observe a curfew and offer up praise to Allah. Then the merry-go-round would start again.

Bud dropped me off on Talaat Harb Street, and headed back to his bachelor flat. I had invited him for a drink, but he didn't want to hang around the city centre. Just in case there might be riots.

* * * * *

I checked into the Hotel Lotus. It was situated on the seventh floor of an office building, and shared its main entrance with the offices of Libyan Arab Airlines. 'We are the best guarded hotel in Cairo', the man behind the reception desk told me, and showed me to a room with peeling paint and a view of a ventilator shaft. He then offered me his services as a moneychanger, but I didn't have time to engage in financial transactions. I had an appointment to keep.

I left the hotel and walked down to Tahrir Square, the geographic centre of the city and perhaps the best vantage point from which to gain a perspective on the modern Cairo condition. Stand on the circular walkway above the square and look to the east and the graceful minarets and citadels of Islamic Cairo dominate the skyline. Turn your back on Islam and gaze westwards and the city becomes a haphazard collection of office buildings and luxury hotels. Down below, a deep cavity has been gouged in the earth. A construction worker is hacking away through some debris, and his mouth is filled with a multicoloured spaghetti of telephone and electrical wires. The hole he is helping to dig has been under excavation for years, as Cairo attempts to build the first underground on the African continent. The construction of the underground is not a symbol of the brave new world of modern Egypt; it is an act of desperation in a city facing up to doomsday statistics. Statistics like an official population of 8 million, with unofficial estimates running as high as 12 million. Statistics like a projected population of over 16 million by the year 2000. Statistics like a population density in certain areas of 150,000 a square kilometre. Statistics that have forced the government to seek some sort of stop-gap solution to a city that has become one vast quicksand of pedestrian and automotive traffic, threatening to swallow up anyone who strays into its midst. And looking at that hole in Tahrir Square. I was reminded of something that Moustafa—the Mahler-obsessed accountant—told me in Alexandria: *Egypt today is like a reverse pyramid*. The Pharaohs of Egypt commemorated their reign with monuments to the after-life that reached for the sky. Their present-day counterparts, however, have no choice but to burrow underground.

I left the circular walkway and hailed a taxi. My appointment was in an outlying district called Matariyyah, but as I had misplaced the address of the person I was visiting, I asked the driver to simply deposit me on the Egyptian equivalent of the Matariyyah High Street. Cairo traffic operates according to the rules of Social Darwinism: only the fittest survive in this automotive jungle. And much of the city has been gutted by flyovers, exit ramps, and suspended concrete strips, all of which have been constructed to appease the four-wheeled mafia who hold the city to ransom. But even this elaborate system of motorways has done little to ease the snarl, and it still took us nearly two hours to travel the twelve kilometres to Matariyyah.

There are many Cairos and Matariyyah is one of them. Twenty years ago, it was a remote, sleepy suburb fringing the fields of the Nile Delta. Enter Matariyyah today, however, and you walk into a street scene reminiscent of the Lower East Side of Manhattan at the turn of the century. Most of the pavements in the district have been dug up, and the human congestion is so dense that you have to compete for your own small piece of the street. I joined the crowd and began weaving my way through the congealed traffic of the market. Up ahead, there had been a collision between a taxi cab and a young boy on a donkey. The side door of the taxi was dented, the driver of the taxi was being physically restrained from attacking the young boy with a tyre iron, and the donkey was looking bemused. Further on, a wedding car, decorated with ribbons, edged its way into the road. The bride and groom, both plump and dressed in co-ordinated shades of maroon, were sitting stiffly between two sets of parents, avoiding each other's eyes. Behind them, an open-back truck was filled with a dozen women dressed in black. One of them shouted over to a butcher who was dismembering a cow. He made a deep incision in the cow's stomach, reached in, pulled out a length of intestine, and then yelled back to the woman, asking her how much she wanted. I moved on, bumping into a bicycle cart filled with chickens, and stopped to ask directions from a man who was sharpening knives on a stone wheel. We had to shout to hear each other over the roar of the car horns, and he pointed me in the direction of a church sealed off from the very public life of Matariyyah by a set of high walls.

The church was Catholic; the priest a bearded tough guy who looked like he could handle himself in a backstreet parish like this one. He dug out a packet of Cleopatras from the folds of his cassock and told me that my bad French was preferable to my bad Arabic. So I spoke French, and explained who I was looking for. This surprised him.

'It's a bit late for a visit', he said. 'Why don't you come back tomorrow.'

'Father, she's family. And it's taken me over two hours to get here.'

'All right', he said. 'I'll take you to her. You'll never find her otherwise.'

We walked back to the main street, then turned down several laneways paved by dirt until we came to a low wall with Arabic graffiti scrawled across it. Two heavy steel doors faced off the outside world. The priest rang a bell, and a voice on the far side of the wall asked us our business. The priest identified himself and the gate was swung open by a housekeeper who greeted him warmly. I explained to her who I wanted to see, and she led me into an immaculate little courtyard and up a flight of steps to a louvred door which she opened. Inside was a functional room with a few chairs facing a set of wooden bars, behind which was a pair of closed curtains. She shut the door and I sat there and waited.

After a few minutes, a light snapped on behind the curtains. Then I heard a voice.

'Well, I was wondering when you'd be showing yourself.'

The accent was vintage Waterford, thick and pure. The curtains drew back and a hand shot out between the bars. I took it and immediately thought: this lady has got some grip.

'Hello Breda', I said.

She was once called Breda O'Keefe, but that was 43 years ago when she was still a girl in the city of Waterford. At the age of seventeen, however, she entered a contemplative order of Carmelite nuns and was re-christened Sister Margaret Therese. In those days, the Carmelites were one of the most enclosed of all religious orders. The nuns never left the convent, and if they put a foot into the outside world, the punishment was excommunication. When visitors came they were brought to a lattice screen behind which they could only vaguely see the daughter, sister or friend now hidden away in the deepest folds of Mother Church. Breda had joined that cloistered world in 1942, entering a convent in the town of New Ross, Co. Waterford. The next time she saw the world beyond the convent walls was twenty-three years later when the call from Rome came. The Carmelite order in Cairo was threatened with imminent closure, due to the fact that there had been no new vocations for several years. The heads of the Order therefore decided to dispatch a few Carmelites to Egypt to keep the convents open. But, as this was a time when mere mention of the word 'Suez' still provoked a knee-jerk response, the Nasserite government wouldn't accept British or French nuns. So the neutral Irish were chosen to fill the gap. It was a voluntary posting, and Breda asked to go. That was 1965. Matariyyah had been her home ever since.

We had never met before, but had exchanged a few letters and had spoken once on the telephone. And now we were related to each other, as I had married her niece several months earlier. My wife had often spoken about her aunt and I was always intrigued by the notion of a group of Carmelites carrying on the contemplative life in the uncontemplative city of Cairo. Not having been raised a Catholic and being somewhat sceptical about most forms of religious doctrine, I could never comprehend the overwhelming faith required to shut yourself off from the world and devote your life to the mysteries of prayer. And I often wondered what sort of vision Breda had of life beyond the convent walls. After all, she had been largely sheltered from the flow of world events since 1942, and to the best of my knowledge, had only been away from her enclosed order for three brief periods in the past forty-three years. And en route to Matariyyah, I envisaged myself being bombarded with questions: Who won the war? Is Stalin still alive? Whatever happened to Harry Truman? Has De Valera retired from politics yet?

I simply didn't know what to expect from this Irish Carmelite who signed her letters to me as 'Auntie Breda'. And I was therefore rather surprised when this energetic woman of sixty appeared behind the wooden bars. The severity of her habit struck me immediately, as it only revealed the oval outline of her face. But her eyes were sharp and alert and, as I quickly discovered, she was a fantastic talker who preferred you not to treat her in an overly reverential manner. Her piety was her own business, and she didn't need to project a sanctimonious image of herself. If anything, Breda was disarmingly worldy and a keen student of current affairs.

'Well, weren't you the smart man not to be on that Italian cruise ship that was hijacked', she said.

'How did you hear about that?', I said.

'On the radio, of course. We listen to the BBC World Service several times a day.'

'You have a radio in the convent?', I said.

'How else would we listen to the BBC?', she said, grinning slightly. And I realized that she was telling me in her own quiet way that, though she was in an enclosed order, she did not have an enclosed mind.

I gave her several letters and messages from her family back in Ireland, and then two of the other Irish nuns—Sisters Veronica and Agnes—joined Breda on her side of the bars. Sister Agnes carried a tray with a steaming pot of tea and home-made scones, and placing the tray on a revolving wooden platform located at the far end of the screened off area, she swung it around to me.

'Now, would you like a fry-up?', Sister Agnes said. 'Bet you haven't had a bit of rasher and egg for a while.'

It was like being in a guest house in the west of Ireland. And, for a moment, I had to remind myself that this was Egypt, and that I was sitting in front of an ecclesiastical Berlin Wall which neither side could cross. Like the medieval Siwans, the Carmelite sisters in Cairo had built their own fortress against the external threat of Egypt. And yet, as Breda told me, Egypt still managed to permeate the convent's walls. The loudspeakers from the nearby mosque invaded their solitude, and there was a running joke among the sisters that, one day, they too would install a loudspeaker on the roof of the convent and start broadcasting their prayers to the community.

'Would the community listen?', I asked.

'We have to be very careful of our position here', Breda said. 'And we're always keeping a close eye on the state of the country to see how it might affect us. I'll give you an example. There was a time during the Nasser years when the government was taking over all foreign property. And one night a group of soldiers showed up at our front gate, saying they wanted to check the building to make certain it was safe. But the Mother Superior wouldn't let them in, and the Papal Nuncio had to be called out, and eventually the soldiers went away which was a good thing because, if they had come inside, they would have sealed off the house and forced us to leave.'

Did she have any memories of the 1967 war with Israel? 'The sound of jet fighters flying low over us.' And the Yom Kippur war in 1973? 'More jets . . . you could hardly sleep with the noise of them.' The autumn of Sadat's assassination? 'That was the time of the riots between the Muslims and the Copts when somebody threw a petrol bomb over our wall which, thank God, failed to ignite.' And now she saw the country moving towards Islamic fundamentalism and sectarian unrest. How had she come to this conclusion? Simple: her Muslim neighbours objected to the convent's hermitage.

'A hermitage?', I said

'The neighbours took us to court over it. They said we were breaking planning laws by constructing a hermitage in our courtyard. And we had quite a legal battle with them until they finally realized that the hermitage was only used for prayer. They accepted it after that, but you can't imagine the fight that hermitage caused. It says a lot about the relations between

Muslims and Christians in Egypt now, doesn't it?'

Though isolated from the mainstream of society, Breda had still been able to gauge the shifting political and social mood of the country by the way in which it affected life in her sequestered community. And given the hardship nature of her post, she was allowed certain freedoms that would have been unheard of in a Carmelite convent in Europe. She could visit her family in Ireland every few years, and could leave the convent grounds from time to time if she needed to make an important errand. The grille had come down, visitors could call at just about any time of the day, and many of the other stringent rules of the Order had been bent to make life in Matariyyah more tolerable.

But now, Breda was worried that their more flexible lifestyle was in jeopardy, as a group of Spanish Carmelites had been actively lobbying Rome for a return to the old draconian ways of the Order. And Rome seemed to be responding positively to their case. Indeed, if Breda was troubled by the Muslim fundamentalists in Egypt, then she was also equally troubled by the fundamentalists within her own church.

'Now the old Carmelite ways are fine for them in a lovely convent in Europe with gardens to walk in and peaceful surroundings', she said. 'But what about an Order like ours in a place like Egypt?'

The heads of the Order—men meeting around a table in the Vatican like a corporation's directorate—would be deciding their fate next year. And the Cairo sisters were praying very hard that they wouldn't side with the advocates of orthodoxy. Prayer would see them through, just as it had seen them through their years in Egypt. Prayer was their vocation in life. Prayer was their bulwark against the outside world.

I looked at my watch. Breda and I had been talking for over three hours, and now it was quite late. Promising to return in a few days, I said goodbye and stepped out into the secular world of Cairo. The laneway was dark, and as I walked towards the main street of Matariyyah, I tripped over a bulky object lying in the dirt. It was a dead dog; its limbs stiff with rigor mortis, a swarm of flies hovering over its carcass.

Breda's enclosed universe suddenly looked very inviting.

* * * * *

Dr Fawsi El-Azziz told me a story.

'I was married once. Egyptian girl. We go to Saudi Arabia

when I get a job in hospital there. One month in Saudi, someone comes to me, says my wife she is selling herself.'

'Selling herself?', I said.

'Getting into the bed with other men for a price. She makes good money. 400 Rials a time. But then, Saudi authorities find out about this, and I have to get her back to Egypt. I tell her, "You crazy. They stone you to death here for adultery. You go back to Egypt." So I put her on the plane. Two days later, soldiers come to my house in Jeddah wanting to arrest her. I tell them she's in Cairo, they leave me alone. Of course, we divorce. She now marries an American, has a kid. But I let her divorce me. I put this in marriage contract. I must be only Muslim man ever to allow a woman to have this right. People tell me, "Fawsi, you crazy." But it doesn't bother me.'

I offered the doctor a beer.

'Of course, I drink a beer', he said. 'I do not make much money in my clinic today. Two pounds only. Bad, huh? But I do not care about money. I make it. I spend it. *Maaleesh.*'

Dr Fawsi El-Azziz drank nightly at the Cafe Riche on Talaat Harb Street. It was a well-known Cairo landmark; a bar and restaurant that was frequented by writers and journalists. Dr El-Azziz didn't care a damn about the literary atmosphere of the place. He went there because it was next door to his clinic, the beer was cheap, and it also stayed open late. I ended up there for similar reasons. It was across the street from my hotel, and after coming back from seeing Breda in Matariyyah, it was the only place nearby where I could find a much-needed beer. Dr El-Azziz was sitting at a table next to mine on the terrace, and when he saw me working in my notebook, he leaned over and said, 'You a writer?'

'I guess you could say that.'

'I tell you what you need for good writing', he said. 'A local medicine called hashish. I use the hashish every day before I work.'

Dr El-Azziz was a paediatrician. A very unlikely looking paediatrician. He was in his forties, and dressed in a shiny brown suit which was covered in food stains. He used his trousers as an ashtray, and clenched his cigarettes between the four teeth still left in his mouth. He hadn't shaved in several days, and when he pushed his hand through his hair, small clumps of it fell away from his scalp and landed on his shoulders. As doctors go, he didn't exactly inspire confidence, especially since he looked like a walking health violation. Still, he told me that he came from a long line of medical men, and that his father was one of the most eminent paediatricians in the country.

'My father, he used to work for Nasser. Taking care of his children in the presidential palace. I work there for a while too. But then, one night . . . why I do it, I do not know, maybe I'm a bit crazy, maybe too much hashish, . . . anyway, one night I am in official car. And I say to Nasser's driver: "Tell the President that he can go fuck a dog." Of course, they put me in a sanitorium after this. And then I go to Saudi with my wife and she begins to sell herself. And then I treat this child who has polio. I give the child an injection, the child dies, and I have some trouble for a while. Terrible place, Saudi. And I smoke hashish all the time when I am there, which in Saudi is worse than drinking alcohol. But the Saudi police, they think I am crazy Egyptian so they ignore me. When my year contract is up, I run to airport, say "Take me out of this crazy country." I drink four whiskys on the plane and kiss Egyptian ground when I arrive.'

Dr El-Azziz evidently led a complicated life. He'd worked for a while in England and France, but couldn't find a permanent niche for himself in the medical establishment of either country. After that, it was off to Nigeria—an experience he didn't like remembering.

'You know Lagos? Worst city in the world. All black people. No water. Sewage in streets. They kill Egyptian friend of mine when I am there. Shoot him with a pistol. No reason. I tell the doctors after five weeks, "You let me go back to Egypt, or I burn your hospital down." They say, "Okay, no problem. We put you on the plane." I think they believe I might actually do it.'

Since returning from Lagos, he now lived in his parent's house. 'I have room of my own, but they do not like I smoke hashish so much. Still, I am happy to be back in Egypt. We are best country in Africa, in Middle East. Sadat, he did a good job. Good nightclubs, good cafes, good television, good clothes shops. When Nasser was in power, Egypt was terrible place. No one had money. No cafes open at night. Everybody goes home at 9pm.'

To explain to me the hardships endured in the country during the Nasserite years, Dr El-Azziz used a rather unusual economic indicator: the price of prostitutes.

'Things under Nasser were so bad you could come to this cafe, find a woman for fifty piasters—that's thirty pence English money. You buy her for fifty piasters, take her in a car to the desert, fuck her, no problems. You could sleep with the best dancer in the country for five pounds and have a virgin for twenty pounds. It was real cheap times.

'But now all the girls want to get married. But I no marry again.'

He lit another cigarette. 'I sleep with no woman now for eight years. I am a good Muslim.'

And with that, he coughed up a lungful of smoke.

* * * * *

Soraya Naafa had lived in the Hotel Rialto for nearly ten years. She was an American of Egyptian extraction: a tiny woman with a tight crop of black hair and a heavily lined face, wearing stretch pants and a leopard skin blouse. She spoke in a husky, tobacco-cured voice and smoked Cleopatras non-stop. At first sight, she could have been a minor Broadway actress who had a few good years in the early fifties playing Manhattan bitches, but had since hit upon hard times and was now living in a transient hotel. Which is exactly what the Hotel Rialto was—a comfortable, down-at-heel establishment located in a *belle epoque* office building near Tahrir Square.

Soraya first came to Egypt in 1960. Her marriage had collapsed in Chicago, and she decided to take her son on a sentimental journey back to the homeland of her grandfather. Cairo had an immediate narcotic attraction for her, and she set up house in the city. She also landed a job teaching English in a small language school, and supplimented her income by writing the occasional piece on Egyptian affairs for a newspaper back in Chicago. The years passed, her son had grown up and returned to the States, but Soraya still remained in Cairo. And then, for reasons she didn't want to go into, she gave up her comfortable flat and moved into a single room at the Hotel Rialto. It wasn't economic factors that made her check into a four pound a night hotel on a permanent basis. Rather, I sensed that it was something to do with the fact that the rootless atmosphere of the hotel held an attraction for her, and perhaps reflected her own status as a displaced person.

An acquaintance of mine in London knew Soraya and asked me to look her up when I was in Cairo. When I came into the main lounge of the hotel, she was sitting in an armchair with a transistor radio held against her ear.

'Trying to listen to Radio Jerusalem'. she said. 'I wanna hear the Israeli reaction to Reagan's interception of the Egyptair jet, so I can talk about it in an article I'm sending off tomorrow. I tell you, I cannot get over what Reagan tried to pull. I mean, *taban*, he thought he could get away with intercepting the plane, but the guy doesn't have a clue about this part of the world. *Inshallah*, he won't be so stupid in the future.'

Soraya peppered her conversation with Arabic words. I asked her if Cairo was the same city she first came to. 'Oh, *taban*. This town has changed completely. Ain't the place it used to be.'

Ain't the place it used to be. A classic Americanism. Spoken by a woman who now taught English to Egyptians, while simultaneously writing about the Egyptian world-view for Chicagoans. Soraya seemed precariously balanced between two worlds and was caught in that dilemma which all long-term expatriates face; that classic syndrome of feeling *at home abroad*, and yet still realizing that you are *abroad at home*.

'Have you ever thought about returning to America?' I said.

'I couldn't go back to the States now', she said. 'How could I? Starting over again at my age? With the kind of money of you need there. This place, the Rialto, it ain't bad. Could be worse. Could be a lot better. But I've got my friends here. Got my work, which I like, even if the money ain't great. Things could be worse. Things could be a lot worse.'

I looked around the faded Edwardian lounge in which we were sitting. Old armchairs, a black and white television with an oval picture tube, threadbare chintz cushions, yellowing wallpaper. And a grab-bag community of guests, many of whom once moved in here for a week and had yet to leave years later. Frugal comfort in the centre of Cairo. It appealed to me. So I stopped by the front desk and booked a room for the next day.

'How long will you be staying?', the desk clerk asked me.

'Does it matter?', I said.

'Not really', he said.

* * * * *

The room I moved into at the Hotel Rialto suited my temperament well. It was a large, genteel junk-shop, filled with curiosities. Like a pair of wooden thrones in Ming dynasty style, with dragons carved into the arms. And a Victorian writing table pockmarked by cigarette burns. The oriental carpet on the floor was threadbare and stained, the big double bedstead had ornamental apples and oranges carved into its headboard, and the mahogany wardrobe was large enough to hide a few bodies in. It was a room designed for a dandy who had gone to seed, and I couldn't think of a better hideout in which to escape the pressures of Cairo.

Once unpacked, I was tempted to hole up in my room for the day and give in to sloth, but outside my windows I could hear the roar of the city and was inevitably drawn to it. Cairo, I discovered, had that effect on me. Any time I slammed the door on its chaos, I would immediately miss the shapeless disorder of its streets. The city was like a massive Victorian novel which forced you to work your way through its broad canvas and complicated sub-plots before it revealed its true meaning. And being an impatient sort of reader I found myself compulsively caught up in its narrative, wondering where it would lead me next. So I left the Hotel Rialto and grabbed a taxi.

'Where you go?', said the driver.

'I'll go where you go', I said.

The driver looked at me carefully. 'You have no destination?'

'Not today.'

'I go Mohandessin', he said. 'Okay by you?'

'Why not?', I said, and climbed in beside him. As I sat down, I felt a large object on the seat and, reaching behind me to pull it out, I discovered that I now had a revolver in my hand. The driver nearly ran us into the back of a bus when he saw the gun, and quickly snatched it away from me, holding it against the steering wheel as he drove.

'Sorry', he said. 'I forget that the gun is on the seat.'

'Do you always carry a revolver in your taxi?', I said.

'I am policeman.'

'A policeman who drives a taxi?'

'It is part-time job. I need the money. Policeman in Cairo does not pay good, so I drive the taxi when I do not wear the uniform.' He brandished the gun in front of me. 'Nice pistol, yes?'

'Lovely', I said. 'Why don't you put it away?'

'Do not be worried. The safety is on.'

'Guns make me nervous.'

'Okay, for you I get rid of the gun', he said, tossing it into the glove compartment.

'Thank you.'

'No problem', he said. 'Are you a Christian?'

'What?', I said, somewhat bewildered by the new direction

that the conversation was taking.

'Are you a Christian? You know, Catholic, Protestant . . . '

'I suppose I am', I said, deciding that this was not the time or the place to explain my rather multi-faceted religious background.

The driver took my hand and shook it vigorously.

'I am very pleased to meet another believer in Jesus Christ', he said. 'I am Orthodox Coptic.'

'A Christian policeman?', I said. 'That's very unusual in Egypt, isn't it?'

'Yes', he said. 'I am what is known as a Coptic cop.'

This gun-toting Copt drove as if he was in a hurry to receive his eternal reward, and it was something of a relief when we arrived in Mohandessin.

'The blessings of God be with you', he said after I paid him off and got out of the taxi. And then he took his revolver out of the glove compartment and began to polish it with a rag.

Ending up in Mohandessin was a happy accident, as I had stayed near this district when I first visited Cairo in 1981. At the time, Mohandessin was an obscure inner suburb, caught somewhere in between the exclusivity of Zamalek—Cairo's own version of Belgravia—and the middle class tower blocks of nearby Sahafayeen.

But the social geography of Cairo had changed in the last four years. The city centre had gone into decline; a victim of Cairo's spiralling population and gridlock traffic. Whereas the area around Kasr el Nil and Talaat Harb Streets was once considered the main commercial and shopping district of the city, now all the smart money was moving to less congested boroughs on the western side of the Nile. The reason for this migration was simple: negotiating the city centre during working hours had become a nightmare. The pavements were packed, the traffic deranged. And since this was a capital where, for most of the year, the mercury was considering the mid-nineties, downtown Cairo had become a parboiled amusement park which constantly tested your stamina for urban living at its most extreme.

Gradually, therefore, the city centre had been stripped of its flashy shops, its restaurants and corporate offices, with the result that districts like Mohandessin had been transformed into North American enclaves; upwardly mobile and affluent.

I wandered down Shehab Street. Past new condominiums and a high-tech Tandoori restaurant. Had I needed a pair of Levis, I could have shopped at Samia Imports—'Egypt's Only American Boutique'—or dropped in for a little workout at the aerobics dance studio on the same premises. French cuisine was available at the Saint Germain Cafe, and a furniture showroom was displaying the latest in Danish design. I stopped at the Tandoori restaurant for an over-priced curry, and was seated near a young Egyptian couple. They both wore leather jackets and—using the language favoured by Egypt's old monied classes—they gossiped in French. About her recent holiday in Paris. And his new Mazda. And how Saturdays were now impossible at the Gezira Club since the government ministries had decided to take the day off.

Their conversation was like the landscape of Mohandessin: smug in its new-found affluence, yet vacuous. The whole district had originally been built as a co-operative by a syndicate of engineers—in fact, the English translation of Mohandessin is 'the city of engineers'—and it looked as if it had been lifted straight off one of their drawing boards. As I left the restaurant and headed towards the neighbouring borough of Sahafayeen, my eyes searched the streets for some visual variation in this apartment block canyon. But all I could see was a dusty prospect of high rise comfort. It was a New World vista which the late Anwar el-Sadat would have approved of. After all, he had been an advocate of a free-market economy. And through his policy of *infitah*—an Open Door economic policy which, for a time, flooded the country with hard currency and foreign investment —a whole new generation of entrepreneurs and speculators emerged during the boom period of the 'seventies. They made fast fortunes in property development and the import/export game, and turned areas like Mohandessin into select *faubourgs* for Egypt's new rich. The boom was now over, and every report I read on Egypt's finances used words like 'hopeless' to describe the country's economic health, but in Mohandessin it was still business as usual: new condominiums under construction, a new health studio due to open next week, the restaurants packed with ladies who lunch. It was as if the residents if Mohandessin didn't want to believe that the party was over; that the lifestyle bestowed upon them by Sadat's laissez-faire policies was now under threat, as Egypt's cancerous economy moved closer towards the terminal ward.

In front of a Kentucky Fried Chicken, I hopped a taxi. The traffic was surprisingly light, so it only took a half-hour to travel from Mohandessin to Matariyyah. As I walked down the laneway towards the convent I could smell something burning— a stench so foul and repugnant that I had to cover my nose and mouth with a handkerchief to avoid an attack of nausea. Turning a corner, I saw what was on fire: the dead dog I had tripped over two days earlier. Three children stood in front of the pyre, watching its carcass burn. They waved to me as I passed by, and then turned back and continued gazing into the dancing flames.

* * * * *

Moving around Cairo was like that. A trip across the city was similar to travelling in a time machine—you started off in the nineteen eighties and ended up back at the turn of the century. Unlike most western cities, Cairo was too congested, too public, to hide its mean streets. And everywhere you turned, you were confronted with the juxtaposition of wealth and poverty, the modern and the primitive—the volcanic disparities of a metropolis in distress.

A few days after my walking tour of Mohandessin, I had a closer look at Cairo's economic incongruities from the back of Brian Barnes's motorbike. Barnes was a maths teacher in the British Council. He'd been living in Egypt for five years, and we first met in Cairo in 1981 when he was working at an English language school and had set up residence in the village of Embaba on the outskirts of the city. At that time, a mutual friend brought me to the village one night to see Brian's set-up, and after negotiating our way through a knot of small alleyways where chickens ran wild and children waded in muddy pools of water, we came to a squat, rudimentary building in which Brian had rented a three room flat. Entering the flat was like stepping into a Habitat showroom designed for the Third World, for Brian had modernized it completely. The walls were newly white-washed, there was cane furniture and rush matting on the floor, a large radio-cassette player, a fridge stacked with Stella, not to mention a small darkroom which Brian had set up in an alcove. And though he was a perfectly amiable host, his Terence Conran environment situated in the midst of a ramshackle village immediately made me suspect that he was a *Third Worlder* having a 'cultural experience' among the natives.

I judged Brian harshly at the time. But when we bumped into each other this time in the bar of the Atlas Hotel in Cairo,

I began to revise my opinion of him. He'd got married to a fellow English teacher since I'd last seen him, and had abandoned his ethnic lifestyle in favour of a flat in Mohandessin. And as we chatted over a few beers, and I heard about his travels in the Sudan, the Yemen and the rest of Egypt, I realized that I had misjudged his reasons for living in the village in the first place. Brian wasn't an unctuous relief worker type who wore his compassion for developing nations on his sleeve. Rather, he was, quite simply, one of those people who had become smitten with the Arab world, and could probably never see himself falling back into the predictable patterns of English life. For a westerner, his knowledge of the complexities of Egyptian society was remarkable, yet he never promoted himself as a professional Arabist who had all the definite answers to the country's multiple dilemmas. If anything, he was the best sort of enthusiast —passionate about his chosen subject, but nonetheless aware of his status as an outsider in an alien culture. And when he offered to take me on an afternoon tour of Cairo's outlying districts, I jumped at the opportunity.

Brian lived on a quiet road in Mohandessin, tucked away from the glitzy consumerism of Shehab Street. When I showed up, he was doing a bit of quick maintenance work on his Jawa motorbike—a Czechoslovakian-made chopper—and after downing a fast glass of lemon juice, he cranked the bike into action and we set off.

Our first port of call was the British Council in an area called Aguza where Brian wanted to collect his pay cheque. The Council's foyer was packed with students, and the noticeboard was filled with leaflets advertising a variety of English language schools in the United Kingdom. For most of the Egyptians who came to study at the British Council (or any of the other language schools dotted around Cairo), a fluent knowledge of English was a potential passport out of the country; a way of escaping Egypt's low-wage structure and lack of professional opportunity. Any time I walked by the American, British, Canadian, or Australian embassies in Cairo during consular hours, I would always notice a long queue of hopeful emigrants waiting to see if they just might qualify for a Green card or a working visa. But, given the tight restrictions that all these countries now imposed on aliens, their chances of success were, at best, nominal. And with the drop in the price of oil, even the Gulf states were beginning to cut back on the number of Egyptian *gastarbeiters* they usually employed. Everywhere they turned, Egypt's young doctors, engineers, technicians and accountants found potential foreign escape routes being sealed off. And as I stood in the main common room of the British Council, watching students darting in and out of classes, the terrible irony of their situation hit home. Here they were studying in an institution that promoted the British language and culture, but should they attempt to live in that culture they would find themselves trapped in a maze of restrictive laws designed to keep them out of the country. It was the same story for an Egyptian at every other language institute in the city. Western governments were only too pleased to propagate their native tongue and social values, but played very hard-to-get when you showed up at their embassies inquiring about a chance to reside in their countries. And looking at all those young students in the British Council, I wondered when they too would be joining the queues outside the consular offices and learning the awful truth about the emigration game as it is played today.

Brian returned with his salary in his back pocket, and leaving the Council, we climbed on the bike and headed north along the Nile. Within minutes, Aguza's elegant apartment blocks were behind us. Passing under a complex network of flyovers, we entered the fringes of Embaba—a township of grim, functional flats packed together to create narrow cul-de-sacs in which kids ran barefoot and laundry dried in a cloud of exhaust fumes; a place of premature mortality and marginal living. But these were hardly the worst slums in the city. Poverty in Cairo has its degrees and Embaba was the middle range. Cramped airless housing may be bleak but it was preferable to the aluminium huts or shanties on the Nile banks in which many people had to make do.

We pushed onwards, past a brickworks with Victorian smoke-stacks, and soon the city simply dropped away as the verdant moist fields of the Delta stretched out in front of us. The Nile Delta must be one of nature's most fortuitous accidents—some of the most fertile land on the entire African continent located in an otherwise largely arid desert state. The deeper we travelled into this agrarian landscape, the further we distanced ourselves from our technological century, for here the past was not a foreign country, but the familiar present. Women washed bundles of clothes in irrigation ditches as their sons and daughters bathed in the same stagnant water. Oxen were used for pushing plows and elderly men wielded primitive hoes against unyielding ground. There was not a piece of modern agricultural equipment in sight. Life in this corner of the Delta remained locked in a bygone era, and as we rumbled past another group of women wading knee-deep in canal water, I had to remind myself that we were only twenty minutes from the centre of Cairo.

'Don't those women risk getting bilharzia from standing in that water?', I asked Brian, mentioning a common disease caused by the bloodflukes which live in stagnant water, and which, when absorbed through the skin, then begin to lay eggs in various parts of the anatomy.

'They probably all have bilharzia already', he shouted back to me. 'It's very common around here. If the doctors can diagnose it early on, there's a good chance of curing it. The problem is that, after they come back from hospital, they start bathing in stagnant water again, which means they immediately become reinfected.'

Turning off down an unpaved track, we bisected a field as flat as an open palm. A group of farm workers stood waist-high in mud and were brought cups of tea by a small boy who had a pair of flies lodged comfortably inside his nostrils. In the distance, the pyramids at Giza could be seen—a reminder that the desert always threatens, always asserts its dominance of the landscape. The dust from the track lacquered our hair and hindered visibility, so Brian executed a U-turn and brought us back to the main road. Up ahead, on the outskirts of a tumbledown village, an expensive new bungalow had been constructed. It stood there like a latter-day feudal manor overlooking a serfdom.

'A number of wealthy people are building weekend places out here', Brian explained, and I could only wonder what satisfaction a rich city burgher would get from erecting a grand modern house within sight of a community who lived in barely adequate conditions.

'Onwards to Giza', Brian said, and we made a cross-country bee-line for the pyramids. Having slipped out of the twentieth century, we now came rushing back towards it, as cracked roads gave way to smoother tarmac, traffic began to thicken, and a strip of tacky hotels and nightclubs heralded our re-entry to the city. Riding on a motorbike in the Cairo rush hour is a bit like taking part in a search-and-destroy mission in which you are the moving target. But Brian was an old hand at this sport and negotiated our passage through this deadly slalom course with ease. Using a ring road, we skimmed the outskirts of the city and then plunged into the convoluted geography of Islamic Cairo—a

skyline of minarets, dominated by that former symbol of auto-
cratic power, the Citadel. Commissioned by Salah ed-Din two
centuries after the foundation of Cairo, the Citadel represented
the triumph of Arab rule over Egypt. Built on a hillside overlooking the capital known in Arabic as *El Qahir*—'The Victorious'—it
later became the principal residence of the sultans and was laid
siege to by Muhammed Ali in 1805 when he established himself
as the pasha of Egypt. Since 1850, the centre of Egyptian power
has been relocated in the Abdin Palace in downtown Cairo, but
the Citadel and its ornate mosque bearing Muhammed Ali's name
still dominate the cityscape—a reminder of Islam's victory in
Egypt; a victory that many Muslim fundamentalists today would
like to emulate.

Like most great works for ecclesiastical architecture, the minarets
of Islamic Cairo reach for the heavens; their slender spires
pointing the way towards the eternal life. Down below them, the
bitter realities of temporal life are on display for all to see. Zigzagging through a spider's web of streets, Brian brought us to a
gate, behind which a community was getting on with the day's
endeavours.

'Welcome to the City of the Dead', Brian said.

At first sight, it looked like any other irredeemably poor
section of Cairo—tiny derelict houses, many of which were
without roofs, packed tightly together like artisan dwellings in a
Victorian slum. But this was no ordinary residential quarter, for,
as its name implies, the City of the Dead is a cemetery. A
cemetery with around 40,000 living tenants who have set up
house in this necropolis.

A few statistics are helpful in explaining why, in the largest
city on the African continent, a cemetery has been turned into a
make-shift housing estate. In the past two decades, Egypt's birth
rate has spiralled out of control, to the point where it is now
estimated that one million new Egyptians are born every ten
months. And given that only 4 per cent of Egypt's entire territory
is habitable, the country simply doesn't have the available space
to house its ever-growing populace. In the past decade, the
government has tried to combat this problem by building a
string of new cities outside the capital. But few people want to
live in a pre-fabricated oasis, especially since most of these
parched satellite towns have yet to develop an economic base
capable of providing employment or essential services. Which
has meant that Cairo the Victorious has become the new mecca

for internal emigration, as the rural poor—the *fellahin*—continue to pour into the capital. But the city and its environs—hemmed in by the desert and already one of the most densely populated areas in the world—simply hasn't been able to cope with the influx. A few years ago, I read an article in *The Middle East* magazine which explained Cairo's crisis with a few cold facts: the city has two million housing units for three million families which means that 42 per cent of the population is living in single room slums. And though the government is building between 55,000 and 60,000 new houses a year, this is still 70,000 fewer than required.

In short, where can the poor find shelter in a city whose resources have been stretched to breaking point?

The answer, for a small segment of Cairo's homeless, has been the City of the Dead. There is a tradition in Egypt that, if you can afford it, you should bury your dead in a sarcophagus and surround it with a small shelter in which you can pay your dear departed frequent visits. And, in keeping with this tradition, many of Cairo's cemeteries are simply row after row of mausoleums—a semi-detached suburb for the deceased. So, somebody got the bright idea to use the mausoleums as squats for families in need of a dwelling place, and soon the City of the Dead became a fully established community, with its own shops and schools springing up beside the crypts.

As Brian and I toured the necropolis, passing cafes where men played backgammon, staring at butcher's shops where sides of beef were suspended over a sarcophagus, I found myself caught in that predictable dilemma which most westerners face when confronted with the extremities of the Third World. Should one, like a good *Guardian* reader, suffer an attack of Islington socialist guilt and, over a glass of Muscadet later in the evening, express outrage at a system that allows such deprivation to exist? Or should one accept the City of the Dead for what it is: a last ditch solution to a housing crisis in a country which essentially doesn't have the economic muscle to meet all its citizens' needs. Brian seemed to be of the second opinion. Judging by his mild-mannered narrative of the sights of the necropolis, I gathered he saw this living cemetery as just another facet of Cairo life. Perhaps his years in Egypt had taught him not to impose his own western values on the country; to avoid immediately assuming that, because social and political conditions within the state didn't correspond with those of a more economically advanced nation, they should be rejected outright. After all, wasn't the City of the Dead basically a more drastic version of Liverpool's Toxteth or Dublin's Ballymun? Certainly one could argue that, at least, in those ghettos such basic facilities as running water, proper sanitation, and electricity were available, but then again wasn't the very fact that such ghettos existed in two relatively affluent western countries a rather damning statement in itself? And therefore, how could I rightfully condemn a place like the City of the Dead? Egypt—a fiscal basket-case—simply had a more brutal and stark form of poverty that our own.

It was an intriguing viewpoint, and one which I could have almost accepted had I not seen a flashy district like Mohandessin or watched Egypt's well-heeled children queuing up for admission to the disco in the Nile Hilton. All societies have such inequities, but driving by mausoleums housing families of five, catching the smell of food being cooked in the little rooms adjacent to the sarcophagus, Egypt's social divisions became chilling in their implications. A journey across Cairo didn't simply drag you in and out of the twentieth century; it also brought you through a series of cantons, some of which were westernized, some almost medieval. And though the citizens of all these cantons shared the same nationality and language, their worlds were so dissimiliar, so at variance with each other, that one could only fear that, given the right set of circumstances, Cario's dangerously primed inequities would one day explode.

We didn't stay long in the City of the Dead, but just before we left we stopped outside an improvised schoolhouse. Crayon drawings were pasted to the latticed windows of the mausoleum in which it was located. A child's sense of wonder in the bleakest possible place. Nearby, in one of the tombs, a colour television flickered on top of a crypt.

Twenty minutes later, we were back in Brian's flat in Mohandessin, drinking tea.

* * * * *

Soraya was sitting in the lounge of the Hotel Rialto talking to Mr Hussainy. It seems that Mr Hussainy—a man in his sixties—recently broke his ankle. This accident occured when he managed to fall out of bed one morning. Since then, he'd got into the habit of dressing only in a faded silk bathrobe and striped pyjamas, spending most the day sitting on a chair outside his room, smoking Cleopatras and working his way through Anwar el-Sadat's autobiography. The book must have been slow going, because nine weeks later—on the eve of my departure from Egypt—I found Mr Hussainy still sitting outside his door and still only fifty pages into the late President's memoirs.

Soraya and Mr Hussainy were two of the 'lifers' at the Hotel Rialto. Another long-term guest was Mr Alwan. He was a senior civil servant from Ismailia who had been transferred to Cairo, but didn't want to move his family to the Big Smoke, so he used the Rialto as his Cairo base, commuting home at the weekends. He was extremely punctillious about his appearance, and was always nattily dressed in a tan business suit or in a golf pro's cardigan which made him look like an Egyptian Perry Como. He also had the habit of repeating the same story several times over, and when he learned that I lived in Dublin, he told me in great detail about his recent holiday in Ireland. In the weeks to come—whenever I was darting in and out of the Rialto from my trips around the country—Mr Alwan always made a point of stopping me and reiterating the fact that he had spent a fortnight in Dublin and Wicklow. By the time I left Egypt, I must have heard about his Irish holiday at least six times.

The other members of the semi-permanent crew at the Hotel Rialto included a young German studying Arabic in Cairo, who had the habit of staring at me with such malevolence that I began to wonder if I had offended him in some former life. Then there was the cheery refugee from Eritrea who was stuck in Cairo while waiting for a western country to grant him asylum, and passed the time by walking around the hotel with a towel wrapped around his waist. Derek, a young kid from Nottingham, was making daily trips to the Sudanese Embassy to see if they might give him a visitor's visa. Derek had taught in the Sudan several years earlier, and upon returning home to England had become a dole queue statistic. After two years of unemployment, he finally decided to escape Thatcherite England and caught a bucket shop flight to Tel Aviv. Then, he crossed into Egypt by bus and landed at the Rialto, where he shared a room with a transient series of guests in order to conserve money. In fact, Derek's finances were getting so tight that he was surviving on a pound a day in Cairo, and was thinking about checking out of the Rialto and moving to a men's hostel that only charged the equivalent of 50 pence a night. Then again, if the Sudanese visa ever came through, he might just travel third class from Cairo to Khartoum, though he didn't seem to be relishing that prospect. Of course, if he could convince the British Council in Cairo to throw a few private students his way, he was thinking about staying on in Egypt and becoming a part-time English tutor. But, according to him, the Council wasn't being exactly helpful in finding him students, so the journey to the Sudan seemed like his best option. That is, if the Sudanese Embassy ever issued him with a visa and if his money held out.

Derek was confused. He'd thought that this trip to Egypt would give his life some necessary focus. But since coming to the Rialto he'd been sucked in by the easy charms of the place, and had succumbed to lethargy. It was a common disease in the hotel. Tad, for example, had stopped by the Rialto for a night and was still here four months later. Then again, loitering without intent in a foreign city was nothing new to Tad. When we met in the lounge of the hotel, I asked him if he was in Egypt on holiday.

'I'm just . . . travelling', he said.

'How long have you been travelling?', I said.

'Four years.'

'Four years?' I said.

'I used to run a big catering business in Phoenix, but then one day I got fed up, so I sold out my shares in the company and just hit the road.'

I didn't know whether to believe this story. So much about Tad aroused doubt. His blond hair tinged with grey that made me wonder whether he dyed it. His fussy precious little voice. And his paternal interest in one of the young porters in the hotel. Even his narrative of his travels strained credibility.

'I was in Thailand for a while, which was just *marvellous*. And then I went to Germany, and some people I knew there said I should stop travelling and do something positive for a change. So they offered me this job as a male nurse.'

'A male nurse in a German hospital?', I said.

'Oh, it wasn't a hospital. It was a Christian Science nursing home.'

'What the hell were you doing in a Christian Science nursing home?'

'Well . . . I was raised as a Christian Scientist.'

'But I thought Christian Scientists don't believe in doctors.'

'They don't. But they do have nursing homes around the world where members of the faith go when they're sick.'

'What sort of nursing home is it without doctors?'

'Well, they have their own form of doctors. They're called

'practitioners' and they come to pray with the patient. And then there are nurses like me who were there to make the patient comfortable. But we couldn't administer medicines or anything like that. It was against the faith. Anyway . . . I nursed for a while in Germany and then I worked in a Christian Science nursing home in England for three years. But after one of my patients died of gangrene because she got a cut on her toe and refused to use an antibiotic on the wound, I lost my faith in the Church. So I quit my job and decided to head back to Thailand. But since the plane first stopped in Egypt, I decided to spend a day in Cairo. That was late June, and here I am, still here in October.'

Talking with Tad was like listening to a displaced person with the funds available to hop a plane whenever he felt like it. His future plans were a series of airports.

'I'm going to Kenya next. Maybe a few days in Nairobi, then a little safari among all those *wonderful* animals. After that, I fly to the Seychelles for a bit—I hear they are just *lovely*. And then it's back to Nairobi and on to Burundi.'

'Burundi?' I said. 'Why?'

'I want to *taste* Central Africa.'

'You'll certainly get a curious taste from Burundi. What's there? I can't even remember the name of its capital.'

'Bujumbura', Tad said. 'It's supposed to be real charming. A little gem. Mind you, it's real poor. The average wage is around sixty American dollars a year. And half the population are supposed to have AIDS.'

'Sounds great', I said.

The 8pm news in English on television interrupted Tad from describing the other delights of Burundi. All the foreigners in the lounge and some of the staff gathered around the old black and white television to hear the official version of today's domestic and international events from the government-controlled broadcasting service. Two newsreaders faced the cameras and began the news summary with the following item:

> *President Hosni Mubarak today headed a meeting of the General Secretariat of the National Democratic Party, in which he briefed the group on his recent tour to Europe and the United States, in addition to discussing ways of facing current domestic problems.*

A film clip rolled, showing the President sitting at the head of a table surrounded by his sober-suited General Secretariat. As the camera panned around Egypt's inner circle, the newsreader listed the names of each member of the National Democratic Party who had attended the meeting. This took three minutes.

Second item on the news:

> *President Hosni Mubarak today laid the foundation stone of the new Beni Suef City, which will emerge to the east of the old Beni Suef City, around seventy miles south of Cairo.*

It was always the same on the 8pm news. No matter what crisis may have befallen the world, the first stories to be broadcast invariably dealt with how President Hosni Mubarak had spent his day. It was a reminder that Egypt was still essentially a one-party state. Though Mubarak, in his attempts to steer a moderate course after Sadat's clampdown, had allowed opposition parties to operate freely once again, his party—the National Democratic Party—still ruled supreme. An election in Egypt was a foregone conclusion: the National Democratic Party were always the winners, always romping home with an overwhelming mandate. Nasser's revolution of 1952 hadn't ended monarchial rule in Egypt—it had simply transferred that rule into the hands of a new political elite. It was a pattern that had existed throughout Egyptian history: the Pharaohs, the ancient Greeks, the Arabs, and the Turks had all established dynasties which controlled the country's destiny until an invasion or a coup wrestled power out of their hands. Mubarak, therefore, was simply the third generation of the Nasserite legacy. He had been Sadat's heir-apparent, and had ascended to the throne after a wave of automatic gunfire abruptly ended his predecessor's rule.

He was, in short, the Pharaoh of the moment.

* * * * *

The Egyptian Television Centre, located on the Corniche facing the Nile, was surrounded by soldiers. Heavily armed soldiers carrying automatic weapons. On a first-floor balcony, two recruits manned a machine-gun turret, and you had to pass through an elaborate system of security checkpoints before being allowed to enter the building. This heavy military presence spoke for itself. The government was taking no chances. They had rendered the state broadcasting system coup-proof.

The International Press Centre was located on the first floor of the broadcasting complex, and it was there that I belatedly registered as a visiting foreign writer and obtained my press credentials. The bureaucrat who was dealing with me seemed rather peeved that I had been in the country for nearly a month and hadn't bothered to get my accreditation earlier. But when I explained that I had been travelling in the north of the country for the past few weeks (not mentioning, of course, that I had been in Siwa), he shrugged his shoulders and issued me with my press card. Once again, Egyptian bureaucracy showed that, however hard it tried, it could never really be officious, and lived according to the principle of *Maaleesh*.

After receiving my credentials, I wandered over to the wire service room and scanned the Reuters teletype. The big story of the day was that the American Deputy Secretary of State, John Whitehead, was in Cairo to meet President Mubarak. It was a fence-mending visit, designed to smooth over diplomatic relations between Egypt and the United States; relations which were still rather strained after the American interception of the Egyptair jet carrying the Achille Lauro hijackers.

Given Egypt's dependence on the United States for military aid, and given America's dependence on Egypt as an ally in the region, I was curious to know how the Egyptians viewed their future relationship with their *padrone* in the light of recent events. So, I asked one of the assistants in the International Press Centre if she could set up a meeting with a government spokesman who would be willing to give me a semi-official reaction to the Achille Lauro affair. After making a few phone calls, she came back to me and said that an appointment had been arranged.

'With a government official?', I said.

'With a senior journalist at *Al Ahram* newspaper', she said. 'He will be able to answer any of your questions.'

Had I not known about *Al Ahram* newspaper, I would have found it strange that I was being sent to a journalist to hear the government line on the current state of Egyptian-American relations. However, *Al Ahram*, besides being the leading 'quality' newspaper in the Middle East, was also a semi-official government publication. And therefore, a senior journalist on the paper was almost as much a spokesman for the Mubarak administration as a press attache in the Ministry of Information would be.

The main newsroom of *Al Ahram* was unlike any other journalistic bullpen I had ever seen. It was actually neat and orderly.

Reporters sat at a tidy row of desks, the floor was free of cigarette butts and the crumpled-up remains of yesterday's copy, and no one looked like they'd been on a bender the night before. The journalist I was meeting—I'll call him Mr Moustafa—had an office adjacent to the newsroom. He was a man in his sixties, immaculately dressed in a dark suit which gave him the cut of a merchant banker. He welcomed me with formal courteousness, and after an elderly servant brought two small demi tasse cups of thick coffee, he said that he didn't mind if I took notes of our conversation as long as his name was not attached to his comments. That agreed, he then launched into a thirty minute lecture on Egyptian-American *realpolitik*.

'We were not expecting this sort of treatment from the United States', he said. 'Egypt only got involved in the hijacking at the request of the involved powers—Italy and America. And the hijacking was brought to a peaceable conclusion without bloodshed. When we made a deal with the hijackers to fly them to Tunis, we were not aware that they had killed an American and pushed him overboard. Had we known that, we would have approached the situation differently.

'Reagan intercepted the Egyptair jet because he wanted to show that he was fed up with terrorism. But, in doing so, he took the risk of alienating his allies in the area. American policy is contradictory. Certainly, they have a policy against terrorism, but this policy collided with their other policy of having strong relations with moderate Middle East countries.

'But the peace process in the region was spoiled beforehand by the Israeli's bombing of the PLO Headquarters in Tunis. For this to be followed by the American interception of our jet was a blow for those working for peace. The Americans always take the Israeli's side when dealing with the situation in the area. They want the PLO to be the scapegoat.

'If the US wants peace in the Middle East, they'll have to work for it. They must begin to make a distinction between terrorism and trouble in the occupied lands of the West Bank and Gaza. The PLO's rights should be recognized—self-determination and the right to retain previous lands as agreed by the United Nations resolutions. 'Land for peace'—it is the only solution.

'Since President Reagan supported the Israeli raid on the PLO headquarters in Tunis, Egyptian-American relations have been strained. And now, after his order to intercept our aircraft, people in the country are beginning to question what the US wants, and why it attacked the sovereignty of Egypt. People wanted Mubarak to take action against the US, but what action could he take? As Mubarak said, the US is a superpower. How can Egypt stand up to that?

'The Americans should remember that Egypt is not only their ally, but a peacemaker in this part of the world. If Egypt loses this role, it will affect its position in the area where other countries are still campaigning against the Camp David accord. If the Americans keep acting this way, it will weaken the position of the moderates inside Egypt and the Arab world. If you weaken the position of Mubarak, of King Hussein in Jordan, and even of Saudi Arabia—which is silently supporting Egypt and Jordan in its peace efforts—then stability will come undone in this part of the world.

'Being dependent on American aid doesn't mean you lose your national will. There is a limit to what a dependant can accept. The Americans should also remember that they are dependent on the Egyptians as a stabilizing force in the Middle East.

'The radicals in Egypt gained a bit of ground after the Tunis bombing and the hijacking. And, believe me, the Islamic fundamentalists would love to initiate an uprising. If they were well prepared, they could take over the entire country. Thankfully, they're not strong enough yet. And the tide is beginning to turn against them, as writers and the intelligensia are beginning to satirize them in the newspapers and on television. But these are dangerous times for Egypt. Very dangerous times. And now, Reagan, through one action, has put a big question mark over President Mubarak's head. Did he not realize that to put a question mark over Mubarak's head in a country like this was an incredibly risky thing to do?'

Listening to Mr Moustafa speak, I was not only struck by the forcefulness of his arguments, but also by the absence of any bitterness or anger in his voice. In expressing his country's frustration with current American foreign policy in the region, his tone was one of disappointment, almost hurt. But perhaps this disappointment was a reflection of an even larger disappointment he felt for the state of the country at the moment. Judging by his years, Mr Moustafa was probably in his thirties when Nasser seized power in 1952, and his career had been undoubtably tied up with Egypt's shifting political currents since then. He had watched Nasser triumph over the British and the French at Suez, and had seen him become a major player on the international stage—'the father of all Arabs' whose dreams of a socialist Egypt and an unified pan-Arab world collapsed around him. Still, there was a boldness to the man, just as there was a boldness to Sadat. The boldness to storm Israeli fortifications on the Sinai during the October '73 war. The boldness to break with the Soviets and link arms with Washington. The boldness to hammer out a peace treaty with the Israelis at Camp David. But, here again, the legacy of Sadat was a jumble of failed dreams. His free-market policies had dangerously widened the gap between rich and poor. His accord with Israel had made Egypt an outcast in the Arab world. His attempts to appease extremist groups like the Muslim Brotherhood only ended up fuelling the fires of Islamic fundamentalism, while alienating Egypt's Christian minority at the same time. And in the final months of his life, his crackdown on those he perceived to be his political enemies inevitably widened the divisions within Egyptian society.

Since that time, Mubarak had been trying to steer a middle course, and had succeeded in cauterizing many of the wounds of the Sadat years. But his country's dilemmas were so overwhelming, so potentionally inflammatory, that his principal task at the moment was to ensure the continuing stability of the state. No doubt, the repercussions of the Achille Lauro affair would die down, but I could sense Mr Moustafa's quiet fear that, given the nation's precarious health, Mubarak could ill-afford such doubts to be raised about his strength as a leader. Egypt had not only suffered a humiliation through Reagan's actions; it has also been shown that, in the eyes of its benefactor, it was considered a welfare case whose sovereignty could be violated since America was picking up its tab. And perhaps what so troubled and saddened Mr Moustafa was the fact that Egypt had never been able to escape that dilemma which almost all Third World countries face—the need to have a superpower as a patron. Thirty-three years after the 1952 revolution, it had all come down to this: Egypt—the traditional head of the Arab world—was a dependent nation facing into an uncertain and troubling future. And all it could do at the moment was hope that the institutions of the state were durable enough to make it through these volatile times.

After leaving Mr Moustafa, I returned to the International Press Centre and learned the outcome of the meeting between President Mubarak and the American Deputy of State. It was predictable. Whitehead had issued a statement saying the United States very much regretted that developments took the course that they did, and spoke of the special relationship between the countries. The Egyptian president, for his part, declined to speak to the press after the meeting, but indicated before seeing Whitehead that Egypt was willing to forgive and forget as long as America began to speed up the Middle East peace process.

Quite simply, he was offering the Americans a way of making amends and they seized it immediately. Later that evening, on the BBC World Service, I heard that the then Israeli prime minister, Shimon Peres, had offered to hold peace talks with Jordan; a move which I interpreted to be a way of appeasing Mubarak and showing him that both Israel and America were serious about peace in the region. Still, Washington never really gave him the apology that he was looking for. Then again, if there was one thing that the whole Achille Lauro business proved, it was that diplomatic relations between Egypt and the United States means never having to say you're sorry.

* * * * *

The dreams of the 1952 revolution may have been dead, but certain legacies of the Nasserite years still lingered on. A few days after meeting Mr Moustafa, I came face to face with a dilemma which had been vexing Egypt for three decades when I went to get my visa extended at Cairo's municipal offices.

The municipal offices were located in the Al Moghamma building on Tahrir Square. The building had been a gift from the fraternal peoples of the USSR and had been designed in that bleak, oppresive Stalinist style which Soviet architects were forced to favour in the fifties. Curiously enough, the Soviet image still clung to the building because if you spoke about the Al Moghamma to anyone in the know in Cairo, they always reacted with horror, probably in the same way that Muscovites trembled when the KGB headquarters—the Lyubianka—was mentioned. Not that the Al Moghamma housed a terrifying state security service. Rather, it was a prison of a different sort—a bureaucratic purgatory that, from all accounts, tested the limits of your patience.

'You're going to the Al Moghamma to get your visa extended?', an Egyptian friend said to me with considerable sympathy. 'Expect to spend at least five hours there. The place is a nightmare.'

He had a point. Entering the building was like walking into a German expressionist film of the twenties: dark grey corridors bathed in shadow; a purposeless mob of people milling around the foyer with no place to go; an endless series of doors, behind which functionaries meandered through stacks of yellowing files; a sense that nobody exactly knew what they were doing in this half-lit snarl of officialdom and had become trapped in an illogical system of their own making. Franz Kafka would have definitely approved of the Al Moghamma. It was his kind of place.

After getting lost twice, I eventually found my way to the room where visa extensions were granted. Had my visa not been expiring the next day, I would have fled the office immediately, as there must have been three hundred people trying to figure out which queue they should be in. Their confusion was understandable, as there were at least four different groups of windows dealing with four different types of visas. What's more, each of these windows had three other windows adjoining it, and you first had to present yourself at all three subsidiary windows before being allowed to proceed to the main window to get your visa.

The drill went something like this: plough your way through the mob and try to discover which queue was for the type of visa extension you required. Then, find the right queue in which to receive an application form. Fill in the form and then join another queue in which the form was checked. Proceed then to the next queue, where you were asked to show proof that you had officially changed the equivalent of $180—the amount required to get a one-month visa extension. After that, it was off to another queue where your accumulated paperwork was double-checked. Then, you finally made your way to the last queue where you paid a small fee and watched with relief as your passport was embossed with a new visa.

Altogether, there were something like twenty queues in that bad dream of an office. But what turned this chaotic scene into a true piece of absurdist theatre was the fact that, behind the windows where a small handful of civil servants attempted to cope with the mob, there were at least fifteen other people sitting at desks, *doing nothing*. One man in particular caught my attention. He was seated at his desk, his hands folded on top of it like a schoolboy, smiling serenely. Nearby, a cluster of women hung around another desk, gossiping and trying on each others' lipstick. At first, I thought they must be on a tea break, but during the hours I spent waiting in a long variety of queues, they never returned to work. What were these people doing here?

The answer is, they were perpertuating a bureaucratic system. A system which guarantees all Egyptian school leavers some form of employment.

It was a system that showed, in miniature, the conflicting ideologies of the Nasser and Sadat years. Under Nasser, there had been socialism. Under Sadat, the free market. Nasser had brought in the Soviets and declared that the only way forward was through *Arab socialism*. Sadat had evicted the Soviets, jumped on the American aid bandwagon, and declared that the only way forward was through *infitah*—his Open Door economic policy. Nasser believed in a nationalized economy. Sadat condemned this doctrine and told Egypt's private entrepreneurs to go back to work. Nasser assured all school children that they never would have to worry about finding a job, and therefore work, no matter how superfluous, was created. Sadat wanted to cut back on this 'jobs for all' system and hoped that a free-market economy would whisk a whole new generation of Egyptians into non-state jobs. Nasser created a monolithic state bureaucracy. Sadat, with the failure of his Open Door policy, had no choice but to maintain it.

Two ideologues, each determined to impose his own vision on Egypt's destiny. Their aspirations were extravagant, yet each failed in his attempt to create a new social order. And if the scene in the Al Moghamma building told me anything, it was this: though Nasser may have left behind the Aswan Dam, and Sadat the Camp David accord, the true legacy of their separate regimes was a bureaucracy of towering waste. Like a genetic disease passed on from one generation to the next, it had now been inherited by Hosni Mubarak. And he too had yet to find a cure for it.

The Egyptian president was not alone in his dilemma. Standing next to me in the queue was a young Italian engineer who had been working in the country for over a year. This was his third trip to the Al Moghamma building within a week, and he was beginning to look like a candidate for a straight-jacket.

'I have spent over twelve hours here in the past four days', he said, the desperation creeping into his voice. 'And everytime I come back, they tell me I do not have the proper documentation. So, I return to my employers and obtain the documents they ask for, but then I bring them back here and they tell me, "No, this is not the documentation we are looking for." Four times they have told me this. Four times I have come back here with the papers they have requested. And they keep telling me this is not the documentation they want, even though it is the documentation they have demanded.'

He suddenly realized he was shouting and that all eyes in the room were upon him. 'You see', he hissed to me, 'they all think I am crazy. But it is not me who is crazy. It is this place. This country. I tell you, even in Rome this would not happen. Even in Rome they would not treat me this way.'

The last I saw of the Italian, he was threatening a civil servant with grievous bodily harm. The civil servant seemed unimpressed, as minor nervous breakdowns in the Al Moghamma building were nothing unusual. There was an unsubstantiated story going around expatriate circles in Cairo that an unfortunate African recently threw himself out of a window of the Al Moghamma. Whether or not this rumour was true didn't seem to worry people, as it was an accepted fact that the Al Moghamma could drive you to such acts of desperation. But I was fortunate to have gotten through the ordeal of applying for a visa extension with few mental scars. Perhaps this was due to the fact that they were working quickly that day, since it only took four hours to obtain an additional month's stay in Egypt.

And when my name was finally called to collect my passport, I caught sight again of the man I had seen earlier sitting at his desk, oblivious to the world around him. He was still there, doing nothing.

* * * * *

Donald Morris knew all about places like the Al Moghamma building. He knew what this 'jobs for all' system had done to the Egyptian economy, and he also knew that Egypt had debts of $31 billion which it was in no position to pay. Donald used expressions like 'no sense of control' to describe the country's financial policies. And, like a doctor informing a patient that he must quit cigarettes, he seemed genuinely worried that, if Egypt didn't give up its bad budgetary habits, it would soon be riddled with a permanent case of fiscal emphysema. Then again, it was Donald's job to be worried about Egypt's economic well-being, as he was external debt adviser with a major international bank.

Donald was originally from Cardiff, but any hint of Wales had been bled from his voice and he now talked with the tickertape precision of a City gent. He was a politely pinstriped man in his early forties, and before coming to Egypt, he had done a stint in Zaire, sifting through the economic debris of the Mobutu regime. After that baptism by fire in Kinshasa, Cairo struck him as a reasonably pleasant place to live. And, unlike many members of the foreign community (who spent much of their time singing one long histronic aria about the city's horrors), he had adapted to the capital's manic cadences and idiosyncracies. But what he couldn't comprehend was the country's economic recklessness. Egypt was like a compulsive gambler who'd had a few good years at the racecourse before hitting a losing streak. And now, the bookmakers it had been dealing with—i.e., some of the world's leading financial institutions—were calling in their chits and getting rather anxious about their client's inability to settle up the score.

Egypt ranks near the top in the world debt league for developing countries. But Egypt is in a far more critical economic position than, say, another developing country like Brazil for one simple reason. It is a desert nation with few natural resources and no real industrial base. In fact, it only has four real sources of income: oil (which accounts for around 25 per cent of its Gross Domestic Product), the Suez Canal, tourism and its expatriate citizens sending money back to their families at home. Not exactly the sort of economic assets to inspire confidence, especially since Egypt, like its neighbours in the Arabian Gulf, has been badly hit by the downward trend in oil prices. Worst yet, with opportunities for foreign employment now severely limited, there has been a fall in the amount of workers' remittances flooding into the country. And, to top things off, little episodes like the Achille Lauro hijacking have not exactly been doing wonders for the tourist trade.

So what you basically have is an economy whose sources of revenue are hitting the skids. But, as Donald explained to me, this crisis has been further exacerbated by Egypt's dizzying population growth. Back when Nasser promised his compatriots that no Egyptian would ever be without employment, he justified the country's low wage structure by subsidizing the cost of such items as bread and basic foodstuffs, petrol and public transportation. At the time, Egypt was a major exporter of food, so the Exchequer could easily offer bread to its citizens for next to nothing, while still earning a considerable amount of badly needed foreign currency by selling its foodstuffs on the open market. Similarly, as an oil producing nation, it could slash the price of petrol for domestic consumption, and still clean up by retailing it internationally at standard OPEC rates.

It was an economic system that worked as long as Egypt's population remained constant. But, when the country began to add a million new citizens to its rolls every ten months, the system began to short-circuit and fuse. More mouths to feed meant less food to export. As the census figures hit staggering new heights, Egypt eventually had to abandon the food export game and begin to buy in its food supplies, to the point where it is now forced to import 50 per cent of all its food; a devastating turn-around for a nation that once was the breadbasket of the Middle East.

More mouths to feed also meant more money spent on subsidies. When Sadat became President and abandoned Nasserite socialism, he still couldn't find a way around this now-established method of offering food to his compatriots at nominal prices. Had he been able to increase wages, he might have been able to reduce the subsidies. But, since the economy couldn't afford to meet a wage hike, he had no option but to keep the system ticking over. At one point, he did try to get away with a price increase on subsidized goods by raising the cost of bread by a penny. This move resulted in riots which got so out of hand that the Army had to be called in to restore order. Recently, the Mubarak government tempted fate through a similar price hike. Within days of its announcement that bread was now three pence a loaf, the Army was on the streets, quelling disturbances in the town of Mansour. For a government conscious of its continuing stability, this incident was bad news. And it pointed up a basic truth about Egyptian society: in a country where 70 per cent of the population is illiterate, the vast majority of the electorate care little about the internal workings of government. What they do care about, however, is the day-to-day business of living. And if they perceive that the government's policies are threatening their stomachs, they can quickly turn into a volatile force to be reckoned with.

The regime of Hosni Mubarak had therefore been placed in a no-win situation. If it removed this system of subsidies, it invited a popular uprising. If it perpetuated it, it invited even greater fiscal chaos. No wonder foreign advisers like Donald Morris were mesmerized by this Gordian Knot of an economy. It had become so entrenched that it defied solution. Certainly, Donald saw ways of containing Egypt's jumbled finances— cutting back on imports, devaluing its exchange rate, providing incentives for domestic food producers—but whether the government was even in a position to act on such advice was a big question. As Donald acknowledged, there was a growing political awareness in international financial circles that you couldn't force Egypt to bite the economic bullet too hard. Because if you did—if you pushed the country that bit too far—it could collapse around you.

Leaving Donald's office, I strolled down to the Egyptian Museum and spent several hours browsing through the world's largest Pharaonic junk shop. And in a room devoted to Funerary Furniture of the Middle Kingdom, I came across an intriguing oddity: a wooden casket, excavated in Luxor, which once housed the remains of the Scribe of the Treasury of the Temple of Amun. The inside of his casket had been illustrated with a momentous scene from his life. A scene which showed him offering flowers to the gods of the West.

Nothing had changed, I thought. Egypt's Scribes of the Treasury still bow down to the gods of the West.

* * * * *

On Fridays, the men who control Egypt's wealth take the sabbath day off and go to the Gezira Club. They enter the changing room where a team of attendants relieve them of their business suits and help outfit them for the day's sporting activities. One man struggles into a pair of jodhpur breeches and highly polished riding boots, tucks a crop under his arm and marches out like a German film director of the twenties heading off to the set. Another pulls on a pair of designer swimming trunks and covers his layers of paleozoic fat with a Cardin shirt. A young executive, fresh from the tennis courts, splashes himself with Christian Dior *après rasage* and snaps his fingers at an elderly attendant for a towel.

Outside, on the verandah facing the pool, their wives and children are already *in situ*. The women sit together in small conspiratorial groups, drinking lemonade served by turbanned waiters. Their nails are lacquered red and their faces are elaborate masks of pancake base, eye shadow, and co-ordinating shades of lipstick. Nearby, Egyptian jailbait—teenage girls wearing jeans that fit them like surgical gloves and Benetton jumpers slung casually over their shoulders—smoke cigarettes and muffle their ears with Walkmans. Their male counterparts carry squash rackets and peer out at the world from behind Ray Ban sunglasses; an aloof touch that comes with the knowledge that they are the future power-brokers of Egypt.

It's a curious scene. The Gezira Club was once the haunt of British officers until Nasser nationalized it. But the well-heeled Egyptians whose recreational needs it now caters for have left its colonial atmosphere intact. There's a whiff of imperial detachment in the air; a sense that within these walls, you can temporarily detach yourself from the clamorous rhythms of Cairo and assert your position as a member of the country's new ascendancy. Like the colonial administrators of the Empire, this governing class also erects barriers between itself and 'the natives'. It stands apart from society at large, imperious and lofty. And yet, beneath the patrician veneer, you can smell the panic. The fear that, one day soon, the walls might come tumbling down, leaving them exposed and vunerable. The fear of being caught up in another Iran. The fear that comes with knowing you're an endangered species.

But still, it's Friday. And the pool is packed. And the waiters are serving up club sandwiches. And the changing room attendants are safeguarding everybody's valuables. And Jidan is just back from Zurich. And Osman and his cronies are playing cards and chewing on extra-large Havana specials. All is as it should be. So, sit back. Put your feet up. Work on your tan. It's Friday, after all.

And on Fridays at the Gezira Club, Cairo seems far away.

On Fridays in Embaba, however, they sell camels. 700 camels which have just arrived from the Sudan, brought overland through the desert by small teams of men. The trek can take up to sixty days, and the going is rough, since sixty days in the sand looking after a hundred camels is no joke. But the journey must be undertaken if you are a freelance camel dealer. For here, in Embaba, is the largest camel market on the continent.

The camels are put on show in an arid fairground. Clustered in groups, packed tightly together, you have to carefully manouevre your way through this four-legged mob, always remembering to avoid stepping on their hooves. Camels take exception to such mistakes and are known to bite. They are also known to be rabid which makes it doubly important that you don't accidently provoke them in any way. And if—as often happens in the market—a camel breaks away from its owner, bares its teeth and charges, you get out of the way. Fast.

The bargaining begins in earnest. A dealer points out one of his camel's attributes to a buyer. Note how well fed it is. Check out its fine unblemished skin. And, while you're at it, take a look at that hump. Now tell me honestly, have you ever seen such a big hump before? Like I said, you're not going to find a better camel on the lot. And I'll tell you what I'm going to do. Since we've done business before, since you know me as an honest guy, I'm going to give him to you at a knock-down price. He's all yours for just £400 cash. And, really, I'm doing myself by offering him at that price, but for you I'll make a sacrifice. Just £400 and you can drive him away now.

The buyer seems unimpressed. He's probably the representative of a slaughterhouse and he's sizing the camel up with a professional eye. How much meat can we get out of him? Is his skin good enough to be tanned and turned into hide? Will his hump yield much camel oil? All these considerations are determining factors in the bartering process, and an unspoken understanding exists between the two parties. The owner, a Sudanese, knows that it's a seller's market, since Egypt's camel stocks are low and it depends on imports from the Sudan. The buyer, on the other hand, realizes that the Sudanese has dragged the camel all the way up to Cairo through the desert and certainly doesn't want to have to drag it all the way back again, which means that he's going to have to settle for an equitable price. And anyway, he's probably thinking, 'This guy's trying to pull a fast one on me. That camel isn't well-fed. It's so thin you can just about see its rib-cage. Does he think I was born yesterday, trying to unload an anorexic camel on me? With poxy skin to boot?'

He offers £300. The seller is outraged. Think of my overheads, he says. This is low-class merchandise, the buyer counters. I leave them as they sit down over a cup of tea and continue haggling.

It's always the same every Friday. The wheelings and dealings of an open market-place. Just a few miles down the road in the Gezira Club, the men with the diamond pinky rings are discussing economic strategy and the devaluation of the Egyptian pound. On Fridays in Embaba, it's all camel flesh.

On Fridays outside the Hotel Rialto, they pray. An impromptu mosque has been set up in an alleyway. Fifty men kneel down on mats and then prostrate themselves to their God. A sheikh chants passages from the Koran through a microphone. His voice crackles on a loudspeaker, rises above the heads of the faithful at prayer and cascades out into the street. A street that is clogged with cars. The dissonant sound of automobile horns counterpoints the melodic incantations to Allah. Two spheres—the spiritual and the temporal—collide.

Fridays in Cairo. The City Victorious is at rest. But its worlds keep colliding nonetheless.

Chapter Five

Faith of Our Fathers

I CHECKED OUT OF the Hotel Rialto and walked down to Tahrir Square. After making several inquiries, I found a collective taxi heading north and asked the driver to drop me off on the desert highway opposite the oasis of Wadi el Natrun. We agreed upon a price and I climbed into his beat-up Peugeot station wagon. Ten other passengers squeezed in after me, including a monk in his late thirties, dressed in black robes and a knitted skullcap. I took a seat in the rear of the motorized coffin. This turned out to be an unwise decision, for as soon as the taxi began to gain speed, I bore the brunt of the vehicle's lack of suspension. Every pothole, every irregularity in the surface of the road, sent me flying. The seat itself was designed for an Indian fakir, with jagged bits of coiled spring sticking up through the vinyl upholstery. And for the next ninety minutes, as we bumped along the dual carriageway, my head made frequent contact with the roof of the taxi, while the seat of my trousers was incessantly perforated by the coiled upholstery springs.

After one hundred punishing kilometres, the driver veered into a lay-by and shouted 'Wadi el Natrun.' The monk and I got out, the taxi drove off, and we were left standing on the side of the road. The monk tapped my shoulder and pointed to the west. At first, all I could see was desert. But then, in the middle of this empty canvas, my eyes fixed upon a blurred configuration in the distance; a medieval fortress adrift in the sand. This was my destination: the monastery of St. Macarius.

The monk said 'We walk five kilometres from here', and we set off down a gravelled side road. After a few yards, we were met by a young boy who greeted the monk solemnly, bending down to kiss his hand. The monk smiled at him, but the boy remained grave and reverential, walking several feet behind us as we resumed our slow march to the monastery gates.

I was hoping to spend several days behind those gates. In a Coptic monastery founded by a camel driver in 3 AD. Before coming to Egypt, I had read of the story of St Macarius; how, one day, he was out roaming through this stretch of desert when an angel appeared before him and bade him found an monastic order on this spot. The Order still remained, as did the Coptic Church—a Christian minority in a Muslim state. The Copts, whose origins dated back to the foundations of the early Christian church, now only comprised around 6 per cent of the population, but still were an important force in the affairs of the country. Indeed, Egypt had always held itself up as a model of religious tolerance in the Middle East: a place where Islam and Christianity co-existed without belligerence. But recently, the rise of Muslim fundamentalism had begun to seriously strain relations between the two communities. As groups like the Muslim Brotherhood campaigned for stricter obedience to the world of Allah and a return to Koranic law, so the Coptic minority had begun to feel increasingly isolated and threatened. Sporadic rioting in mixed Muslim/Coptic neighbourhoods was no longer major news, and though the government media tried to play down this rise in sectarian violence, it was generally acknowledged that the spirit of ecumenical *detente* was eroding fast in Egypt.

And yet, anytime I broached the subject of sectarian tension with people I met in Cairo and Alexandria, I was usually told that it was only a handful of fanatics who were poisoning the atmosphere; that the majority of Muslims and Copts lived together harmoniously. There was not universal agreement on this matter, however. On one of my last nights in Cairo, I visited the home of a young doctor who had nursed me through a particularly explosive dose of food poisoning. He was interested in doing a post-graduate degree in Dublin, and after my insides finally stopped trying to qualify as an Olympic gymnast, he invited me around to learn more about the benighted city which had become my adopted home. He said he wanted to study in Ireland because it was a Catholic country, and he too was a Catholic. There weren't many followers of the Church of Rome in Egypt—perhaps 140,000 at most—making them a tiny sub-section of an already tiny Christian minority. And the doctor left me in no doubt as to how he felt about his Muslim compatriots.

'You can feel the discrimination by the way they look at you. When I was in university, they stared at me as if I was a foreigner. They pointed out to me that my name was different, that I didn't look typically Egyptian. Even the professors treated me differently because I wasn't a Muslim.

'I will tell you something you have probably not heard before. The greatest danger in the Middle East is Islam. It holds back everything—especially freedom.'

His vehement bitterness surprised me, and made me question all those declarations of inter-faith cordiality I had been hearing. It also made me realize how little I understood about the complexities of spiritual politics in Egypt today. Though I knew that the country had a variegated religious landscape, I had yet to venture out into that field. Walking down this desert road was, therefore, the beginning of my journey into the realm of Egypt's faithful.

The monk introduced himself as Father Archiloas and welcomed me to *Deir Abu Magar*—the monastery of St Macarius.

'Do you often go down to Cairo?' I asked him.

'No, we are not supposed to leave the monastery without the permission of the head of the Order—the Spiritual Father. But I had to see a patient who was in hospital, so I was allowed to go for a day.'

'You're a doctor?', I said.

'We have eleven doctors in the order, as well as thirty engineers, several of whom specialize in petroleum. There are also quite a number of agronomists, some teachers, and a few lawyers. We are not a contemplative order. We have many projects. We are doing much work in desert agriculture and cattle breeding, and we have a farm with around 600 workers, many of whom are from Upper Egypt. And the workers are both Muslim and Coptic. We have built housing for them and also take care of their health needs in a medical clinic which we run. The Spiritual Father says it is our duty for each of us to feed 1,000 people. This is our goal.'

I asked him if he felt there was active discrimination against the Copts by the Muslim majority in the country. 'I think there are problems between Muslims and Copts', he said, 'because the Copts do not love the Muslims enough. From a young age, we— the Copts—are told not to buy anything from a Muslim merchant. A child at the age of five cannot tell the difference between a Muslin and a Copt, but his parents put this idea in his mind. In the monastery, we show love to anybody who needs it. I do not think the Muslims hate the Copts. Only the extremists.'

He paused for a moment and pointed to a small mound in the middle of the desert. 'This is where St Macarius had the angel appear before him. On the other side of the monastery are caves where hermits live. It is an important part of our training—to be sent out by the Spiritual Father to live as a hermit for a while.

'In 1969, there were only six monks in St Macarius, and the monastery was in ruins. Now we have rebuilt the monastery and we have 100 monks in the Order. All throughout Egypt, there has been this revival of monastic life, this spiritual awakening.'

He had touched on an important point, for unlike many Christian faiths in the West, the Orthodox Coptic Church did not have to worry about a declining membership or a questioning congregation. If anything, the Copts' position as a minority religion in Egypt had only served to increase their steadfast devotion to the faith. This 'spiritual awakening' which Father Archiloas spoke of manifested itself not only through a renewal of religious piety, but also through a closing of ranks. A mighty fortress was their God; a bulwark never failing.

The midday sun had become uncompassionate, turning our measured walk into a true desert trek. A lorry piled high with soil passed us by and Father Archiloas flagged it down. We climbed into the cab and the young boy who had been walking behind us jumped on to the lorry's running board and braced himself against the window frame as we drove through the main gates.

The gates were deceptive. They announced our arrival in the oasis of Wadi el Natrun, but the monastery itself was still two kilometres away, perched on top of a small hill that overlooked a desert farm with huge patches of sugar beets swelling in the sand. The lorry careered up the road, bringing us closer to the restored stone walls of St Macarius. The walls were circular and smooth and some 30 feet high, giving the monastery the look of a gentrified ampitheatre. Father Archiloas asked the driver to stop and then told me to walk along the walls until I came to an archway. There, I would find a rope which, when pulled, would ring a bell in a tower and summon a member of the Order to let me in. We shook hands and I disembarked.

The archway was a monolith; a narrow stone tower which loomed over the monastery, with a plain granite cross adorning its summit. At the bottom of this structure was a small iron door, perhaps four feet high. Its design was intentionally humbling, as it forced you to enter the spiritual world as a supplicant, dwarfed to the glory of God.

The door was opened by an old monk with a thick grey beard. He was called Father Jeremiah and when I handed him a letter of introduction (provided for me by a Greek Orthodox priest in Cairo who was a friend of my Carmelite 'Auntie Breda'), he beckoned me in. I stooped down to pass through the door and then he closed it behind me, securing it with a wooden bolt. For the next two days, I would remain inside this enclosed universe.

After reading the letter, Father Jeremiah asked me to take a seat on one of the benches in the courtyard while he went off to consult the Spiritual Father. Left alone, I inspected my new surroundings. The initial impression I had of the monastery being a renovated ampitheatre proved correct, for its open-air interior was built on two tiers. The courtyard where I sat formed the upper level. It was laid out like a small public park with groves of trees and benches. Surrounding this area was a circular sweep of buildings containing guest quarters, assorted work-shops, and a kitchen and reception area for visitors. The monk's cells were on the far side of this ecclesiastical arena, and off-limits to all visitors.

Below this tier was the medieval centrepiece of the monastery —four small chapels with rounded domes and an ornate church, all of which dated back to anywhere between the fourth and seventh centuries. As I later learned, all the chapels were in ruins before the necessary five million Egyptian pounds was raised to rebuild the monastery, and the workmen involved literally re-discovered the chapels while digging through the rubble. Now, seen in their rehabilitated form, they took on the appearance of a separate village within a village; the doctrinal heart of a walled community.

Father Jeremiah returned and said that I should go get something to eat in the kitchen and then I would be shown to my quarters. The Spiritual Father had evidently granted permission for me to stay. I thanked Father Jeremiah for his assistance, he acknowledged my thanks with a nod of the head, and then hurried off. It was a characteristic I began to notice about all the monks. They were welcoming, they would stop and talk to you, but their conversation was never spendthrift. Their day was rigourously defined by work and prayer and, like men in a perpetual 'time and motion' study, they seemed always aware of the clock and the need to maximize their productivity.

In the kitchen, a young monk offered me lunch: baked beans served in a plastic bowl, a plate of bread rolls, a bottle of water.

'The water here is very sweet', he said, 'We have dug deep on the grounds of the monastery and have found a mineral spring.'

Before I had time to reply to this statement—to ask him how the Order managed to locate a mineral spring in the middle of the desert—he was gone. No small talk. No idleness. Only work and prayer.

I began to eat, aware of the deep silence of the place. After a few minutes, however, I looked up from my plate of baked beans and saw that I had company: an American who was pushing forty, with long wiry hair, an equally long beard, and thick spectacles which shielded a pair of eyes that were frozen over like a lake in winter. A backwoods prophet cultivating the Jesus Christ look.

'Howdy', he said in a soft accent that hinted at the Ozarks. 'I'm Glenn. Are you here on a spiritual mission?'

'Not exactly', I said. 'Is that your line of work?'

'I'm hoping to do a prayer vigil here for the Reagan-Gorbachev meeting. That is, if the Fathers let me stay.

'This is a very holy place. I knew I was coming here for a long time', he said, his voice thick with other worldliness. 'When I was working on a Quaker farm in Vermont, I had this dream. Train tracks going north. Haley's comet shooting across the sky. You know the comet's supposed to appear this year which means bad times ahead. The last time it appeared, World War One began. It gets me worried thinking about that.'

He fell silent, his eyes fixed upon a bread roll.

I said, 'Train tracks going north and Haley's comet brought you all the way from Vermont to the monastery of St Macarius?'

'Egypt is the centre of the world', he said. 'If you bunched all the land mass of the earth together, it would converge at the pyramids in Giza. And the pyramids are on the same longitude, less five degrees, as Stonehenge. You see? Egypt is the spiritual capital of our globe.'

'I never thought of it that way.'

Another awkward silence passed between us. Then Glenn said, 'I'm thinking of becoming a monk here. It would mean learning Arabic and the Coptic liturgy, and it would all depend on whether the Spiritual Father thought there could be a purpose for me in the Order.

'The Spiritual Father is like a Zen master. The monks have given him the authority for the spiritual guidance of the Order. He instructs them in the stripping away of the self; in the death of the ego. I would like to convince the Spiritual Father that I could obey him and kill off my ego completely. But maybe he'll want me to go back to the States and train for a year. I was thinking about joining a monastic order in L.A.'

'There's a monastery in L.A.?', I said.

'It's a very holy place.'

Glenn's magical mystery tour was beginning to wear thin, so I excused myself and asked one of the monks to show me to my 'cell.' It was an austere chamber located two floors above the kitchen. Bare stone floors, unadorned walls, a bed, a naked lightbulb, a porthole for a window.

I flopped on the bed and browsed through several pamphlets I had picked up in the reception area. They were all written by the Spiritual Father and dealt with such subjects as the meaning of fasting and the demands of the ascetic life. After reading about casting off your ego, controlling self-will and giving in to a spirit of obedience, I decided that I would be a disastrous monk.

Then I slept for an hour. When I woke, a narrow shaft of sunlight was streaking through the porthole, disorientating me completely. For a moment, I was convinced that I was aboard a ship cut adrift in calm tropical waters. But the illusion was only momentary. As if a switch had been pulled, the light suddenly blacked out and I was back in my darkened cell staring out through the circular window at the sand.

At the end of the corridor of guest cells was a small lounge, and it was there that I met two young novices: Michael and Magit. Michael told me that he had been a teacher, while Magit once practised law. But all that was in the past now, as they had given up the secular world to spend the rest of their lives in St Macarius. They had only been in the monastery for several weeks, and still seemed rather self-conscious and anxious about their status within this new community, waiting for the day to come when they would divest themselves of their street-clothes and don the habit of a monk.

I asked Magit when he discovered he had a vocation.

'I have always known that I was to be a monk', he said.

'Always?', I said.

'Ever since I was a boy.'

A bell rang in the courtyard. Michael and Magit heeded its call and left. Wandering downstairs I met Father Jeremiah, with whom I attempted to have a conversation.

'Where do you come from originally?', I said.

'I come from St Macarius', he said.

I passed that one over. 'And how long have you been with the Order?'

'It is not the quantity of time that counts', he said, 'only the quality of that time.'

I had overstepped a boundary. In an Order dedicated to the death of the self, personal history did not matter. Your home, your family, your former life no longer identified you within these monastical walls. You had to rid yourself of any individualism in order to serve the Holy Spirit. Your past and your future was of no concern anymore. Only the temporal present counted.

The bell rang again, and Father Jeremiah asked me to join the community at its evening payers. I walked with him to one of the small chapels, and following his example, removed my shoes before going inside.

The chapel was severe and dimly lit—a narrow stone cavern divided into two parts. There was a small ante-chamber near the doorway, and beyond this was an iron gate ornamented by Coptic crosses. Within the gates was a simple altar and an inlaid wooden door in front of which prayers were offered. The main body of the chapel was an open space containing no pews or seats. In keeping with the asceticism of the Order, you didn't take the weight off your feet to pray, but stood throughout the entire ceremony.

As the monks entered the chapel, they knelt down and kissed the floor and then approached the alter where Father Jeremiah and another senior monk were waiting. After bowing to kiss each of their hands, they formed a line against the wall facing the altar and pulled the hoods of their habits over their heads.

Once enough monks had assembled, Father Jeremiah began reciting a prayer and the others joined in. Then another monk broke into a chant which was taken up by the gathering. The chant had a distinctive Gregorian texture to it—a plainsong from the Coptic liturgy that was sung in unison; its melodic line resonant and starkly powerful. Occasionally, the chant would stop, a prayer would be uttered, and then one of the monks would walk by each of his brethren and whisper to them, as if passing on a divine secret. The chanting began again in earnest, more prayers were murmured, more secrets passed along that row of hooded clerics. A *Kyrie eleison* was sung and then repeated several times over. As the monks filed into the small ante-chamber and continued chanting with even greater force, pushing the *kyrie* towards a crescendo, I caught sight of one young monk with his head against the wall, his entire body nearly convulsed as the chant took him over; a raw, unbridled form of spiritual ecstasy that was as hypnotic as the repetitive chant that now hit a fevered pitch, turning the chapel into a echo chamber reverberating with religious devotion.

And then, suddenly, it was over. The stone walls of the chapel absorbed the last peal of voices, there was a moment of silence, and the monks left. Outside, night had come and I lingered for a moment, staring up into a tantalizing empty sky. No stars tonight, no celestial fireworks. Just sheer infinite blackness. A dome of darkness enclosing a fortress in the desert.

Returning to the kitchen, I found Glenn already seated at the table, mumbling a short prayer over his bowl of yoghurt and plate of hard-boiled eggs. He opened his eyes as I began to crack the shell of one of the eggs.

'Were you praying with the Fathers?', he said.

'No, watching them pray.'

'You don't pray yourself?'

'Not really.'

'You mean, you're not considering becoming a monk?'

'I don't think my wife would be too thrilled with that idea.'

'You're married?'

'Got it in one.'

'Marriage is a sacred responsibility, of course', he said.

'That's one way of looking at it', I said. 'You ever try it?'

'I lived with someone once.'

'For how long?'

Glenn gazed down into his bowl and began to form circular patterns on the surface of the yoghurt with his spoon. 'Three months', he said.

A change of subject was definitely needed, so I asked Glenn what sort of work he used to do back in the States. It turned out that he'd had quite a career in civil disobedience and was an old veteran of countless peace marches and anti-nuclear protests. A slight hint of bravado came into his voice when he told me about his string of arrests at assorted sit-down demonstrations, and he was full of jail-house stories and memories of meeting such heavyweights of the American left as Daniel Ellsberg and the brother Berrigan. A stint as a medic in Vietnam, he explained, had decided him on this career as a professional Pentagon adversary, though I sensed that his time in south-east Asia had also turned him in on himself and damaged his sensibility. Like so many other veterans of that campaign, he now came across as a member of the walking wounded, still trying to cauterize the mental scars ten years after being demobilized.

'I think my involvement in the anti-war movement eventually killed my father', he said. 'He was a career soldier in the Army. But when he died in 1980, I suddenly felt that I was being taken over by some higher force, that I was attaining a new spiritual level. Have you ever spent time in a Zen monastery?'

Pacificism, Gandhian civil disobedience, Zen buddhism—Glenn had tried them all. His past history sounded like a consumer's guide to counter-culture idealism, and he was obviously a compulsive shopper, still hunting around for an identity that would fit him. Behind his thick rimless spectacles was a hurt which his relentless search for a spiritual niche had failed to dispel. And like so many of life's marginals, he kept hoping that the next Quaker farm, the next Zen master, the next monastery would give him the focus he craved.

'I'm 39 now and I really need to start figuring out what my real purpose is', he said. 'Maybe I'll find it here in St Macarius.'

'But do you really think you're cut out for this sort of life', I said. 'Could you handle the isolation?'

'Well', Glenn said, 'I was a forest ranger once.'

* * * * *

Back in my cell, I began to have a craving for news of the outside world, so I dug out my radio and tuned in the BBC World Service.

The headlines were dominated by one story: a monastery in East
Beirut, the venue for a meeting of right wing Christian leaders,
had been attacked by a squad of suicide bombers.

I fell into an uneasy sleep.

* * * * *

The monastic day begins at three in the morning. A bell rings,
summoning the community into consciousness. For the next
hour, the monks pray silently in their cells. Then, at four, a
second bell rings and a procession of hooded figures crosses the
half-lit courtyard and enters the chapel for morning prayers—a
daily two hour ritual.

The nocturnal chill made me shudder as I made my way to the
chapel. Inside, the oratory was cloaked in shadow; a few candles
and a chandelier providing the only illumination. Glenn was
already in place against the wall, his eyelids at half-mast. Standing next to him were the two novices, Michael and Magit, both of
whom were yawning without shame. How would they ever get
used to a lifetime of three a.m. wake-up calls? More monks filed
in, and would continue to do so even after the prayers had
begun. As Glenn had explained to me the previous evening,
attendance at this pre-dawn rite was not obligatory, and many of
the monks actually left half-way through the service to return to
their assorted duties. The spiritual did not take precedence over
the practical in this Order, as work was considered to be just as
much a holy obligation as prayer.

Matins followed the same format as the evening worship. A
celebrant sang a prayer and the congregation responded with
liturgical plainsong, chanted with an intensity that made the
controlled passion of last night's service look Unitarian by
comparison. Perhaps this accentuated zeal was due to the hour of
the morning—a time when the consciousness is numbed, yet
still imbued with a peculiar clarity; the sort of mental state that
heightens one's receptivity to the mysteries of the Spirit. A
hooded monk passed in front of us whispering the almighty
secret, and as most of the brethren formed a group inside the
altar gates, their voices swelled to such an extent that it seemed
like they were no longer simply singing, but had fallen under a
liturgical spell.

An hour into this ritual, my head was swimming. It was too
forceful, too overpowering to be observed cooly at five a.m. Next
to me, Glenn now had his eyes snapped shut and was swaying

madly, ready to blast off. Bruised by a lack of sleep, I slipped into a reverie which deepened as the chanting shifted into an even higher gear, and headed into over-drive. And when Glenn nudged me out of my stupor and whispered, 'Let's go, it's finished', I realized that for the last half hour of the service I had lost all track of time, and had been caught somewhere between wakefulness and repose. It was like having been fed a powerful sedative, the after-effects of which left me muddled and drained. And as I blinked into the first light of morning, I couldn't initially decide whether I had just witnessed that two hour ritual or was simply coming out of a narcotic sleep.

The monks donned their sandals outside the chapel and headed off to their day's labours. There was no respite for them; no tea break or rest period. They would now work until their one main meal of the day at noon and then return to the tasks at hand. Evening prayers would interrupt them again at five, and then it was back to the job for as long as they could remain awake. A Victorian robber baron would have definitely approved of this form of spiritual workaholism, as the monastery was the ultimate sweatshop, staffed by a voluntary workforce with an insatiable appetite for long hours.

As I walked away from the chapel, Father Jeremiah greeted me and said, 'As you are a writer, you should see our printing press where we publish all our literature.' He pointed me towards a block of buildings next to the guest quarters, where I expected to find a room with the sort of old metal typeface press which Johann Gutenberg used to print his Bible. It came as a bit of a surprise, therefore, when I walked into an office where a young monk was seated in front of a word processor with an impressive array of software nearby. Assorted floppy discs were spread out on his desk and a bank of terminals were stacked flush against a wall. In a bookshelf on the far side of the room, copies of the Bible in English were lined up alongside thick computer manuals; a juxtaposition of the sacred and the hi-tech.

'Would you like to see how the word processor operates?', the monk asked me, pointing to the screen on which a section of the Spiritual Father's latest book was being typed out in Arabic. Pressing a few buttons, the monk then turned to the printer, out of which came a typeset page ready for the press.

'It is a very efficient system', he said. 'I can also use English or French programmes if we are printing in one of those languages.'

Adjoining this office was the actual print shop, the focal point of which was a new state-of-the-art colour press, turning out a selection of St Macarius postcards. Nearby, one monk was overseeing an electric guillotine that trimmed copies of a recent book, while another was running pages through a high speed collator. Watching them work, I had to remind myself that only thirty minutes earlier they were chanting prayers as part of a medieval ritual. The monks of St Macarius straddled these two worlds with dexterity. Their spiritual lives may have been bound up in liturgical mysteries, but when it came to the business of running their farm, their medical clinic, their print works, they became tough-minded pragmatists and advocates of new technology. And by reconciling the traditional with the modern, they were reflecting, in miniature, the vision which Sadat had of a new Egypt—a society which retained its conservative values, yet still embraced the age of technocracy. In the secular world of modern Egypt, that vision had led to a crisis of identity, in which Arab self-image was pitted against westernization. But here, within the confines of an ascetic religious order, the dream had been realized.

But, while recognizing the achievements of the monks, I still wondered whether their success in adapting to the modern world had been due to their isolation from the pressures of secular society. It was an isolation that would soon be coming to an end, as a new city—Sadat City—was currently being completed opposite St Macarius on the far side of the desert highway. Sadat City was one of a string of new towns which had been commissioned by the government in an attempt to curb the population growth of Cairo. During my stay in the capital, I took a day trip north to see this sandy metropolis in the making, and came away doubting whether anyone would ever agree to build a new life in such a nowhere town. At first sight, Sadat City had the architectural flavour of an unfinished state university campus in mid-America. Empty office blocks, a bunker-like hotel, half-built apartment towers, and signs pointing to a city centre that didn't exist. It was as if some urban planner had decided to play with a Lego set in the middle of the desert, yet forgot to include any amenities that would break the drabness of life for those who were exiled to this artificial city.

Considering Sadat City now from the perspective of St Macarius was like peering down from a monastic Shangri-la and discovering that a new Babylon was under constuction in the valley below. And I wondered whether the monk's model community would eventually suffer from this exposure to new-style urban blight. Later that day, I put this question to Father John, a senior monk in his sixties whom I met in the guest lounge near the kitchen.

'We have no objections to Sadat City', he said. 'There is a terrible need for housing in this country, so it is a good thing that such new cities are being built. The problem will be how we will be able to cope if the city expands; how we can help and assist the people of the city. This is why the Spiritual Father says we must try to feed 1,000 for every one of us, and why we must also try to make the farm grow faster. The day is not long enough for the work we have to do. You know we are trying many experiments in desert agriculture. And we have even done the first embryo transplant on cattle in Egypt. The Spiritual Father, he sent one of the monks to West Germany to learn this technique, and he has had a remarkable success rate with these experiments so far. It is almost a miracle, you know.

'The Spiritual Father is a remarkable man. You have heard about all the books and pamphlets that he has published? He is renowned throughout Egypt as an important thinker on spiritual matters, and one who has always counselled for moderation. You know that we have our own Pope in the Coptic Church—Pope Shenouda—who was banished to a monastery near us in Wadi el Natrun during the time of Sadat. Well, God forgive me for saying it, but our Pope has been too politically active. Telling the government that he will not put up with this or that. It is not the role of the church. We must remain moderate and show love.

'The conflict between the Muslims and Copts was very bad a few years ago, but with the exception of a few fanatics, it is much better now. And many Muslims I speak with hate these extremists. Sadat tried to appease them and they ended up destroying him. Sadat was a man of courage, but he was impulsive in his opinions and he made many enemies. Mubarak is wiser. He is trying not to speak out against any one group, and to steer a moderate course in dangerous times.

'Look at that group of men seated at that table', he said, pointing to a half-dozen farm workers drinking tea in a corner of the lounge. 'They are all Muslims, but they work here and we offer each other mutual respect. This has always been an ecumenical country. I only pray that it stays that way.'

I asked Father John if he had heard the news about the bombing of the monastery in East Beirut. He blinked in shock.

But when I mentioned that it had been the venue for a Christian militia meeting, he said, 'You see! When you let politics near you, it will destroy you. We must have peace between Muslims and Copts. Otherwise, we will all be destroyed.'

A bell rang, and Father John excused himself, saying he hoped we could talk again later. I wandered back into the courtyard and ran into Glenn who mentioned that evening prayers were about to begin.

Inside the chapel, there was a distinct tension to the proceedings. A sense that something was deeply troubling this community and they had their minds on matters other than prayer. They went through the motions of the ritual, but when it came to the singing of the liturgy, their voices were flat and uninspired, never once hitting the emotional pitch which I had heard on previous occasions. The service was over within fifteen minutes and I left quickly. The monks also began to disperse, but stopped before the door to allow one member of their community to pass first. He was a grey-haired man in a habit that was no different than those worn by the other brethren, but I sensed immediately that his presence was special. He saw me pulling on my shoes and we caught each other's eye for a moment. He bowed his head gravely to me, a slight smile forming on his lips. Though I can't confirm it—especially as Glenn had earlier told me that he was indistinguishable from the rest of the community—I was almost certain that I had made brief contact with the Spiritual Father.

Father Jeremiah came out of the chapel and whispered to me, 'I was hoping to show you the rest of the monastery now but we must go to a meeting.' He shook his head sadly and then joined the other black robed figures as they followed their Spiritual Father back to their quarters.

* * * * *

I never did find out what was the cause of that communal tension during evening prayers. Nor did I ever get a straight answer as to why, at nine p.m. that night, the lights in the monastery suddenly blacked out and stayed off until dawn. Over breakfast the next morning, Glenn told me that he was convinced that it was all to do with the attempted assassination of the former Libyan Prime Minister at his home in Alexandria. He'd heard on the BBC World Service that a hit squad had been sent from Tripoli to murder the man, but had been foiled yesterday by the Egyptian secret police. And this news led him to conclude that the government had told the monks to black out the monastery for the night, just in case there was a reprisal bombing raid by Libyan fighter jets.

It was an absurd scenario, and I said so. After all, though Col. Qaddafi had his wayward moments, I doubted that he would risk war with Egypt just because two of his stooges got caught trying to kill one of his political opponents. And anyway, even if he had ordered his airforce to strike an Egyptian target, why should he choose a monastery that was over 1,000 km away from his territory? I think Glenn knew that his theory strained credibility, yet he continued to embellish it.

'After what happened last night, I think it's looking very bad for me here. Maybe the Fathers will get worried about having an American in the monastery. They might consider me a security risk and ask me to move on.'

Glenn was obviously preparing himself for an eviction notice. Following their established tradition of offering shelter to any stranger who showed up at their gates, the monks had taken him in when he had arrived unannounced, saying he wanted to pray for the Geneva summit. But now, I think he sensed that he had overstayed his welcome. And so, if he was asked to leave, he was going to soften the blow by believing that, because he was a security risk, he was being given the push. It was yet another of Glenn's fantastic scenarios; a way to avoid confronting the fact that he was using St Macarius as a temporary haven against a world in which he had yet to find his place.

'You know', he said, 'I was in Alaska once. Spent an entire winter in a trailer in a state park outside Juneau. Park rangers kept moving me on because I couldn't afford the camping fees. But then, I hid out all alone in the middle of the woods. Just me and my trailer. Would have stayed there if the cold hadn't gotten to me. It was 40 below, and I'd used up all the heating oil in my trailer, so I had to leave. Imagine that: if it hadn't been for the cold, I might never have come to the desert.'

It was time for me to go, so I stood up from the table and said goodbye, leaving Glenn still thinking about his winter in Alaska and his own spiritual desert. After putting a contribution in a box marked 'Donations', I met Father Jeremiah in the courtyard. He wished me well on my journey, but when I asked him about last night's black out, he became evasive. 'Just a power failure', he said. 'Nothing more than that.' His tone encouraged me to press him no further, so I dropped the subject. As I had discovered in Siwa, an isolated community has many secrets and builds its own ramparts against the outside world. Even in this monastic order peopled by worldly technocrats, there was the need to maintain that fortress mentality. And if, as Glenn had theorized, the power failure last night had been a precaution against a possible external threat, I certainly wasn't going to be informed about it, because that would have been an admission of vulnerability to secular tensions. *When you let politics near you, it will destroy you*, Father John had told me. Perhaps all 'model communities' like this one had to cloister behind their walls in order to survive. Perhaps that was the only way the monks could preserve their regime of work and prayer—by distancing themselves from the crazed dance of modern Egypt.

Father Jeremiah took my hand and gave me his blessing. Then, he unbolted the main door of the monastery and we both looked out into the desert. Once again, I had to crouch down to pass under the narrow archway, dwarfing myself this time not to the majesty of the Almighty, but to the complexities of the society that lay beyond here. A German tour bus was parked outside and, with some reluctance, the tour leader—the aptly named *Gruppeführer*—agreed to let me cadge a lift down to the desert highway. As we pulled away, she barked a commentary through a microphone while her charges—a sunburnt party of burghers from Bremen—aimed their Nikons and portable video cameras through the tinted glass for one last shot of the battlements of St Macarius. Having just left one cocooned world, I now found myself temporarily in another, drifting across the desert landscape in an air-conditioned, north European bubble.

The bubble burst when we reached the main road. I left the bus and immediately flagged down a collective taxi going south. It looked like it had just taken part in a demolition derby and wobbled precariously on its four wheels. Climbing in beside the driver, I heard barnyard noises and turned around to discover a wicker basket full of chickens seated next to several women dressed in black. The driver plugged in a cassette, and to the accompaniment of Om Kalsoum—the legendary 'Nightingale of the Nile'—and a not so legendary chorus of hens, I headed back to the bright lights of the big city.

* * * * *

In Cairo, I had a day to kill before venturing south, and used the time to run assorted errands in the city centre. While walking down Adly Pasha Street en route to lunch, I stopped in front of a building which I must have passed dozens of times during my weeks in the capital, but failed to notice before. It was a curious structure, built out of buff-coloured stone, with art deco features. A bas-relief of pineapple trees spanned the length of the building, and was flanked by two ornamental pillars. At first, it reminded me of the old Picture Palaces which still existed in the New York of my early childhood. But then, I caught sight of the Stars of David carved into the pillars and the armed soldiers stationed in a sentry box by its main gate, and I suddenly realized that this was one of Cairo's few remaining synagogues.

As it was Friday, I gambled on the fact that there would be evening prayers, and dropped back at sunset to discover the front gate open and lights on inside. The military presence had been strengthened by two to three soldiers, and a caretaker sat at a table by the door. He handed me a yarmulke as I entered and pointed the way in. I had planned to sit quietly in a back pew and watch the service, but when I came through the swing doors, five heads turned around and an elderly gentleman stood up and greeted me like a lost member of the tribe. There were smiles all around from the other men, a prayer book was thrust into my hands, and when I tried to explain that I didn't read Hebrew, I was told not to worry, as it didn't matter what language I prayed in. They were simply pleased to see a visitor in their midst.

My arrival had swelled the entire *kahal*—or congregation—to six. A mere half-dozen worshippers in a synagogue that could accommodate at least two hundred. A synagogue with gold inlaid ceilings, marble floors, mahogany pews, magnificent brasswork, and no signs of deterioration or neglect. A synagogue that was one of the most stunning houses of worship I had ever seen.

The five assembled men were an eclectic bunch. One of them was young, dressed in a button down shirt, levis and runners. Definitely not an Egyptian but, more than likely, a citizen of a neighbouring country. The other four formed a distinctive group. They were well over seventy, and sported baggy woollen pin-stripe suits of the type worn by Eastern European emigres in the thirties. Seen together, they were like faded figures in a sepia photograph—the few remaining members of a once-flourishing Jewish community in Egypt. After the Suez war—in which Israeli forces, invited into the conflict by the British government, captured much of the Sinai peninsula—life became impossible for the Jews living under Nasserite rule. Though Ben Gurion, at the request of the United Nations, eventually withdrew his troops from the peninsula, this did nothing to quell the wave of anti-semitism which had seized Egypt. Altogether, over 11,000 Jews had no choice but to leave the country during this period, forced out by laws which nationalized their assets and their means of a livelihood. Their numbers dwindled away to nothing, to the point where there were now only a handful of survivors left. Relics of a dying community, soon to become extinct altogether. And judging by the ages of the pensioners in the front pew, I wondered who would be left to pray in this synagogue in ten years time.

The young man stood up and glanced at the door in the hope that a few more worshippers might be coming. We waited for several minutes and the silence was terrible. Every footstep in the corridor, every sound of an outside door opening immediately raised expectations of the late arrival of another member of the community. But no one ever did show up, and finally the young man opened his prayer book and began singing the *Kabalat Shabbat*—the Friday evening prayers. The others soon joined in, and the singing was as spirited as possible under the circumstances—the young man's voice becoming passionate and almost defiant. I looked around at the row of unoccupied pews, the balcony where women would have been seated, the Hebraic lettering on the walls, and listened to these elderly voices in broken harmony with one young tenor. It was melancholic, yet moving—the left-behinds of Egyptian Judaism still clinging to their faith, still praying in an empty immaculate synagogue that was guarded by armed soldiers.

My mother is a Jew; my father a Catholic. And though I was raised in neither faith, I nonetheless felt a curious kinship with those elderly men, remembering my German great-uncles who traded Bavaria for Flatbush, and used to dress in similar pin-stripe suits. I thought about a photograph I had at home in Dublin of my late Uncle Al in the company of one Haille Sellasie, taken when Al was the head of the U.S. North African mission after the Second World War. The kid from Brooklyn meets the Lion of Judah, and as that photograph reassembled in my mind, I recalled the jacket Al was wearing when he posed with the Emperor: baggy and pinstriped. And, most of all, I mourned the loss of my grandfather; a classic New Yorker of the old school who, had he seen this synagogue, would have probably reacted in true Manhattan style by saying, 'Quite a classy joint. Too bad about the business.' The sense of loss that pervaded this spectral temple—the feeling that I was witnessing the death-knell of a community—magnified that of my own, as their ghosts and mine intermingled.

The *Kalabat Shabbat* prayers drew to a close, a small brass cup of wine was passed among us, and then we said 'Shabbat Shalom' to each other and shook hands. I introduced myself to the young man. His name was Aaron and, as I had thought, he was an Israeli.

'It breaks my heart to see this, the most beautiful synagogue in Egypt, so empty', he said. 'It is a tragedy.'

One of the elderly gentlemen asked me if I could come to Saturday morning services. I said that, unfortunately, I was leaving Cairo tomorrow. Dismay was registered. One more member of their *kahal* lost.

As we were leaving, Aaron mentioned that he was a student at Tel Aviv University, doing research here in Cairo. I never found out what kind of research he was engaged in because, as soon as we reached the street, Aaron saw something that immediately made him jumpy.

'Care for a coffee somewhere?', I said, wanting to prolong the conversation.

'I can't. Anyway, we're being watched.'

'By whom?'

'Whom do you think?' He quickly indicated two men dressed in sharp suits standing by a car. When they saw me glance at them, they turned away.

'They follow me everywhere', Aaron hissed. 'Perhaps it is not a good idea if you are seen with me.' He began to walk towards the kerb and apologizing for his hasty exit, he yelled a 'goodbye' that was drowned out by the traffic into which he disappeared.

I look back at the plain clothes policemen. Once again, they averted my stare by showing me their backs. I was planning to return to my room at the Hotel Rialto, but decided that that might not to be a wise move at the moment. So I walked down to Talaat Harb Street and fell in with the crowd, never once turning around to see if I was being tailed.

* * * * *

Ramses Square at seven in the morning was a three-ring circus without a tent. The traffic was already coagulated, the symphony of car horns was in full swing, a cop halted the flow of oncoming cars to let a herd of goats pass by, and the poor were waking up from another night on the street. One woman and her children were stretched out on a sheet of cardboard that served as their mattress. Nearby, a man in rags lay motionless on the ground. A soldier came over and nudged him with his boot, but there were no signs of life. When he bent down to examine him, removing the newspapers that covered his head, the dead man's frozen stare met his own, and the soldier jumped back, thoroughly spooked. I shared his sentiments and crossed quickly into the Victorian splendour of Ramses Station.

On track 8, I boarded the morning express to Upper Egypt and took my seat in the First Class compartment. The class distinctions on Egyptian trains are striking. First is grubby luxury: large cushioned armchair seats, badly stained, with worn out carpet on the floor and smudged blinds shielding you from the sun. Second class is simply a more crowded version of First, only the seats of vinyl and there's a prevailing atmosphere of petit-bourgeois discomfort. And then there's the cattle car known as Third Class. A few wooden benches, no light, broken windows, no sanitary facilities—a deliberately designed hell-hole which is usually so overloaded with passengers that floor space becomes luxury accommodation, while the late arrivals must either stretch out on the luggage racks or sit on the edge of the open doorways with their legs dangling over the side.

The train departed on time, and for the next four hours, I worked on my journal, occasionally peering out of the window at a landscape of small villages and arable fields. A pair of dacroned American tourists seated in front of me couldn't get enough of this fleeting panorama of Egypt at its most bucolic. Every grove of palm trees, every oxen struggling against the weight of a plow, every women washing clothes in an irrigation ditch was faithfully recorded by their instamatic cameras. 'It's so archetypically African!', one of the women exclaimed upon seeing a shanty town with kids running barefoot, making me think that poverty always looks pastoral to western eyes if it's shaded by palm trees.

Though the train was travelling the full 879 km to Aswan, I got off after a mere 247 km to spend two days in the town of Minya. It was a place few people outside Egypt had ever heard of. In Baedeker's *Egypt 1929*, it merited only a few lines, calling attention to its position as the capital of the Upper Egyptian cotton industry. Its attributes sounded rather meagre: a

British war cemetery, a handsome bridge spanning a canal, a market which 'presents a gay picture of oriental life', and little else. But friends in Cairo insisted I go there for two reasons—it was one of the few towns left in Egypt which retained its colonial character, and it was also a mixed community of Muslims and Copts living together in cautious harmony.

On leaving the station, both aspects of the town came into view. At eye-level, the large dusty mansions in mock Louis XIV style, the gently senile hotels with their shuttered French windows, the small central square with its collection of palms, and the cafes where men huddled over dominoes all conspired to give Minya a 'down on the plantation' atmosphere. The British landowners may have been long gone, but the scent of their cotton was still in the air. Looming above the venerable townscape was an ecumenical skyline of Christian crosses and Islamic crescent moons; a hint that, at least, there was an architectural co-existence between the two faiths.

The porter behind the reception desk of the Hotel Palace wielded a fly swatter at an unsuspecting victim and told me that rooms were available. I liked the feel of this establishment immediately. It was a New Orleans brothel done up in ersatz Pharaonic style. Two fantastically garish wall murals of Cleopatra and Nefertiti looked down upon a thirty foot lounge furnished with once plush sofas and a collection of Edwardian four-folders. My room was a jumble sale of Victoriana, with peeling floral wallpaper and a mammoth double bed. Opening the French windows, I stepped out on to the balcony that overlooked the main square and decided that Minya and I were going to have a very agreeable relationship.

I left the hotel and wandered down to the Nile. In Cairo, the Nile is an urban waterway; a wide dark effluent smear that splices the city in half. But here in Minya, the river assumed an epic grandeur. The water was almost still, a slight current rippling across an otherwise flat mirror. Sunlight interplayed with the reflective surface, giving it an incandescent glow. On the far bank—over 1,000 yards away—there was a long expanse of granite cliffs fronted by palms and a small village. A felucca piled high with cotton drifted by, embellishing this vision of the river as myth. In its wake came a Nile steamer of the Swan Hellenic line—a square box of a vessel with luxury cabins and a party of holidaymakers sunning themselves in deckchairs. No doubt, they had booked passage on this floating hotel enticed by the mythology of a Nile cruise. And seeing them was a reminder that, in the late twentieth century, bygone romance is a marketable commodity.

I strolled along the riverfront, passing an amusement park where a group of gentlemen invited me to sample the chunk of hashish that was roasting in their hookah. It wasn't the sort of amusement I was looking for, so I declined the offer and cut down a muddy boulevard that led into the town's main market. It was a normal workaday souk; a place where just about every domestic need was catered for. I stopped by one stall where a gentleman earned his living by refilling cigarette lighters. Next to him was a small shop that housed the local *maquaggi*, with whom everyone deposits their clothes for ironing. As I watched him heat up his old flat iron, I was tapped on the shoulder by a bootblack seeking custom. He motioned me over to a table in a cafe where I removed my shoes and he lay a sheet of newspaper on the ground so my feet would not make contact with the pavement. As he restored some sort of lustre to my badly scuffed brogues, I ordered a coffee and watched a shoemaker at work in his shop, hand-stitching a leather upper. Nearby, a confectioner poured a glutinous pink liquid into a mould that, when hardened, would become one of the garish candy statues which are sold annually on the birthday of the prophet Mohammed. This was the service sector of the Egyptian economy. Unlike the West, when mass production and chain stores have edged out small merchants, the tradesman still plays a crucial role in Egyptian mercantile life. The plug-in domestic steam iron has yet to replace the *maquaggi* in his shop, and few would think about shining their own shoes when there are people whose livelihood depends on this function. Here in the market, your business—no matter how humble—has its role to play in the commercial life of the community.

My shoes were returned to me, I paid off the bootblack, and left the souk, hiking through another complex network of alleyways. Martial music could be heard in the distance, and as I approached a squat stone building, high-pitched voices began to accompany this brass band, shouting *Misr!. Misr!* (Egypt! Egypt!). Intrigued, I wandered inside and found myself in the courtyard of a primary school. The music was being blared over a loudspeaker and a group of children in tan uniforms and red scarves were marching in formation to its militaristic beat, extolling the virtues of their country. I looked on, fascinated by the indoctrination of the young into a regime of discipline and blind patriotism. There was an office off the courtyard and I knocked on the door and was met by a matriarchal woman who turned out to be the head-mistress. Her office was decorated with collages made by the children, all of which depicted great moments in the career of President Hosni Mubarak. I explained that I was a writer travel-ling through the country and would be very interested in seeing her school. This perplexed her a bit ('I have never had a request like this before'), and after making several phone calls, she told me that I would first have to go to the State Information Office who, in turn, might send me to the appropriate Ministry who, in turn, might supply me with the necessary documentation which would allow me to return to the school for my tour. The bureaucratic belly dance was evidently alive and well in Minya, but with time on my hands and no fixed itinerary for the day, I decided to use up some shoe leather and set off in search of the State Information Office.

I found it in a side street off the main square. Its director was a middle-aged man with an unfortunate squint. Tea arrived, cigarettes were proffered, phone calls were made, my passport and press card were scrutinized, questions were asked about my work and why I was interested in visiting an Egyptian school, the director wrote a letter, and then assigned one of his young assistants, Samir, to guide me to the Ministry of Education. After a twenty minute walk, Samir and I arrived at a broken-down administrative centre and entered an office where an obese man sat behind an obese desk. More tea arrived, more cigarettes were distributed, more phone calls made, and then Samir was told that we had come to the wrong building. So, we set off on another twenty minute walk, made our way to yet another decaying building, entered yet another office, and were offered yet another round of tea and cigarettes by a middle-aged woman seated behind yet another obese desk. She was dressed in a severe suit and regarded me with the glacial indifference of an *apparatchik* in an Eastern bloc country. Samir tried to engage her in conver-sation, but she didn't seem to be in a talkative humour and drank her tea in sullen silence. I was beginning to wonder whether we had ended up in another wrong office when a man dolled up in donnish tweeds, his hair slicked back in the style of a forties bandleader, breezed into the room. He pumped my hand vigour-ously and introduced himself as 'Radwan Afify—public relations director for the Educational Authority of Minya. And you are Mr

Kennedy the writer, yes? I shall be happy to accompany you on a tour of our excellent educational facilities in Minya.'

News obviously travelled fast in this town. 'And I see you have made the acquaintance of our delightful Madame Director of Education', Mr Afify said in his melodious voice. 'Would I be interrupting your conversation by suggesting that we leave now?'

Madame Director scowled. I said that I had no objections to starting the tour right away, so we made our goodbyes and left.

'We will now go to a secondary school that trains primary school teachers', Mr Afify said as we walked to his car.

'Is this a Muslim or a Coptic school?', I asked.

'There is no such thing as a "Muslim" or "Coptic" school. We are all brothers. There is no problem between the two religions in Minya, or in the whole of Egypt.'

Mr Afify could have made it big in Madison Avenue. His patter was as slick as the tonic in his hair, and he was determined to sell Minya to me as a model of ecumenical harmony. As we drove off in his Seat, he re-emphasized that the school we were about to visit had students of both faiths; a comment he regretted when we pulled up in front of the school's gates and were greeted by seven young women in traditional Muslim dress. They were grouped around a piano in the courtyard and formed part of the welcoming committee that had gathered for our arrival. A heavy-set woman with a pillbox hat stepped forward and was introduced to me as 'Madame Dean.' Then, there was 'Madame Assistant Dean'—a wallflower with coke-bottle glasses—and 'at the piano . . . Madame Music Teacher.' As Mr Afify played the compere, Madame Music Teacher hit a chord on the piano and the seven young women burst into song.

'These are the primary music teachers of tomorrow', Mr Afify said.

Inside Madame Dean's office, the usual glasses of tea arrived and then Mr Afify told me that Madam Dean was ready to answer any questions I might have about her school.

'Could you tell me about your curriculum?', I said. Madame Dean adjusted her pillbox hat and replied, 'We teach the usual subjects.'

'What are "the usual subjects"?', I asked.

'What are they anywhere else', Madame Dean said. Mr Afify, sensing that the interview was not getting off to the most auspicious start, jumped in quickly. 'It is like a secondary school in your own country', he said. 'We teach reading, writing, arithmetic and history. Any other questions?'

I wondered out loud whether women in Egypt today were becoming more career-minded or simply accepted the inevitability of marriage. 'Of course, the girls will one day marry', Madame Dean said, 'but they will have jobs first'. There was another awkward pause which Mr Afify immediately filled. 'That is the great thing about Egypt', he said. 'Each student here is assured of a job. There is no unemployment like you have in Europe. Next question, please.'

How about training teachers to deal with hardship areas? Mr Affify danced over this one: 'The Authority decides where the teachers are placed, and there is no difference between the education offered to anyone.' But surely, I reasoned, a teacher working in a deprived area must be more adaptable than one working in a middle class community. 'Our teachers are very adaptable', Mr Afify said. Madame Dean nodded her head in vigourous agreement, and deciding that this dialogue was turning into an exercise in Newspeak, I asked if I could be shown around the school. Madame Dean didn't like this one bit and whispered something quickly to Mr Afify. 'Unfortunately, all the students have gone for the day', Mr Afify said. 'Perhaps we go back outside and hear the young girls sing.'

So we adjourned to the courtyard where the chorus of young Muslim women were practising scales, their headscarves and long flowing shifts making them look like the Islamic cast of *The Sound of Music*. Madame Dean asked Madame Music Teacher to give us a song and the chorus obliged. It was a sentimental dirge which Mr Afify accompanied with a simultaneous English translation.

'It is a song for the birthday of the Prophet Mohammed. They sing that Allah lights up their life and brings them great joy. It is a very religious song.'

'Do they teach this song to Coptic children as well?' I said.

Mr Afify smiled thinly and dodged the question by pointing out the plaster frescoes that adorned the external walls of the school. They were reproductions of bas-reliefs from Pharaonic burial chambers; a bit of mock ancient art ornamenting a breeze-block institution. Here again was a collision of two worlds. The frescoes reminded all students who passed through these gates that theirs was a monumental heritage, while the functional architecture spoke of the boxed-in realities of Egypt today. The grandiose past met the utilitarian present in this school.

Goodbyes were said, and we departed in Mr Afify's car. Before dropping me back to my hotel, he gave me a quick motor tour of the city, showing me the old Governor General's residence, the 'new town' (a mismash of jerry-built flats), and a bridge built by the British which spanned the Ibrahimia Canal. En route to these various sights, I discovered that Mr Afify was a figure of renown in Minya, as every third person we passed seemed to recognize him, and he shouted greetings to policemen on the beat, merchants in their shops, and former students. This small town familiarity put Minya in perspective for me. It was a large village in which everybody's business was common currency, and where the communal image was all important. And if an outsider like myself came to call, it was imperative that he be treated to an out-pouring of civic pride. Mr Afify had been entrusted with that task, and was performing it wonderfully. Seen through his eyes, Minya was Main Street America with Arabic sub-titles: a cosy, secure repository of all that was good and upstanding about the country.

Being in Mr Afify's company was therefore like attending a meeting of a one-man Chamber of Commerce. When we met again at seven thirty the next morning outside the Hotel Palace, his brillantine hair was glistening in the sunlight and his publicist's voice was as melodious as ever.

'Really, it is a lovely day', he said. 'A lovely day to visit the biggest military school in Minya, our first stop this morning.'

The military school was a few streets away from the hotel. It was a dark, imposing institution, smelling of cleaning fluid and gym socks. At a side entrance, we were met by 'Mr Headmaster'; a thin, chain-smoking man with receding hair and the look of a prison guard. He was accompanied by three deputies—'English Teacher Mafouz, Physics Teacher Mahmoud, English Teacher Hassan'—and together we marched to his office, our heels reverberating percussively on the marble floors. The now-predictable ritual of tea and cigarettes followed, and Mr Afify gave me a short run-down of the school's attributes—2,000 male students, ('Of course, a mixture of Muslims and Copts'), with a curriculum that placed a strong emphasis on sciences and maths as well as 'discipline and patriotism.'

Through the windows of the office, I could hear martial music and commands being barked, and after finishing our tea, Mr

Headmaster invited me to join him for an inspection of the troops. We walked through the main door, stepping out onto a portico with Greek columns and stone steps leading down to a large parade ground. The entire student body was assembled on that ground, marching in formation. They all wore blue trousers, blue shirts and blue jumpers with epaulettes, and followed the directives of their commanding officer with masterful precision. The music stopped and the students grouped themselves into four platoons as officers carrying batons moved among the ranks, scrutinizing their appearance. Then, the entire assembly snapped to attention, two students marched down to the flag-pole, and as the band played the National Anthem, the Egyptian flag was slowly hoisted up to its lofty position above the school. Mr Headmaster stood directly in front of the flagpole, his body rigid, his eyes gazing at his nation's banner with an intensity that approached religious devotion. I thought back to the little children I had seen yesterday shouting *Misr! Misr!* in the courtyard of their primary school, and decided that Mr Headmaster had learned the lessons of his youth well.

After the anthem, a student came to the microphone and sang a prayer from the Koran. My eyes searched those four platoons of uniformed adolescents, hoping to find someone yawning or looking bored or whispering to a mate; a small sign of schoolboy irreverence towards matters spiritual. It was a fruitless search, for their attention to the Koranic reading of the day was complete and unswerving. Standing there on the portico, I felt like a member of a military junta reviewing the obedient forces of the state. But, as I had to keep reminding myself, these were not soldiers. These were just kids and, as Mr Headmaster later told me, only five per cent of them would eventually choose the military as a career. The rest would enter university and then take their place in civilian life. But, before they reached adulthood, a love of nation and of Allah would be instilled in them. From the moment their mothers first dressed them in their tan primary school uniforms, the conditioning would begin. Their first teachers would teach them songs about Allah lighting up their lives, and march them in formation. Later on, they would be handed over to Mr Headmaster and his subordinates for a course of no-nonsense discipline which would teach them to be loyal sons of Egypt. I now understood why so many Egyptians I had met spoke about their country with such passionate devotion. Nationalism in Egypt wasn't simply an in-built reverence towards the homeland. It was a course of study which all had been forced to take.

The prayers ended and then Mr Deputy Headmaster took the microphone and began to address the student body. In the midst of his booming lecture, I heard my name being mentioned and grew somewhat uneasy as 2,000 set of eyes focused upon me. Mr Afify leaned over and whispered, 'Mr Deputy Headmaster is saying that you are a writer from Ireland who has come all the way to Minya to visit our school, and that the students must demonstrate to you the excellence of their school.'

I stared at my feet, and was greatly relieved when the band struck up a march and the students paraded by us in tidy formation. We returned to Mr Headmaster's office where I complimented him on the decorum of his troops. This pleased him, and he explained that this was a highly selective school which only accepted the best and the brightest. And, of course, there was never a problem with discipline. To reinforce this statement, Mr Headmaster waved his forefinger in the air and then slammed it down on his desk top. There was no need to ask Mr Afify for a translation of this gesture.

As an 'honoured guest', I was invited on a walkabout of the school and discovered to my considerable embarrassment that I was the head of a ten-person entourage. We toured a series of classrooms where English exams were in progress, and Mr Headmaster took one of the papers from a student and pointed to a fragment of Arabic that had to be translated into English. It read: 'We all know that smoking is bad for your health and intelligent men refrain from this bad habit.' Mr Headmaster coughed with distaste.

Walking down the corridor towards another classroom, I asked one of the English teachers whether his students found English a difficult language to master. 'Our job is made a lot easier by all the imported television programmes that are shown on Egyptian television', he said. 'They all watch them, so they pick up the vocabulary very fast.' This comment was greeted with a scowl by Mr Headmaster who made a point of showing me three student posters cellotaped to a wall, on which were drawn maps of Egypt with white doves looming overhead. 'These show that we are a land of peace', Mr Afify said. While we stood admiring these pacifistic sentiments, I heard the sound of wood whistling in the air followed by a sharp cry. Turning around, I saw a student being caned on the hand by a master. The members of my entourage became slightly embarrassed and Mr Headmaster barked, 'That's enough' as the cane came down the second time.

Mr Afify attempted to make light of the incident. 'What do you say in your country? Spare the rod, spoil the child.'

'That's one way of looking at it', I said. Mr Afify gave me a public relations laugh, and then suggested it was time we were on our way.

Leaving the military school, we walked around the corner to a group of low pre-fab buildings which catered for educational needs of the under-nines. The man in charge here was fantastically overweight and wore a purple safari outfit which would have suited a Las Vegas habitué, but didn't exactly seem like the most appropriate garb for a headmaster. More tea was poured down me, and then it was off to another classroom where the teacher ordered the children to stand and I was greeted with an a capella rendition of 'Good morning, how are you?' Two sisters were brought forward to meet me. They were both dressed in gingham uniforms and wore thick horn-rimmed glasses which made them look like a pair of spinster librarians.

'We used to live in Indiana', one of the said.

'Do you know Indianapolis?' the other one chimed in. 'Our Daddy worked there for seven years, but then we were brought back to Egypt.'

'And do you prefer Indiana or Egypt?', I said. They both grew uneasy, but then one of them quickly whispered to me, 'Minya is nice, but it's not Indiana.'

In another classroom, I fielded the occasional question in English. 'What your name?' I wrote it on the blackboard. 'Where you live?' I drew a map of Ireland. 'Egypt good?' Yes, I said, Egypt was good.

Throughout this school, basic English was being taught at an early age. It was a reminder that English was now the unofficial second language of the country—the language of its patron, the United States; the language of its imported culture; the language needed by its would-be emigrants who were searching for a berth in the West. The love of country which forms an intrinsic part of an Egyptian education may have been an exercise in romantic patriotism, but the study of English was a course in the politics of reality.

The tour completed, there was the usual round of handshakes and farewells, and then we set off in Mr Afify's car. 'I am always at your service in Minya', he said when we pulled up in front of the Hotel Palace. 'Any time you are here, you will find me willing to help you.' It was genuinely felt, and for all his glossy talk, I was grateful to him for giving me a glimpse of Egypt's educational system at work. I never did get a straight answer from him when I asked if Copts resented attending schools with a Muslim orientation, but perhaps his attempts to play down any tensions between the two communities were simply a reflection of Minya's wary religious tolerance. In this pleasantly parochial town, whatever sectarian conflicts did exist were generally concealed from public view. Minya basked in its languid atmosphere, and to understand its temperament you simply had to go down to the Nile banks. Which is what I did after leaving Mr Afify. Perched on a rock, I found myself transfixed once again by that passive, sedate waterway. Perhaps the Nile had a tranquilizing effect on Minya, mollifying any internal frictions that simmered below its patrician veneer. With such lazy beauty ebbing by you, who would want to go looking for trouble? Especially when you could sit here and watch the river flow.

A man in his twenties approached me and asked if he could share my rock. I motioned to a place beside me, he dug out a packet of Cleopatras, and we smoked and chatted. His name was Ahmed, a typist in a government office. The job didn't pay much, he told me; a fact that was beginning to worry him as he had been engaged for the past three years, but still couldn't afford the finance required to set up house for himself and his future wife. It was a problem that was shared by most young adults throughout the country who were getting by on meagre civil service wages. And Ahmed said that he'd felt depressed today just thinking about the amount of cash he still needed to put a deposit on a flat. 'I got upset, so I came down to the river', he said. 'It's nice here, yes?'

'Far too nice', said. 'I'd like to spend a few more days here, but I'm leaving for Assyut tonight.'

'Assyut?' he said and began to laugh. 'You leave this for Assyut? My friend, I do not envy you at all.'

It was not the first time I'd heard derisory laughter at the mention of Assyut. Every country has, at least, one city which is universally loathed by all but those who live there. In Egypt, Assyut holds this honour. No one I met ever had a good word to say about the place. It was a dump, it was unfriendly, it was suspicious of strangers, it could turn nasty on you, and its only redeeming feature was the next train out of town. From what I

155

could gather, Assyut had only established this reputation as a city to be avoided in the past few years. Before that, it was primarily known as the largest city in Upper Egypt and a big university town with over 60,000 students. But then, the trouble started. In 1981, Muslim fundamentalists clashed with riot police on the streets of Assyut following the assasination of Anwar el-Sadat. Jubilant that the infidel president was now dead, they unsuccessfully attempted to take control of the local radio studios and besieged various police barracks. Since that time, the city had become notorious as the mission control centre for Egypt's Islamic revivalists. Moreover, given the fact that over one-third of Assyut's population was Coptic, it had also been the scene of intermittent sectarian violence, thereby embellishing its reputation as an Egyptian Belfast.

But could it really be as bad as everybody said? Trouble spots always seem nightmarish when considered from a safe, cosy distance. When viewed close-up, however, they often end up being suprisingly ordinary centres of human endeavour. And wagering that Assyut would prove to be far less extreme than I had been led to believe, I hopped a train going south.

It only takes ninety minutes to travel by rail from Minya to Assyut, but the train was delayed by three hours, so my first view of Assyut was of a nocturnal cityscape which immediately lived up to its charmless reputation. The main street fronting the station was a clutter of decaying cafes and concrete office blocks, and the policemen on the beat were dressed in riot gear. I asked one of them to direct me to Sabit Street where I was hoping to look up a German teacher named Stefan. He was a lecturer in the University of Assyut; a diminutive, thirty year old Austrian from Linz. We'd met at a party given by a mutual friend in Cairo, and when I mentioned that I'd possibly be passing through Assyut, he'd given me an address on Sabit Street where he said he could be found, hinting that I might be able to avail myself of a spare bed in his flat. So I followed the policeman's instructions and walked on through a faceless commercial district, my eyes trying to adjust to the dim, lustreless glow of the city's street lamps. They seemed to be operating on low voltage and provided only the most nominal illumination. There was something almost mean-spirited about the quality of light, and it bathed Assyut in a miserly glow. Though it was still reasonably early in the evening, the streets were almost deserted and an uncomfortable silence hung over the city, as if everyone had gotten wise and gone home. Turn into Sabit Street, the sight of shabby store fronts protected by heavy steel shutters reinforced this image of Assyut as an urban ghost town and made me wonder if the three nights I planned to spend here was going to be three nights too long.

The address Stefan had given me was not, as it turned out, the address of his flat, but rather that of the parents of a friend of his. I found this out when a man wearing an elegantly tailored white *galabiya* answered the door. We had a curious conversation. I asked him if Stefan Stutterheim lived here and he looked at me blankly. I asked him if he knew Stefan and he said that Stefan was a friend of his son, Hussain. I asked him if I could have a word with Hussain, and he replied that Hussain was in Minya. I asked him if he had any idea where Stefan actually lived, and he invited me inside while his wife phoned Hussain in Minya.

I was ushered upstairs to a sitting room that had been done up in the suburban dementia school of interior decor. There was cheap beauty board covering the walls, framed pictures of children with big eyes, a three-piece suite upholstered in imitation fur, and a wall-to-wall Axminster that looked like a Rorschach test. My host turned on his colour television and a rock video filled the screen. His heavily made-up wife came into the room carrying a tray filled with tea and cakes. She said that Hussain should be calling back from Minya shortly, but the gentleman seemed oblivious to this news as he was engrossed in watching Madonna sing, 'We are living in a material world and I am a material girl.' I sipped my tea and ate a slice of baklava, rather bemused by my new surroundings. There was a sense of deep confusion in this room, as the owner and his habitat simply didn't mesh. This gentleman obviously had money and had used it to recreate a vision of western luxury right in the centre of downtown Assyut. It was a troubling vision, for it showed what he perceived to be the height of imported culture: Axminster carpets, children with big eyes painted on silk, the material girl in the material world. And I thought somewhat sourly: like the empire builders of the past, we in the West continue to bring enlightenment into areas of darkness.

Mick Jagger was doing his usual strut-and-stride number on the television screen when Hussain finally rang from Minya and gave his father Stefan's address. The gentleman insisted on driving me there, saying I wouldn't find it on my own. His car was a bright yellow Mercedes and as we cruised through the empty streets of the city, he told me that he was in the shoe business with outlets in Paris, Milan, Cairo and, of course, Assyut. We said little else until we reached Stefan's flat which was located on the far side of town. There was no answer when I knocked on the door, so I left a note and then drove back with the gentleman to the city centre and found a hotel. My room was a small overpriced box with a narrow bed and a colour television. I flicked the set on and watched the last ten minutes of an American medical drama. A woman doctor told a patient that he had the Big C and then went on to say that life was a bitch. A few minutes later, she confronted her live-in boyfriend with the news that she was leaving him. He looked at her meaningfully and said that he understood her need for 'personal space'. Outside my window, the city was filled with the voices of muezzins, high atop their minarets. As the credits rolled on the television set, the faithful of Assyut prayed.

* * * * *

Stefan showed up at my hotel early the next morning, having searched every other hostelry in the city for me. He was running late for a class, so he had little time to talk, except to say that I could have a bed in his flat for the next few nights and that I should meet him and another German teacher for lunch at the Lawyer's Club on the Corniche by the Nile. Then, relieving me of my bag, he drove off at a dangerous speed. This, as I came to discover, was Stefan's style. He charged around Assyut like someone who feared standing still for too long and had to keep himself perpetually in motion. An edgy man in an edgy city.

With time on my hands, I turned away from the drab asphalt jungle of the commercial district and headed towards the Nile. The closer I got to the river, the more I realized that Assyut had hidden charms, as shopping mall architecture and hard angular streets yielded to spacious boulevards and old colonial mansions. By the Ibrahimia Canal, I strolled along a path shaded by trees, pausing to watch a group of fishermen casting nets upon the waters. More stately mansions lined this route, the greenery was lush and tropical, and sunlight streamed through the foliage. Assyut's downtown may have looked like a jerry-built suburban precinct, but here, by the waterfront, the city threw off its ugly cloak of modernity and became a turn-of-the century patrician, graceful and at-ease with the world.

A bridge of considerable length and Edwardian design spanned the canal. I crossed it, stopping a student to ask directions to the university. And this is how I met Mohammed.

He was a first-year student in the Faculty of Law who dressed like a Mediterranean smoothie—designer jeans, a Cardin shirt, Ferrari sunglasses. Immediately adopting me as a westerner with whom he could practise his English, he cast a critical eye over my down-market wardrobe and said, 'You are wearing Levis, yes?'

I complimented him on his powers of observation.

'Which do you think is the better jeans? Levis or Wranglers?'

I said that I didn't really have any preference towards either brand of denims, and asked him again for directions to the university. Mohammed insisted on taking me there, saying that he would be honoured to give me a tour of the old campus. And linking his arm with mine—a traditional sign of camaraderie among men in Egypt—he led me forward.

Like Mr Afify in Minya, Mohammed cast himself in the role of press agent for his city and was eager to please.

'You like Assyut?', he asked me.

I said that the canal was very beautiful.

'Everything is very beautiful in Assyut. We are the most beautiful city in Egypt.'

I decided not to contest that point and nodded in polite agreement as we entered the old univeristy. It was imitation Oxbridge—a quadrangle with mock Gothic buildings, shaded walkways, manicured lawns. Hundreds of bicycles were parked by its front gates, students were lounging in the grass or dashing to lectures, and there was that air of inspired idleness which one associates with universities everywhere. But then, in a pleasant little open air cafe where Mohammed and I sat drinking Cokes, I began to notice something strange. The cafe was exclusively used by male students, while all women sat at another cafe far away from the men.

'Aren't women allowed to use this cafe?', I asked Mohammed.

'This is the cafe for boys. Over there is the cafe for girls.'

I ventured a 'Why?'

'Assyut habit', Mohammed said.

We finished our drinks and wandered over to a modern building that was used by the medical faculty. Mohammed said that he wanted to show me this new lecture theatre, but as we approached a doorway he saw a cluster of women standing outside it and stopped abruptly. 'We cannot enter here', he said, leading me to the other side of the building. 'That is the door for girls. We go to the door for students.'

'There is a difference between girls and students?', I said.

'Assyut habit.'

Inside the lecture theatre, this sexual segregation continued, as all the women were seated in an isolated corner of the hall.

'Don't the women complain about this?', I said.

'It is the regulations here', Mohammed said.

'But they don't have these regulations in universities in Cairo and Alexandria. Men and women mix freely there.'

'There are Cairo habits and there are Assyut habits.'

Islamic fundamentalism had evidently triumphed in the University of Assyut. Rejecting the more tolerant and liberal traditions of universities in the north of the country, the Muslim student groups on this campus had succeeded in forcing the administration to adhere to the most orthodox forms of Islamic doctrine. The clock had been turned back; the influx of infidel western ideology halted. Good Muslim girls dressed with appropriate decorum, negating their femininity by bandaging their hair in headscarves and wearing long shapeless gowns that covered their arms and legs. Good Muslim girls were quarantined from male students. They had their own cafes, their own separate areas in classrooms, their own doorways which only they could enter. The sexes did not fraternize here; they were wedged apart and kept in separate isolation wards. And though the Coptic minority in the university had often complained about these draconian regulations, there was little they could do to stop the new-found fervour of the Islamic revivalists. They had seized upon Assyut as their showpiece. Here they would show the rest of Egypt how to fend off corrupting foreign values and return to the purity of the faith. Here they would reinforce the traditional role of women in Muslim society. Here, one feared, they would spearhead a vanguard that would eventually attempt to impose its own pietistic vision on the rest of the state.

It struck me as ironic that a university was the centre of such a fundamentalist backlash. After all, students the world over usually agitated against society's moral policemen. In Assyut, however, they cast themselves in that role. Perhaps geography had something to do with their innate conservatism. Assyut is a midlands town, and draws many of its students from the backwaters of Upper Egypt. And like so many provincial cities hemmed in by land and unable to see a world beyond its own rural outskirts, it is suspicious of big city cosmopolitanism. Just like all those born-again Christians in the American Bible Belt who consider New York to be the Sodom and Gomorrah of our times, so many of the good citizens of Assyut probably look askance at Cairo's tinsel glamour. Not only do they see its chintzy commercialism as a sign of moral decay, but also as a threat to the traditional standards which they, as a community in the heartland of the country, strive to uphold. The 'Assyut habits' which Mohammed defended were not simply a repudiation of Egypt's uncomfortable liason with the West; they were also an act of fear, designed to keep the confusing forces of modernity at bay.

Mohammed led me out of the old university and insisted on bringing me to the new campus; a twenty minute walk along the banks of the Ibrahimia Canal. While strolling there, he told me that he loved Egypt, that Egypt was a great country. I wondered if he had been educated at a military school similar to the one I had visited in Minya, and decided to test his blind patriotism by asking him if he didn't recognize certain problems within Egypt today—for example, the tensions between the two religious communities in Assyut.

'All Muslims and Copts love each other', he said. 'I am a Muslim, but all the Egyptians are brothers.'

More empty statements. Mohammed played the loyal son of Egypt to perfection. And yet, he wasn't totally convincing in his role. His designer wardrobe hinted that he fancied himself to be something of a westernized dandy, and he was totally mesmerized by American pop culture. As we walked, he kept humming a medley of Michael Jackson songs and later asked me if I liked the way John Travolta danced. One moment, he was the devout Muslim who condoned the segregation of women in his university; the next, he was just another eighteen-year-old kid who had seen *Saturday Night Fever* four times and was saving up for Prince's new album. Like his country, he seemed to be caught between two identities: trying to conform to Islamic tradition, yet tempted by the vicarious pleasures of the West.

'How many wives do you have?' he asked me.

'Just the one', I said.

'Why do you only have one wife?' I tried to explain that, in Ireland, polygamy was not exactly a popular practice.

'In Egypt, it is very difficult to marry', he said, echoing a statement that I had been constantly hearing. 'But one day, when I have the money, maybe I have two or three wives. You think

161

this is good?'

'I wouldn't be against it if women could have two or three husbands.'

He looked at me and laughed. 'You're a funny man. Are all people from Ireland so funny?'

The new university was laid out like an industrial park and had just about as much visual appeal. Glancing at my watch, I told Mohammed that I had a lunch appointment to keep and we exchanged addresses.

'Maybe someday I visit you in Dublin', he said. 'Maybe someday I find a job there. I want to work outside of Egypt.'

'But I thought you loved Egypt?'

'I love Egypt', he said, 'but I don't love the money they pay for work.'

* * * * *

I was early for my meeting with Stefan at the Lawyer's Club, so I wandered across the road and entered what I presumed to be a Christian church. Once inside, however, I realized that I was in some sort of grand presbytery and encountered a patriarchical figure in black robes sitting behind a desk in a wood panelled office. His beard was full and grey and he must have been a remarkably striking man in his youth because, even now, he still projected great authority. I apologized to him for my intrusion, saying that I had mistakenly thought this to be a house of worship, but he motioned me to join him on a bench outside his office and introduced himself as Johannes Nouer. When I asked him if he was the local parish priest, he smiled benignly and said, 'I am the Coptic Catholic Bishop of Assyut.'

He was a Fransciscan who had been in Assyut for twenty-one years and his face showed it. Near where we sat was a photograph of him being presented to Pope John Paul ii during a public audience in Rome, and I presumed from both his ecclesiastical rank and his forceful presence that he was the authoritative leader of the Christian community in the city.

'What do you think of Assyut?', he said, his tone suggesting that he wasn't interested in my thoughts about its merits as a tourist attraction. I said that the segregation of men and women in the university seemed rather chilling in its implications, and recounted for him Mohammed's statement that all Muslims and Copts love each other. Bishop Nouer shook his head, as if to say, 'I've heard that line before.'

'This is a city of fanatics.'

'On both sides?', I said.

'There are bad Christians everywhere. But in Assyut, we have too much tension, too much militancy, though no one likes to admit that there are problems between Muslims and Copts. They want to keep it all under the table. Still, the fundamentalists make life impossible for us here. There was a Chrisitian girl killed just a few days ago. I do not know exactly what happened, but I do know that she had spoken out against Muslim associations in the university and that she was murdered by Muslim students in the university housing where she lived.' (I later asked several people about this story, but could not get it substantiated by anyone.)

'But violence is not the only problem we have. I wanted to build a block of flats for the younger members of my church who want to get married, but cannot afford an apartment. First I had to get permission from the municipality, but then I had problems with the police who accused me of trying to build a new church by disguising it as an apartment block. Can you believe such logic? Now, I have to go to Cairo to make an appeal before a tribunal to see if the construction can go ahead. I tell you, in Assyut Christians are always regarded with suspicion.'

The lights blacked out for a moment, and Bishop Nouer mentioned that constant power cuts were another of Assyut's habits. Low voltage was the norm here, except when it came to sectarian conflicts. Mutual fear, mutual suspicion gave Assyut the extra burst of electricity that its generators failed to provide.

'I say this much for the Muslims', the Bishop said. 'You see the mosques, they are always full. But in our own churches, many Christians spend Sunday mornings in bed.'

Power was restored, but then failed again. The Bishop rose with great difficulty, explaining that it was now difficult for him to walk. On his desk were assorted medicine bottle and hypodermic needles. He was evidently not a well man and Assyut's internal climate perhaps exacerbated his ill-health. An invitation to lunch was offered and I regretted having to turn it down. He gave me his blessing and then struggled back to his office. As I left, the Coptic Catholic Bishop of Assyut was sitting alone in the dark.

The scales of justice had been sculpted into the front gates of *Nadi Houkoukiym*—the Lawyer's Club. The club itself was an uninspired modern building, but it had one splendid attribute— an immaculately groomed garden with cane chairs that looked out over a commanding sweep of the Nile. There was something unashamedly colonial about this setting. It was a memsahib's paradise; a place to take tea on the lawn and gossip about the frail young thing from Somerset who'd just come out to join her husband and was having problems with the heat. I looked around, hoping to find a latter-day wife of the Empire, but all I could see were solicitors in sharp suits. I joined a table where three prosecutors who worked for the police were talking shop with a local detective. The detective packed a gun under his jacket and drank a Coke by the neck. He downed a bottle in one go and then called for another. It had been a long morning, he said, and work was wearing him down. I asked him what sort of crimes kept him most occupied. 'Murder', he said.

Stefan showed up several minutes later in the company of Christa Pippig. She was the new German teacher in town; an attractive bookish woman in her twenties, recently arrived from Tübingen. She'd only been in Assyut for three days, but had already succumbed to a stomach virus, and was on a medicinal diet of white rice and black tea. Hairshirt rations in a hairshirt city.

Over lunch upstairs in the club's dining-room, Stefan said that I should not take everything I heard in Assyut too seriously. But on one point he was firm—the Muslims and the Copts of Assyut were like neighbouring states engaged in an endless Cold War. Both sides had their bellicose factions, both sides were responsible for occasional acts of violence. The Copts, however, did have one major disadvantage—they were the minority community and they suffered blatant discrimination, especially in the university. For example, there was the case of two brothers who graduated from the medical school near the top of their class (which according to Stefan, was quite a feat for a pair of Christians, as many Muslim professors supposedly feared giving a Coptic student too high a grade). However, on the day of their conferring, a group of Islamic militants whistled and booed them when they went up to receive their diplomas. Then there was the business about the Christian folk group who came to play on the campus. A Muslim organization objected to their spiritual music-making and registered their dissatisfaction by smashing their instruments before the concert.

Of course, Assyut was full of tales like that. Divided communities generate their own mythologies and build up their own distinctive repertoire of horror stories. As Bishop Nouer had

164

pointed out, Assyut hid its tensions behind a façade of normality. Yes, you saw occasional policeman in riot gear. Yes, the bias against women in the university was blatant. Despite that, however, a peculiar sort of equilibrium still existed in the city. The explosive undercurrents between the two communities were now an accepted, if unwanted feature of the metropolitan land-scape, and I gathered most people simply hoped that the tensions could be contained.

Stefan headed off to teach another German class, and Christa and I took tea by the river. She told me a splendid story. It seems there was a girl from a wealthy Muslim family who had enrolled as a student in the American University in Cairo. However, her parents were staunch traditionalists and not only made her wear the veil and a long gown, but also insisted that she be chauffeured to and from the university daily. And being a dutiful daughter, she assented to their wishes. But, as soon as she got inside the walls of the university, she immediately went to the loo and removed the veil, behind which her face was fully made-up. Then, she pinned up her gown so it now looked like a simple dress cut fashionably above the knee. Her transformation com-plete, she went off to classes disguised as a typical student. And when her lectures were finished, she returned to the loo, scrubbed off her make-up, covered her face again with the veil, unpinned her gown, and was whisked back to her parents in a black Mercedes.

Christa delighted in the hypocrisy of this story, and seemed to be using it to illustrate her own misgivings about Assyut. She frankly wondered how long she would be able to stick the place. The educational authorities had yet to inform her whom she should be teaching, and the city's orthodox astringency was already getting to her. She had to dress carefully and could only wear skirts and modest blouses when walking outside. And then there was the business of Stefan. She was currently staying in a room in his apartment, which meant having to tell anyone who asked (and many did ask) that she was married to him and had only recently joined him here. This deception bothered her, but she had no choice: an unmarried couple sharing a flat in Assyut was simply not on, even if the man and the woman weren't sleeping in the same bed. And Christa had absolutely no inten-tion of sleeping in Stefan's bed, though she gathered he was hopeful that their current 'room-mate' situation would develop into something more interesting. This also bothered her, because while she found Stefan pleasant, she also considered him a little odd. Then again, four celibate years in Assyut would make anybody odd, and perhaps that explained why Stefan marched around the city like he was being powered by high-octane fuel. Sexual tension was very much in the air, and that was something Christa hadn't bargained for. Still, she was trying to maintain a positive attitude. After all, she was only planning to stay in Assyut for six months, and she did have a degree in Arabic and Archaeology, and she did love this corner of the world, and she had lived in Cairo before and had been happy there . . .

But this was not Cairo. This was Assyut. And as Christa was beginning to realize, six months was a long time to spend in Assyut.

After tea, we walked back to Stefan's flat. It was spacious, yet spartan and painted in an institutional colour scheme. For all his years in Assyut, Stefan had accumulated little in the way of belongings. Lightbulbs had been left bare, no pictures hung on the mid-brown walls, and the furniture was Early Bedsitter. It was the flat of someone who was still trying to convince himself that he was just passing through town.

Christa, succumbing again to stomach complaints, slept for the afternoon and I worked. Around eight that evening, Stefan arrived back and stormed into his room, slamming the door. After a moment, the door flew open and he stomped into the kitchen, clattering a few pots and pans as he boiled water for coffee. The coffee made, he marched into the sitting room, drained his cup in one extended gulp, and then announced that it was time for us to go out.

Behind the wheel of his Peugeot, Stefan became James Dean. His own internal combustion found expression in that of his engine's, and we flew at low altitude through the city. I was reminded of the way West Berliners drive—burning across their metropolis as if they were trying to defy their enclosed boundaries. Stefan possessed a similar toxic energy. He was like the get-away driver of his own prison break, only the prison was of his own making. And he betrayed his sense of entrapment in Assyut by pushing his accelerator to extremes.

We landed with a skid in front of the Assyut Cultural Centre. Christa went off with Stefan to speak to a local bureaucrat who would hopefully tell her some details of her teaching schedule. I loitered without intent in the foyer and then noticed that the Cultural Centre was screening a film this evening and wandered into the auditorium. It was packed with men and they were watching a fifteen-year-old Japanese science fiction cheapie, *Legends of Dinosaurs and Monster Bones*. The film was dubbed into Hawaiian English and subtitled in Arabic. The crowd followed the plot with minimal interest, but suddenly became animated when a geisha girl came on the screen, dressed in a postage stamp bikini. Catcalls filled the auditorium. In the all-male preserve of the cinema, this flickering illusion of foreign sexuality was greeted with approval. But had that geisha girl walked the streets of Assyut in such a costume, she would have been run out of town.

* * * * *

There was another cultural centre in Assyut; a centre devoted to the study of Islam. It was located on the Corniche near the Bishop's Palace and was a recent addition to the cityscape. As new Egyptian buildings go, it was pleasing to the eye. Though constructed out of white concrete, it followed the traditional principles of Islamic architecture and featured lofty arches, curved windows and a graceful minaret. There was an elegance to its austerity; a harmonious balance between the modern and the ecclesiastic which succeeded in projecting a contemporary, yet sober image of Islam in the late twentieth century. Stepping through its main entrance, I found myself in the *sahn*—an enclosed courtyard, where men washed their feet in a shallow trough before entering a small mosque to pray. A reverential hush filled the courtyard and was broken by the voice of a caretaker asking me my business. When I mentioned that I would be interested in having a tour of the centre, he escorted me down a long corridor and presented me to the man in-charge, Dr Mahmoud Mehanni.

Given the puritanical nature of Assyut, I had expected the director of its Islamic Centre to be adorned in the garb of a sheikh—long white robes, a thick flowing beard. But Dr Mehanni contradicted such stereotypes. In his sharp blue blazer, red polo-neck jumper and horn-rimmed glasses, he looked more country club than fundamentalist. He also didn't speak much in the way of English, so an elderly gentleman with a military moustache and a Harris tweed jacket was brought in. All he needed was a bull terrier and he could have passed for a retired English major. And when he introduced himself as Mr. Christopher, I did a double-take.

'You are surprised by such a name', he said. 'I am a Copt. There is a club here for retired men which both Muslims and Copts belong to.'

The director asked a question which Mr Christopher translated. 'Dr Mehanni wishes to know your religion.'

'Christian', I said for want of a better word. Another question followed.

'And the director wishes to know what is your understanding of the Islamic faith.'

I said that my knowledge of Islam was basic: I was acquainted with the historical foundations of the faith, and knew a few biographical details about the prophet Mohammed. Dr Mehanni seemed pleased with my response, but continued to probe my attitudes towards his faith. 'The director is also interested in knowing', Mr Christopher said, 'what aspect of Islam pleases you most.'

I paused and chose my words carefully. 'The great devotion to the faith shown by the people.' Dr Mehanni nodded in agreement and we all relaxed. It had been a casual, yet pointed interrogation and I realized that I was being carefully sounded out. Perhaps few foreigners ever visited the Islamic Centre, and therefore the director was simply curious to learn how an outsider perceived Islam. But I also sensed that Dr Mehanni was slightly wary of me as well, wondering if my reasons for visiting his Centre arose out of a genuine interest in the faith, or out of a concern with the dominance of Muslim tradition in this community. He was quick to point out that the Centre existed to promote an appreciation and understanding of Islam to anyone who was interested, and he used Mr Christopher as proof that his was a truly ecumenical institution. Mr Christopher backed him up on this point.

'As I told you, I am a Christian, but I come here every day', he said. 'These problems you hear about the Muslims and the Copts in Assyut, they are isolated incidents and they usually only take place in the university. Muslims love all religions. We are all brothers here.'

Was everybody in Upper Egypt taught that line? Mr Afify had used it, Mohammed had used it, and now Mr Christopher was repeating it almost verbatim. Rather than coming across as an expression of fraternal good-will, it now began to sound to me like a defensive statement; a way of masking an uncomfortable truth. Few, it seemed wanted to admit to a foreigner that the spirit of religious tolerance was endangered in Egypt. Any time I was told about a sectarian incident, it was in hushed tones, as if I was being let in on an appalling family secret; as if the person was saying, 'This can't be happening to us.' Egypt had yet to become a fratricidal country like the Lebanon, but in Assyut you could see the warning signs of escalating divisiveness. A statement like 'We are all brothers' therefore had two meanings. It maintained the image of an *entente cordial* between the two faiths, yet it also expressed the fear of unspeakable consequences should that fragile peace ever disintegrate.

Dr Mehanni suggested that Mr Christopher show me the Centre's library, so we marched down two flights of stairs and entered a small functional room lined with a haphazard collection of books. Next to a stack of scholarly volumes on the Islamic faith was a row of dog-eared foreign titles, including Dale Carnegie's *How to Win Friends and Influence People*. No doubt, the future sheikhs who studied in this library found this a most essential reference book.

The librarian—a large and cheerful woman on the fringes of fifty—approached me with three large tomes and said that these were the most prized volumes in the Centre's collection. I expected to be shown a special illuminated edition of the Koran, or something of similar gravitas. Instead, I was urged to leaf through a collection of photographs which recorded King Farouk's visit to Assyut in the 1930s. Turning the pages was like taking a trip down a monarchial Memory Lane, as every page lovingly featured the King—a young man dressed in a cut-away suit—going through the tedious tasks of royalty: opening the city's new train station, being presented to assorted local officials, and greeting the usual groups of schoolchildren. Judging by the perpetually bleak look on His Majesty's face, the King had found his trip to Assyut something of a chore. The staff of the library, however, took delight in this glimpse of their nation's regal past, and crowded around me as I browsed through the album. When I opened another photographic collection, featuring formal portraits of the Egyptian royal family, the librarian was able to identify every prince, princess, dowager aunt, and distant cousin who now gazed out at us with the accusatory stare of the dispossessed. Not only that, she also knew all the dirt behind the throne, and could recount stories of historical intrigues at court. And it struck me as curious that here, in a centre for Islamic studies in the most orthodox city in

Egypt, such affectionate nostalgia was being shown towards a long-defunct monarchy. If there was a strong undercurrent of fundamentalism in Assyut, then it also seemed to be tempered by a quirky secularism—Mohammed swearing his allegiance to Allah while humming Michael Jackson's *Thriller*; a collection of royal photographs forming the centrepiece of a library devoted to the study of the Koran. In this landscape of incongruities, it was difficult to gauge whether the city's stern 'habits' were merely a way of asserting Islam's traditional identity in the face of accelerated social change, or whether they were the first step towards the rejection of all infidel values. Some weeks later, while sitting in the *sahn* of the Al-Azhar mosque in Cairo, I got talking to a student from Chad who was studying to become a sheikh. And he was in no doubt about which road Egypt would eventually choose to travel.

'The problem with this country today', he said, 'is that the people want Islam, but the government will not let them have it. Islam is not a religion. It is a way of life. It does not look into the past. It always looks forward. It answers all the questions. Iran is good because Khomeini understands Islam and follows it. Egypt is very bad because the men who run the government only think of life now. But, one day, the people of Egypt who want Islam will have a chance to take power. And they will seize that chance and build a true Islamic society.'

Islam—the way of life; the answer to all questions. Having tried socialism and failed, having tried the free market and failed, would *a true Islamic society* become Egypt's only alternative? That threat—as so many people had told me—hovered over the country like a vulture waiting to swoop. In Assyut, I had seen a glimpse of what an Islamic Egypt might be like and it was troubling. But even here, in this bastion of Muslim conservatism, the Egyptian love of the worldly still seeped through the fundamentalist veneer. And listening to that librarian chatter on about the antics of King Farouk and his family gave me a peculiar sort of reassurance that Egypt was as yet unwilling to embrace the stark precepts of a theocratic state.

But might it accept Islamic rule in time to come? Might the purity of the faith be seen as the simplistic answer to all of Egypt's dilemmas? After leaving the library, Mr Christopher brought me to a small kindergarten located in the basement of the Centre, and it was there that I witnessed an incident which starkly symbolized the shape of things to come. A class of five-year-olds stood up when we entered their classroom and were commanded by their teacher to recite for us the lesson of the day. The kids obliged, chanting the lesson in unison and acting out what they were saying by first pointing to the ceiling and then to the floor. Mr Christopher translated it for me in a hesitant and uneasy voice.

'The children say: *"We are Muslims. We are the one true faith. We will go to Heaven when we die, and everyone else will go to Hell".'*

Mr Christopher fell silent and turned away.

'Who are all the other people who will go to Hell?', I asked him.

He attempted a smile and said, 'That is open to interpretation'.

'But I thought you said that Muslims love all religions?'

'They do, of course. But every religion thinks that they will be the only ones to go to heaven'.

And at the age of five, the young Muslims of Assyut were being taught that they alone would enter paradise.

* * * * *

On my last evening in Assyut, I met a Pole who had become an Egyptian. He was a priest in his fifties with the tough, weathered face of a shipyard worker in Gdansk. He'd been in Assyut for two decades and, after some struggle, had taken out Egyptian citizenship. But Poland still pervaded his flat. Polish books lined his shelves, a Solidarity sticker adorned one wall of his loo, the collected sermons of Fr Jerzy Popiluzsko were prominently displayed on his coffee table, and a photograph of the murdered priest was given pride of place in the sitting room. He had even turned his spare bedroom into a small private chapel, complete with ikons and a roughly hewn wooden altar. There was something almost clandestine about his set up; the sort of place, one imagined, where proscribed literature was exchanged and the government in-exile met in secret conference.

The priest made me coffee and spoke about his reasons for leaving his homeland. 'How could I ever go back to Poland?', he said. 'Solidarity was the great hope, but the hope is now dead. Had I remained I would now be a dissident and I could never have lived under that regime. So my work as a priest brought me to Egypt, and I stayed'. He laughed; a quiet self-depreciative laugh which seemed to say, 'And look what I got in exchange for Poland . . . Assyut'. But then, the laughter stopped.

'You know there is little hope left for Egypt', he said. 'The economy here will eventually lead to revolution, there is no political choice, and the majority of people are paid next to nothing. What is the future in such a country? What is the future in a city like this where the fanaticism runs so deep? Where there is no trust between the two communities? Where the fear begins so young? How can we undo all that conditioning?'

I had no answers to his questions. Nor had he. Nor had Egypt. We finished our coffee in silence and, as I got up to leave, the lights failed. Outside his window, the city was black.

'That is Assyut', he said. 'The dark.'

I walked back to Stefan's flat. Halfway there, power was restored and light burst upon the city with the dazzlng intensity of a Roman candle. But then, after one brief illuminating moment, Assyut went black again. And under cover of darkness, I left town.

Chapter Six

Some Time on the River

O N THE EVE OF the fourteen-hundred-and-fifteenth birthday
of the prophet Mohammed, I took a train south to Luxor.
Halfway there, a rumour began to circulate around the First Class
compartment in which I sat. Someone had heard that an Egyptair
jet had been hijacked, and within minutes at least three different
versions of this story were being spread among the passengers.
One businessman said that the flight had originated in Italy and
had been seized by Syrians. Another insisted that it had taken off
from Madrid and was now en route to Tripoli. The Nubian waiter
who served me tea agreed that the Libyans were responsible, but
was certain that the plane had been flying from Casablanca to
Cairo. And, showing a definite flair for the gothic, he also told me
that the hijackers had cut the throats of eight passengers.

To put an end to this Egyptian Rashomon, I dug out my radio
and attempted to tune in the BBC. Static filled the wavelength
where London should have been, so I switched to Radio Cairo.

The announcer was terse and solemn. I asked my neighbour to translate the bulletin. It went like this: an Egyptair jet with over 80 passengers had been hijacked shortly after take-off from Athens and had been forced to land in Malta. The identity of the gunmen was unknown, but they had already killed several passengers and were threatening further carnage. No other details were available at the moment, and we now return you to our regularly scheduled programmes . . .

'Athens again!', said the young man sitting next to me. 'The Greeks, they are terrible when it comes to security. All the madmen in the Middle East use Athens Airport because they know its security is so bad. I tell you, the Arab world is full of crazies. Look at Libya, Sudan, the Lebanon—all insane countries. Only Egypt and Jordan are sane.'

We introduced ourselves. My travelling companion's name was Fuad Aziz Abu-Sidah, but he told me to call him 'Freddy'. He explained that he had given himself that nickname after a party of Japanese tourists found that saying Fuad Aziz Abu-Sidah was a formidable task. That was Freddy's job—shepherding groups of package holiday-makers through the Valley of the Kings, the Temple of Amun, and all the other archaeological debris upon which the Luxor economy depended. It was trying work, he said, especially when it came to putting up with arrogant Parisians ('Why do French people complain all the time?') or double-knit Americans who thought that their dollar could buy anything. Still, the pay was fantastic, and he needed the money because he was getting married next summer. His engagement had been dragging on for years—he'd met his future wife when he was fifteen—and he reckoned that after a few months in the tour guide game, he could put a down-payment on a flat and then start thinking about a career in international business. That was Freddy's goal—to run an import/export operation out of Luxor and become a man of commerce. Egypt needed businessmen who were committed to the country, yet versed in the world at-large. And Freddy saw himself as the ideal local entrepreneur—well-travelled, fluent in four languages, comfortable in the cosmopolitan swirl, but still retaining his traditional identify as a pious Muslim. Though the intensive mercantilism of the West attracted him, he didn't want to become too seduced by its value structure, as it ran contrary to that of his own. He wanted to be urbane, yet faithful to his own background; the sort of wheeler-dealer who, when closing a sale in Frankfurt, would always retreat to his hotel room to pray five times a day. Like the monks in St Marcarius, he believed that the only way to maintain one's internal equilibrium in Egypt today was by merging spiritual devotion with software.

But, for the moment, the days of deal-making in Frankfurt were still in the future and he was trying to steel himself for the task ahead of him tomorrow: leading a party of Spaniards through the sites of ancient Thebes. He asked me if I wanted to tag along on this tour, but when I said that I had little interest in Pharaonic monuments, he expressed surprise.

'If you don't like monuments', he said, 'then you will not like Luxor.'

Freddy was right. From the moment I arrived, the awfulness of Luxor seized me. An aroma of horse dung blanketed the town; the horses hitched up to carriages which cruised the streets touting for touristic custom. Leaving the station, I was immediately surrounded by three local sharks, offering their services as foreign exchange dealers, hashish salesmen, and tour guides. I shrugged them off, checked into a cheap hotel, and then continued walking down the main thoroughfare—Rue Saad Zaghlul. The street was black with people prowling through the warm November night, and everywhere I turned touts would approach me, saying 'Hello, my friend . . .' and insist that I accompany them to their souvenir bazaars. Once again, I dodged their advances and weaved my way through the congealed crowd. A small platoon of Japanese tourists wearing imitation Arab headscarves were being enticed into a shop that traded in plastic pyramids, pictures of Cleopatra on silk, and mother-of-pearl daggers for the entire family. Further on, a young American couple, kitted out in designer tropical clothes and designer rucksacks, were cornered by a pair of touts.

'How much you want for your woman?', one of the touts asked the gent. 'How much you sell her for?'

'Beat it, assholes', the gent replied.

Little scenes like this were being played up and down the street. Having so far avoided the meretriciousness of the Egyptian tourist trade, I now found myself plunged into its spiritual centre. Then again, Luxor had always been a tourist town; a city that owed its livelihood to a group of ruined temples and ancient tombs. In the literature of early twentieth century travel, no grand tour through Egypt would have been complete without at least a three-day visit to the site of the Theban kingdom. Karl Baedeker, writing in his 1929 guidebook, became almost lyrical when describing the pleasures of its environs:

> The verdant crops and palms which everywhere cheer the traveller as soon as he had quitted the desert, the splendid hues that tinge the valley every morning and evening, the brilliant, unclouded sunshine that bathes every object even in the winter season, lend to the site of ancient Thebes the appearance of a wonderland, richly endowed with the gifts of never-failing fertility.

Of course, when Baedeker was writing, jet propulsion had yet to democratize travel, and only those with sufficient funds and time on their hands could afford a journey to this archaeological amusement park. Luxor, therefore, was the haunt of *the haves*, escaping the icy grey hue of a north European winter. And Baedeker, preparing his well-heeled readers for a dose of Edwardian culture shock, devoted a short section of his book to the matter of deportment among 'the natives':

> The average Oriental regards the European traveller as a Croesus, therefore as fair game, and feels justified in pressing upon him with a perpetual demand for bakshish *(bashish, bakhshish)*, which simply means 'a gift'. The number of beggars is enormous, but bakshish should never be given either to adults or children, except for services rendered or to the aged and crippled . . . A beggar may be generally silenced with the words *'al Allah* or *Allah yihannin aleik* (God have mercy on thee) or *Allah ya tik* (May God give thee). The best reply for more importune cases is *ma fish, ma fish* (I have nothing for you) or *mafish bakshish* (there is no present), which will generally have the effect of dispersing the assailants for a time.
>
> It is of course, inevitable that cabmen, guides, donkey boys, and the like should expect a gratuity in addition to the stipulated fee for their services, and the traveller should therefore take care to be amply supplied with SMALL CHANGE at all times, and especially with pieces of half a piaster. Payment should never be made until the service stipulated for has been rendered, after which a deaf ear should be turned to the protestations

and entreaties which almost invariably follow. Even
when an express bargain has been made, and more
than the stipulated sum paid, they are almost sure to
pester the traveller in the way indicated . . . and if the
attacks which ensue are not silenced by an air of calm
indifference the traveller may use the word *ruh* or *imshi*
(be off) or *uskut* (be quiet) in a quiet but decided and
imperative tone . . . While much caution and firmness
are desirable in dealing with the people, it need hardly
be added that the traveller should avoid being too
exacting or suspicious. He should bear in mind that
many of the natives with whom he comes in contact are
mere children, whose demands should excite amusement rather than anger, and who often display a
touching simplicity and kindliness of disposition.

Considered now, Baedeker's code of conduct comes across as
an artefact from the colonial past; a classic piece of jingoism *in
extremis*. And yet, as I made my way through Luxor's garish
streets—ducking the touts who looked upon any foreigner as
decidedly easy prey; mingling with the coachloads of overfed
German and Swiss—I couldn't help thinking that Baedeker's
attitudes still had a disturbing validity in Luxor today. It was as if
both the *hawagahs* and the locals had entered into an unspoken
agreement to play-act traditional roles—the foreigners assuming
the part of latter-day sahibs; the locals, the wily, unscrupulous
natives. The tourist-based economy of the city reinforced these
stereotypes. Westerners were treated as fly-by-night colonialists
because they possessed hard currency. And though the locals
pandered to them, there was a distinctive undertone of hostility
to their obsequiousness *(How much you want for your woman?
How much you sell her for?)* Watching the touts at work was like
observing a peculiar form of schizophrenia, for beneath their
sycophancy was what I detected to be a surly nationalistic pride.
'We will grovel to you because of your dollars and deutschmarks',
they seemed to be telling the tourists, 'but don't think for a
moment that we look up to you as our masters. We're the masters
now.'

And being the masters, they took every opportunity to swindle
the hapless *hawagahs*. I stopped by a cigarette kiosk where I was
asked to pay a pound for a packet of Cleopatras that cost 30
piasters. And when I pointed to the price in Arabic on the side of

177

the packet and asked the vendor why he was trying to cheat me, he smiled and said, 'Not every tourist can read Arabic numbers.' Later on, a kid in a news stand wanted three times the normal price of an *Egyptian Gazette*, and when I stopped by a telephone exchange to book a call to my wife in Dublin, I was told that the fee would be fifteen pounds—nearly double the standard rate I had been paying in Cairo.

It wasn't simply avarice that compelled the merchants of Luxor to overcharge: rather it was a way of expressing contempt for their passing trade. They needed the tourists, and yet I sensed that they despised them for their naïvety; their package holiday vision of the country. In turn, the tourists—harassed and shortchanged—probably came to the same conclusion as Baedeker: the natives were nothing more than gangsterish children whose protestations could only be silenced with words like *imshi* or *beat it, asshole*. Neither side had any comprehension of the other's sensibility. The hucksterish rough and tumble of tourism made them regard each other as cartoon figures, equally infantile.

This was the worst of the western influence in Egypt. The quest for the almighty dollar (or any other major monetary unit) had robbed Luxor of any self-esteem. Its colonial ambience had simply been updated to meet the demands of contemporary tourism. Sanitized Victoriana was a strong selling point. Along the Corniche stood two of the great nineteenth-century hotels of Egypt—the Old Winter Palace and the Luxor. On first inspection the Old Winter Palace was pure Somerset Maughan—a central corridor long enough to serve as a cricket pitch, 30 foot ceilings, a lingering perfume of *noblesse oblige* in the air. But a muzak system had been installed to pump Stevie Wonder into its empty hallways, and a new Spanish-style apartment block had been umbilically attached to the original manse. The Luxor, on the other hand, retained its turn-of-the-century flavour, but still pandered to the 'explorer in the tropics' fantasies of many of its guests by calling its bar *The Africa*, and doing it up in mock safari style. I took a seat at the cane and bamboo bar, ordered a beer, and found myself within earshot of the two American couples grouped around a table. The men were wearing double-knit sport shirts and nylon trousers, and had been trying to cultivate designer stubble without much success. The women were heavy in the thigh and dressed for Miami in plaid bermuda shorts and tee-shirts depicting the Roman Coliseum and the Tower of

London. They began to talk. Loudly.

'I think that camel driver was trying to rip us off', the Roman Coliseum said. 'And *gawd*, did you see his teeth? Don't they have any good dentists in Egypt?'

'I hear it's one of the worst countries in the world for gum diseases', one of the guys said.

'I'll tell you what really got me', the Tower of London said. 'It was that guide we hired last night. I mean, he had the potential to bring Luxor to life for us. But he couldn't care less about fulfilling that potential.'

'Egyptians never fulfill their potential', the other guy said. 'They don't understand what it means to achieve excellence.'

'Boy you can say that again', the Roman Coliseum said. 'I mean, take that guide. Think of what he could have done for us. Like, I've shown people Dallas and have given 'em a real good time. Why couldn't he have done the same for us? Especially since we were paying him?'

Egyptians never fulfill their potential. The First World looks at the Third World and is dismayed. It manifests its dismay in two ways: (1) The 'Why Can't the Natives Be Like Us?' approach, in which rampant gum disorders, corrupt camel drivers, and uninterested tour guides are all cited as examples of why countries like Egypt are nothing more than perennial down-and-outs who refuse to get off the dole; (2) The 'Look at the Downtrodden People' school of western shame, in which—to use V. S. Naipaul's line—'revolutionaries who visit centres of revolution with return air tickets' fly in for a little tour of backstreet deprivation, express solidarity with the oppressed masses, and speak about their affluent guilt.

In Luxor, these two visions of Third Worldliness seemed to merge together. The foreigner could discover latent imperial tendencies and complain about native fecklessness. Alternatively, he could express outrage that tourism had turned many of the locals into fawning menials. Either way, he would be conveniently classifying Egyptians as 'types'.

I left the bar and continued walking along the Nile banks. Groups of feluccas were tied up for the night and cocktail music could be heard aboard several floating hotels. Voices from the shadows kept calling to me—*Taxi? Change Money? Hashish?*—but I ignored these clandestine whispers and strolled on past the endless jewellery shops, the bazaars stocked with cheap trinkets, until I eventually ran out of road. Surrounded by trees, I now found myself in a small woodland; a quiet sanctuary tucked away from the oppressive familiarity of Luxor's streets. Or, at least, I thought it was a quiet sanctuary until two men asleep in the nearby weeds suddenly jumped to their feet.

'You have cigarettes?', one of them asked me. I tossed him my packet of Cleopatras, he bade me goodnight, and disappeared with his friend into the undergrowth.

Retracing my steps, I returned to the city centre and, cutting up a side road, headed in the direction of a mosque outside which several hundred people had gathered to celebrate Mohammed's birthday. The atmosphere resembled that of a street carnival, a riotous jumble of children, car horns, street merchants, and the voice of a muezzin rising above the din. Once inside this tightly-wedged crowd, it became impossible to move, so I sought refuge with a family who were standing on top of a wooden bench. Trumpets sounded in the distance, and a manic procession began to push its way up the street. A huge wooden float drawn by donkeys and ablaze with gaudy lights led the parade. On top of it were a group of men in drag and singing along to a ghetto blaster. What exactly they were singing I couldn't tell as they were drowned out by a marching band which followed them. It was unlike any marching band I had ever heard, as this group of trumpeters and percussionists followed no set musical score, but simply blew discordant notes into the night. Behind them was a solid wall of men pointing sticks in the air and looking like a dancing baton charge. Then came several more floats. On one, a nightclub star in an electric red shirt crooned into a microphone. He was followed by a kid in boxer shorts doing a homoerotic bump and grind act, and then there were more trumpeters, more dancing men with sticks, more percussionists beating out an unsyncopated rhythm until, finally, the whole hurly-burly passed us by and faded from view as it snaked its way towards the city centre.

In the West, we tend to perceive Islam as a medieval monolith; socially repressive, absolute in its doctrines. But the sight of this Mardi Gras momentarily altered that view. The birthday of the prophet was a cause for unrestrained festivity; a chance to cast off the rigorous orthodoxy of the faith and give in to a spirit of earthiness. Here was the theatrical, celebratory face of Islam, and a reminder that beneath the puritanism lay a sense of frivolity and mischief.

In the wake of the parade came a gang of youths on horseback.

They tore hell for leather down the street, oblivious to anyone who was in their way. I just managed to jump on to the pavement before being trampled, but a young kid on a bicycle wasn't so lucky, as one of the marauding riders plowed right into him. The bicycle went flying, the horse collapsed, and both the cyclist and the cowboy were showing signs of accidental wear and tear. Immediately, a crowd gathered and a kangaroo court of inquiry was set up to apportion blame. Opposing counsels for the defence and prosecution were chosen, witnesses came forward with their account of the accident, and a free-for-all argument raged. I left this judicial circus and strolled back to my hotel. In the lounge, several members of the staff were watching an old Stanley Kubrick film, *Paths of Glory*, on the communal television. I arrived in time to watch the scene where three innocent French soldiers during the First World War were about to be shot for an alleged act of cowardice. But just as the firing squad was raising its rifles, the film broke and a newsreader filled the screen. She smiled at us and said that the Egyptair hijack was over. A team of Egyptian commandos, sent earlier that day to Malta, had stormed the plane. All the hijackers had been killed, but the passengers were alive and well.

Upstairs in my room, the BBC World Service had a different version of the day's events. Yes, a squad of Egyptian commandos had stormed the plane, but over 57 people had died in the attack.

* * * * *

The next morning, the BBC had further details of the bloody finale to the Egyptair hijacking. It made for a grim beginning to the day. It seems that the Mubarak government had decided to send a commando team to Malta after hearing reports that eight passengers had been murdered by the gunmen. However, when the commandos blitzkrieged the plane—blowing off the doors with explosives—the hijackers counter-attacked by detonating phosphorus grenades which set fire to the aircraft's cabin. Most of the passengers killed were alleged to have died from the effects of smoke inhalation, though several survivors said that the Egyptian troops fired indiscriminately at anyone fleeing the jet. All but one of the hijackers was shot dead, the captain of the plane felled the only surviving gunman with an axe, and the final death toll was 57 with several survivors still critically injured. But perhaps the most terrible irony of the whole incident was the news that only one passenger had been killed prior to the storming of the plane; a revelation that raised doubts about Egypt's decision to order their commandos into action at such an early stage of the crisis. Had they been misinformed about the number of dead, and therefore concluded that the hijackers would execute more passengers if they didn't act quickly and decisively? Or had they pushed the panic button prematurely and now stood accused of using force with haste? Like the Achille Lauro affair, the aftermath of the carnage in Malta was riddled with ambiguities.

Down in the breakfast room of the hotel, I shared a table with an engineer from Alexandria who was buried in that morning's edition of *Al Ahram*.

'Heard the news?', he said. 'Sixteen killed on the plane. Terrible, yes?'

'Only sixteen dead?', I said. 'I thought that the final count was 57.'

'Impossible', he said, pointing at the front page of his newspaper. 'Look at the headlines—it says sixteen dead. Radio Cairo reported the same number earlier this morning.'

'Well the BBC reported 57', I said, and proceeded to fill him in on what I had heard. He looked at me with incredulity.

'You are certain about this?', he said.

'I heard it.'

'I hope it is not true', he said. 'I do not want it to be true.'

His sentiments were evidently shared by the government of Hosni Mubarak. They too didn't want the final death toll to be true, and they were stalling for time before informing the public of the actual dimensions of the tragedy. It was as if they wanted to believe their own fictions and couldn't bear the thought that an Egyptian commando raid had resulted in the deaths of 57 innocent people. To admit that would be to admit that the apparatus of the state had failed. And in a one-party state, the regime in charge could never be held accountable for an incident that injured national pride, because it feared that it would call into question its self-imposed mandate to rule. The public, therefore, could not be trusted with news that presented the government in a bad light. It was better to lie to them first ('our brave commandos have stormed the plane and all the passengers are alive and well'), and then gradually reveal the truth. By following this strategy, the men-in power would not immediately have to defend their actions. They could take their time to formulate an official response that would absolve them of any wrong-doing or poor judgement. In a state-controlled media, the illusion of factual reporting is coupled with the illusion that the regime is always right. And had I not heard the BBC report last night, I too would have gone to bed believing that the hijacking had ended without the loss of innocent lives. I too would have accepted this fiction.

The engineer excused himself to catch the morning flight back to Alexandria. 'I hope airport security is better today that it was in Athens', he said.

I finished breakfast and then went out and rented a bicycle. It was an old-style 'sit up and beg' Raleigh with high handle-bars, a wide seat and defective brakes. After zipping along the Corniche and having a near-fatal encounter with a donkey cart, I cycled down to a dock and loaded myself and my transport on to one of the ferries that plow back and forth across the Nile. The ferry was packed with tourists, heading off to explore the archaeological ruins on the West Bank of Thebes. And when we landed on the far side, we were immediately surrounded by little kids and professional flim-flam men, all offering their services as guides to the Valley of the Kings. Bearing down on the pedals, I pushed my way out of this side-show and soon found myself in open countryside: a tableau of lush vegetation, the occasional small dwelling, and a sheer stone cliff demarcating the horizon. It was an impossibly hot day, but the agrarian sun was a welcome relief after the airless commercialism of Luxor. I pressed on, passing two Pharaonic statues posted like sentries at the side of the road, and then began to struggle gradually uphill until the outline of a village came into view. The road forked, the hill became a downward slide, and I coasted at speed into the hamlet of Medinet Habu. Had I been on the monuments trail, I could have stopped off and spent time scrambling through the Temple of Ramses III. Instead, I parked my bike in front of a small hotel and, following a map drawn for me in Cairo, I crossed a moist irrigated field and walked down a narrow gravel path until I came to a small box of a house built entirely out of dried mud brick and looking like a piece of cubist sculpture.

The house belonged to a doctor named Darwish. The amateur cartographer who had drawn the map for me was the French journalist I had met in Siwa, Patrick Godeau. While in Cairo, I had looked Patrick up and spent an evening at his flat, during which I dented a bottle of his Benedictine. I remember little about the evening (though the after-effects the next morning were unforgettable), but before I left I did recall Patrick thrusting a hastily scribbled diagram of Medinet Habu in my hand and saying that if I happened to find myself on the West Bank of Thebes, I should look up his friend, Dr Darwish.

Darwish, he said, was a young general practitioner from Cairo who had escaped the world of big city medicine to set up a practice in the small rural enclave of Medinet Habu. His reasons for this radical career change remained unclear, but I was intrigued enough by the notion of an urban Egyptian doctor coming to work in a backwater that I decided to pay him a visit. And as I knocked on the door of his mud-brick house, I wondered if he was going to turn out to be one of those sanctimonious missionary doctors who oozed commitment and humanity as he talked about his work among the *fellahin*.

The door was opened by Darwish's assistant—a young kid around eighteen—and when I asked to see the doctor, he led me into a small living area that was the height of indigenous chic. It was an open-plan space with an intricately crafted mud brick floor, hand carved benches covered by brightly coloured local rugs, exposed wood beams, an adjoining roofless courtyard thick with greenery, and a small studio kitchen neatly wedged into an alcove. *Better Homes and Gardens* would have definitely approved of this ingenious use of local building materials to create a fashionably 'native' environment.

After a few minutes, Dr Darwish emerged from a bedroom, still half-awake. He was around thirty, with a floppy moustache and hang-dog eyes, dressed in jeans, a tee-shirt and sandals. Like the decor of this house, he was stylishly casual; a hint that, though he might have traded the city for a village, he still maintained his sense of urban flair. I mentioned that I was a friend of Patrick's, he offered tea and, apologizing for his state of semi-conscious-ness, tried to kick-start himself awake with a cigarette. He'd been up late last night dealing with an emergency case and hadn't slept much. It was one of the problems of being a local doctor in a small community—you were always on twenty-four hour call. Not that he minded that aspect of the job. He'd worked in a university hospital in Cairo before coming to the West Bank of Luxor, and I gathered he decided that the life of a provincial physician was eminently preferable to the chaotic rough-and-tumble of a big city hospital. Anyway, if he missed the noise and hubub of a city, Luxor was just across the river, and was also equipped with a hospital where he could refer patients for treatment that he couldn't provide. His set-up evidently pleased him. In his custom-built house—designed by himself, executed by a local mason—he could enjoy the comforts of tasteful interior design while still being situated in the heart of a mythic landscape. It wasn't every doctor who had the Temple of Ramses III as his neighbour, or could step out of his front door and see the arable fields of the Theban kingdom laid out before him. But, while acknowledging that his was a pleasing lifestyle, Darwish's central concern was the business of running a surgery in a tiny parish. There were no special health problems in the area, and he and his assistant were able to cope with most ailments that didn't require hospitalization or the specialized skills of a consultant. But when I asked him about the standard of health care in Egyptian hospitals, his early-morning fog evaporated and he suddenly became animated. Nurses, he said, were the biggest problem facing medicine in the country. Nurses, in his mind, symbolically embodied the dilemma of Egypt today.

'You must understand that a nurse in Egypt is considered socially very low. This is because she has to stay out at nights, away from her family. And in Egypt—a sexually retarded country—it is considered very bad for a single woman to not come home to her parents in the evening. Also, everybody thinks that all nurses just want to marry doctors, so they are considered prostitutes as well. This means that many women who might have a talent for nursing will not go into the profession because they are afraid of the stigma that is attached to it.

'But the problem is that nurses have no education beyond secondary school, which basically means they know nothing. I am in a hospital dealing with a premature baby in an incubator. I say to the nurse, "Give him five mg of this medicine, dilute it in saline, and then inject it". What does she do? She looks at me blankly. I have to write it all down, go through it with her several times to be certain that she does not make a mistake. They cannot do anything by themselves.

'Of course, there is a college for nurses in Cairo and Alexandria which gives them a B.A., but as soon as they finish their studies, they become supervisors in the hospitals because they have more education than any of the other nurses. So, a nurse with a B.A. is immediately promoted to sergeant without ever having been a private, which means that she has never got her hands dirty and has little practical experience. And, of course, because she has the B.A., she thinks she knows everything. She almost thinks of herself as a doctor. But this is a common attitude here. It is like this: a man who fixes a car may know how to change the oil, but he has no idea about the principle of internal combustion which makes the engine work. The man who wired this house, the only thing he knows about electricity is that there are two wires, one of which is positive, the other negative. I know of a surgeon in Luxor who has an assistant who has no medical education, but has assisted the surgeon in operations for over fifteen years. And now he thinks he can perform an operation! Sure, he could probably remove an appendix, but if something went wrong during the surgery he wouldn't know what to do. Still, he thinks he understands surgery, even though he doesn't understand the workings of the human body.

'But that is the biggest problem in Egypt today. Everyone who has a little education thinks he is an expert, but no one understands the workings of the country.'

And having given me his diagnosis of Egypt's internal health, Dr Darwish excused himself to see a patient with less vexing ailments.

* * * * *

I returned to the east bank of Luxor and cycled out of the city. Past new blocks of flats and the Club Mediterranean and the Isis Hotel. Everywhere you looked, Luxor was Miami Beaching itself with luxury resorts. But what was most interesting about this stretch of holiday spots was that, seen from the road, they all took on the appearance of colonial enclaves: a place for sahibs to escape the natives and luxuriate in western comfort. Was this the ultimate aim of tourism the world over—to filter out all that was potentially alien and therefore disquieting about a foreign culture and shroud the visitor in a neutral airport lounge environment? Has the ease of jet travel actually turned us more insular by making us demand western standards in any place that could afford to pave a runway? Looking at those fortresses, behind which lay chlorinated swimming pools and air-conditioned lounge bars and gift shops trading in suntan oil and local arts and crafts, I wondered whether Third World tourism today was essentially an exercise in mass deodorization, designed to remove all the noxious odours of an economically developing nation. We no longer 'civilize the natives' through colonization. Instead, we allow the Hiltons and the Sheratons and the Holiday Inns and the Movenpicks to do the job for us.

Running out of road, I cycled back to the city centre, returned my hired bicycle, and walked back to my *declassé* hotel. As I entered the foyer, I was called over by a desk clerk.

'I heard you said that 57 passengers died on the plane', he said.

This stopped me short. 'I simply told someone over breakfast what I'd heard on the BBC.'

'You think this is true?'

'I doubt the BBC would lie about the number of dead.'

'You know, we have not been told about this', he said. 'Do you think Egypt was right to do this?'

'I think the loss of life was appalling', I said.

'Maybe we move too fast. I do not know.'

Later, that night, on the 8pm news in English, Egyptian television finally admitted that 57 passengers had been killed in the storming of the aircraft. This was followed by an interview with the pilot of the plane. His head was swathed in a bandage, and he said that, given the hijackers threats to kill everyone on the plane, the commando raid had been the only action Egypt could have taken. After this, the American Secretary of State, George Schultz, filled the screen. Terrorism, he said, had to be stomped out. It was all beautifully stage managed.

After the news bulletin, I went out for a stroll along the Corniche. The Nile was empty of traffic and dark. In my journey south, I had been following the route of the river, but had yet to spend any time on it. So I resolved to find a boat heading out of town the next day.

* * * * *

I left the hotel and headed towards the Corniche, sauntering down a river bank to where a cluster of feluccas were docked. A man in his sixties wearing a striped *galabiya* approached me and said, 'You want boat?'

'How about going to Aswan?' I said. The man smiled the sort of knowing smile which creeps across the face of a taxi driver who has just landed a big fare, and invited me aboard his felucca. I negotiated a narrow gangplank and took a seat on a mattress on the deck. We exchanged names. His was Mr Abdul Mohammed, and while brewing us a pot of tea on top of a small camping stove, he insisted on showing me a packet of letters and post-cards that he had received from past satisfied customers. 'Thanks for making the Nile so beautiful', wrote an American couple from New Jersey. A Christmas card from a family in Hanover wished

Mr Mohammed a *Frohe Weihnachten*, while a pair of English schoolteachers had sent him a Buckingham Palace postcard, expressing their gratitude for a 'super' time on the river. These were his letters of recommendation, his proof that he ran an honest ship. 'I get you to Aswan in five days, no problem', he told me. But as we drank tea from small shot glasses, I could sense that he was carefully sizing me up, trying to estimate the state of my finances, wondering whether I was an easy dupe or the kind of *hawagah* who works out exchange rates with a pocket calculator and argues over every misappropriated five piasters. I too was trying to get the measure of Mr Mohammed. On first inspection, he came across as what a writer of tourist brochures might call 'an archetypal Nile boatman'. His face was predictably craggy and weather-beaten, he wore a traditional *galabiya* and turban, he was the perfect holiday snapshot—a venerable man of the river. When the subject of money was broached, however, he became a no-nonsense car salesman with his eye firmly on the bottom line.

'You travel alone?', he asked me.

'That's right', I said.

'Why you no find seven-eight other tourists to travel with you? It is cheaper that way.'

'I'd rather go on my own.'

'Okay by me', he said, 'but you must pay the full price for the boat.'

'What's the price?'

'When I bring seven tourists to Aswan, I charge £30 each, including food and bedding. That's £210 for the five day trip.'

'That's a little steep for one person', I said.

'It's the price.'

'But you'll only be feeding one passenger, not seven.'

'Okay, I can give you small reduction—£190, with food and bedding.'

'Try £130', I said, knowing that I was chancing my arm.

'Impossible', he said. 'I stay in Luxor, do daytrips, I can make £130 in two-three days, no problem. I go with you to Aswan, I am away five days, then I must find new passengers to come back to Luxor. I lose valuable revenue being away so long. So I must charge you £170—final offer.'

Mr Mohammed refilled our glasses and we continued bartering. It was a ritualistic form of doing business. He had a service to sell, I was an interested buyer, and we would share refreshment together and dicker over a price until one side eventually capitulated. It was the age-old tradition of the market-place transposed on to a tourist-based economy. Though feluccas were still used as a small time commercial transport on the Nile, the boatmen of Luxor now almost entirely depended on a steady influx of foreigners to maintain their cash flow. And a tacit understanding existed between Mr Mohammed and myself as we bargained. He knew that the initial price he asked for was an inflated one. I knew that he was doing a bit of market research and seeing just how much a *hawagah* would be willing to pay at a time when tourism in Luxor was in a depressed state. He was thinking about profit margins; I was trying to calculate what his base figure would be.

It was a game that not only allowed us to test each other's resolve, but also gave us the chance to see whether we could exist in close quarters for five days. A felucca is, after all, an intimate vessel. It only stretches 15 feet in length, its bow is just long enough to house the roughly hewn wooden mast up which its triangular lateen sail is raised, and its passenger deck is simply an open-air sunken platform surrounded on three sides by raised planks that serve as benches. Altogether, the living area is a 10 foot by 5 foot space, which means that you want to be on cordial footing with your fellow travellers, as there is no escaping their presence during the entire journey. This was the main reason why I was willing to pay over-the-odds to sail alone to Aswan. It wasn't just a desire to be on the Nile only in the company of local boatmen. It was also the fear that, had I joined a 'felucca party' of fellow foreigners, I would have inevitably been drawn into the sort of group dynamic that occurs when strangers are thrown together in cramped conditions. And rather than getting caught up in the progression of the river, my instinct would have been to concentrate on the politics of transient relationships—making mental notes about personality quirks, watching factions form, hoping for the odd late-night confession about a fractured marriage, trying to detect any sexual tension in the air. Undoubtedly, it would have made for good copy (toss seven foreigners together in a small boat and you're bound to end up in a floating encounter session), but I would have ended up seeing the Nile from the same filtered perspective as passengers on a tour bus. With Mr Mohammed, however, I doubted that we would be exchanging nocturnal secrets or trespassing into each other's lives. There would be no need to make conversation, or to concern ourselves with the whims of others. I would be his sole fare and the voyage would have no supporting cast of characters. The Nile would be the one-man show.

Or, at least, that's what I thought when Mr Mohammed and I finally agreed on an all-inclusive price of £150. But when I returned to the boat after collecting my bag from the hotel, I discovered that Mr Mohammed had decided to amend the rules of the game we were playing.

'I need half the money in advance', he said.

I dug into my pocket and counted out £75 in withered bank notes. I attempted to hand the cash over but he refused it, saying 'You give me £100 now, £100 in Aswan.'

'That's fifty more than we agreed.'

'The fifty is for food', Mr Mohammed said.

'You said food was included in the price.'

'Okay, £150 for the boat, £30 for food.'

I got up and grabbed my bag.

'Sit down, sit down', Mr Mohammed said. 'Okay, we agree £150 with food.' We shook on that, but then came the sting. 'And £10 for water.'

'Wait a minute . . .'

'You want to drink Nile water?'

'Not particularly', I said, 'but you didn't mention anything about charging extra for water.'

'We agreed £150 for the boat, food, bedding. Not water. You want fresh water, it is £10.'

'Ten quid will buy a lot of water.'

'You'll need it', he said. 'We buy one case.'

'Twelve bottles for a tenner? It costs fifty piasters a bottle in the souk. What's the extra four quid for?'

'Transport.'

'That's crazy.'

'Okay', Mr Mohammed said, 'You can bring it yourself.'

'When do we leave?'

'You do not go with me. You go with my brother.'

'Your brother?'

Another elderly gentleman with a constant scowl on his face walked up the gangplank. 'This is my brother, Mr *Ahmed* Mohammed', Mr Abdul Mohammed said. 'He has a very nice boat. We go there.'

So, we disembarked, walked along the river bank and boarded Mr Ahmed Mohammed's felucca, the *Thebes*. It was a carbon copy of Mr Abdul Mohammed's felucca except, of course, that it belonged to Mr Ahmed Mohammed who scowled all the time and looked like he went through life giving everyone a bad time. Five days alone in his company struck me as a daunting proposition. And though I could have bailed out at this point, I couldn't face another round of protracted negotiations with a new boatman, so I stowed my bag under one of the benches and sat in silence with the two brothers. Two minutes passed, then five, then seven, then finally I said. 'What happens next?'

'We wait for the police', Mr Abdul Mohammed said. 'They want your passport number before we go. It is the regulations.'

'So after the police come, we leave?'

'No. After the police come, we take the form back to the police to be stamped.'

'How long will that take?'

'One-two hours.'

'And then we leave?', I said.

'No', Mr Abdul Mohammed said, 'then we go to the bazaar to get food.'

'And how long will you be in the bazaar?'

'One hour, *inshallah*. Then we go to Aswan.'

Patience—the true religion of Egypt. After ten weeks in the country, I had become used to encountering bureaucratic folly everywhere I turned, so it only made sense that the boatmen of Luxor also had to wander through their own maze of red tape before setting sail on a voyage south. With time to kill, I left my bag on the *Thebes* and headed off looking for a stand-up lunch. As I walked down the Corniche a boy of around ten began to follow me. 'Mister . . .', he shouted, but I walked on. 'Mister . . . you want a boat?' I turned around and said that I already had a boat, thanks anyway. 'Mister, I give you a good price.' I continued walking. 'Mister . . . fuck you.'

I was pleased to be leaving Luxor.

In the souk, I bought a couple of felfella sandwiches and then found a shop where a case of mineral water cost a fiver. Struggling back with it to the boat, I did a tight-rope walk up the narrow-plank and loaded it on. Mr Abdul Mohammed sat alone on the deck and when I asked him for an estimated time of departure, he said 'We wait two-three more hours. You give me half the money now.'

'But shouldn't I pay your brother, since I'll be going with him?'

'I take care of the family money', he said, and I forked over the

191

cash. Then I sat on the deck, working on my journal, sweating in the sun. Mr Ahmed Mohammed eventually came back in the company of a plain clothes policeman who inspected my passport, filled in some forms and disappeared. Meanwhile, the two brothers huddled together and talked conspiratorily.

'What's going on?', I said.

'No problems', Mr Abdul Mohammed said.

Another hour passed. Mr Ahmed Mohammed went off to the police station to collect my stamped letter of transit, and I nodded off in the sun. When I came to, I saw that another felucca had pulled up alongside the *Thebes*. It was commanded by two young men — one around eighteen, the other no more than eleven — and I quickly noticed that my bag and the case of mineral water had already been shifted over to their craft.

'You go with them to Aswan', Mr Abdul Mohammed said to me.

'Who are they?', I said.

'My brother's sons.'

'Ahmed's sons?'

'No, my other brother's sons. You get on the boat.'

I had evidently fallen into the hands of the Luxor felucca mafia, of which Mr Abdul Mohammed was the undisputed *capo*. And the Boss and his brother had obviously decided that I wasn't going to be the most profitable customer, so they had unloaded me on 'the nephews'. Their names were Adel and Tayeb. Adel was the eldest of the two, and spoke fluent English. After climbing on board his boat — the *Al Aslam* ('Islam') — he asked me to take the tiller while he and Tayeb took up oars and rowed us across the river. I immediately felt something close to horror, as I envisaged the journey turning into a floating rickshaw ride — the sahib lolling in the stern while the coolies did the slave labour.

'You're not going to have to row a great deal, are you?', I asked Adel.

'If I row to Aswan', he said, 'I die'.

'Why can't you use the sail?'

'No wind', Tayeb said, pulling on an oar. We glided across the Nile, docking on the West Bank near the launch for the cross-river ferries. Adel looked up into the sky, shook his head, and offered me a cigarette. 'We have a problem', he said. 'As my brother told you, there is no wind. And we cannot go far without wind.'

'What does that mean?', I said.

'I do not know. Maybe there is more wind later, maybe not. If it was up to me, I would tell you to go to a hotel in Luxor and we try to sail tomorrow when, *inshallah*, there is better wind. But it is not up to me because my uncle Abdul runs the business and has already taken a £25 commission for this journey.'

'He what?'

'He always takes a commission on any journey. I do not like it, but what can I do? He is the boss. So I must try to get you to Aswan in five days, but I cannot promise that we make it in that time. And because we are going *up* the river, we are travelling against the current which makes the trip more difficult. You must understand that only Allah controls the wind, and only He will decide how long it takes us to get to Aswan.'

Put your hand in the hand of the man who makes the wind blow. At the moment, he seemed thoroughly uninterested in getting us moving. Had we been travelling north—*down* the river—at least the current would have been on our side. But by embarking on an up-river journey, divine providence in the form of a constant breeze was definitely required to counteract the downstream flow. It was a no-win situation, but as Adel pointed out, it was too late to call the whole thing off. Money had exchanged hands, 'Don' Abdul Mohammed had gotten his rake off the top, and by venturing the far side of the Nile, we had already, in a sense, departed. So I decided to gamble with my timetable and told Adel that I was willing to risk the possibility of a windless voyage against the current.

That agreed, he went off to get supplies and I walked along the river bank to a small kiosk where I loaded up on cigarettes. When I came back to the *Al Aslam*, Tayeb was busy at work, swabbing down the deck with a rag drenched in Nile water. He gave me a shy smile and returned to the task at hand. Though barely into two figures birthday-wise, he deported himself with a maturity that belied his age. He wasn't simply the kid brother along for the ride; rather, he saw himself as a full member of the crew, in training for the day when he would command his own felucca. The training had obviously begun very young because when I asked him if he went to school, he said, 'No school. Must work. Family needs me.'

Adel returned several minutes later, accompanied by two new crew members—his father, Gabar, and his cousin, Mahmoud. Gabar was a patriarchical figure with a few battle scars. His left eye was missing, he had a skin disease which had turned his face into a lunar landscape, his two front teeth were made of steel, and half of the middle finger on his left hand appeared to have been misplaced. With the exception of the skin disease, all of these injuries seemed to have occured in unfortunate circumstances. But despite his shocking disfigurements, he still managed to exude a statesment-like dignity; a sense that, within the tight little community of Nile boatmen, he was an authoritative figure. Mahmoud, on the other hand, was something of an enigma. He was in his late twenties and hardly ever spoke. Taciturn and brooding, it would be a full day on the river before we heard a word out of him.

We all shook hands, the sail was raised, and Adel pushed us off, remaining on shore as we drifted away from the river bank.

'Isn't he coming with us?', I asked Tayeb, getting somewhat confused by the constant change of crew.

'He stays behind', he said. 'We go Aswan.'

That is, we should have been going to Aswan, but the lack of wind impeded our progress. We sat listless in the middle of the Nile for over ten minutes until the sail caught a meagre breeze that sent us drifting for about a half-kilometre. Having expended its energies, the breeze died and we came to a near standstill once again.

'This doesn't look too good', I said.

'We must wait until Allah gives us wind', Tayeb said. Gabar, seated on the stern, nodded in agreement. The stern was to remain his domain throughout the voyage. It was the captain's wheelhouse; a perch from which to navigate and oversee the smooth running of his craft. Mahmoud was his first mate and chief. He tended to the sail and looked after the larder and kitchen equipment which were housed in a storage space underneath the bow. Tayeb, meanwhile, was the all-purpose deck hand, and as we sat waiting for another gust of wind, he stowed my bag underneath a bench, rolled out a thin cotton mattress and covered it with a brightly coloured sheet. This was to be my living area. Just as the crew of the *Al Aslam* had their own predefined areas on the boat, so I too was being assigned my own small patch of deck space. Given the close confines of a felucca, it was necessary to divy up the available space from the outset of the journey; to establish territorial boundaries which would prevent us getting in each other's way. The *Al Aslam* may have been a one class boat, but it still had its own on-board hierarchy.

A big Nile steamer packed with holidaymakers plowed by, rocking us in its wake. It also got us moving, as a small puff of backwind sent us a further half-kilometre upstream. Then we came to a standstill. A quarter of an hour passed. Then there was another brief gust and we coasted a little further out of Luxor. It became a predictable pattern—a short glide followed by an extended period in the doldrums. The day was absurdly still and we hugged the shore, occasionally getting grounded on the river bed, forcing Mahmoud to use a long wooden pole—like that found on a punt—to push us clear.

By sunset, we had docked opposite Banana Island—a nature sanctuary on the outskirts of Luxor and now also the site of a Movenpick hotel. I consulted my map and discovered that in four hours we had travelled a mere five km. With around 200 km still left to cover, Allah's disposition towards us was definitely going to have to improve if we were to make Aswan by Saturday. Across the river, I could see the lights of the hotel and hear disco music. On board the *Al Aslam*, there was silence and darkness. Tayeb dug out an old oil lamp, but discovered that it was lacking a wick, so we sat there watching the last hues of twilight fade to black. The arrival of a full and luminous moon brought with it a nocturnal chill, so I pulled on a jumper and cloaked myself in a blanket, but still found myself shivering. Mahmoud began to prepare dinner. His cooker was a small camping stove housed inside a cut-up biscuit tin, and he quickly cobbled together a tomato and potato stew, tossing in a few handfuls of Nile water to give it body. My hunger forced me to overlook the potential health dangers of river water cuisine, and I ate with relish, pleased to learn that Mahmoud was an accomplished short-order cook.

After dinner, Tayeb washed the tin plates and cutlery in the Nile, and then changed into a heavy black *galabiya* and headscarf made out of thick blanket. Gabar and Mahmoud also clothed themselves in similar night-time vestments, giving them the look of latter-day Crusaders. I dug out my radio and was immediately popular. Gabar took charge of it and tuned into a station which was featuring the golden voice of Warda—an Algerian singer based in Cairo and perennial favourite in the Egyptian hit parade. As she pushed her vocal cords into all sorts of uncharted territories, I rolled up in a blanket and attempted to sleep. But the cold penetrated the blanket and I began to shiver. Gabar, realizing my discomfort, found a sleeping bag stowed beneath the bow and I climbed into it fully clothed. Cucooned by its warmth, I quickly passed out, waking briefly an hour later to find that the crew of the *Al Aslam* had also bunked down for the night. I looked at my watch. It was nine o'clock and the Nile was a lunar-lit sheet of glass. A fish broke this immobile surface, caught a brief glimpse of the hotel on the far side of the river, and showing excellent critical judgement, dove back to safety. I did the next best thing: I went back to sleep.

* * * * *

The sun rose at six thirty and I woke with it. Gabar was already seated in the stern, shouting orders to Mahmoud to hoist the anchor and get us cruising. Tayeb brought me a glass of tea and a plate of bread and apple jam. It was still numbingly cold, so I remained wrapped up in the sleeping bag while eating breakfast. Our lateen sail was mildly fluttering; a hint that it was going to be another slow day on the river. But sitting there, feeling rested and very much awake, the tea warming me, the sun slowly gaining altitude, I decided to temporarily abandon my time-table. As I was beginning to discover, travelling on a river in a slow-moving craft works a kind of alchemy. Cut adrift from the world of adult responsibility, out of touch with any social order beyond that of the waterway's, you drift upstream, oblivious to personal obligations or professional burdens. It's a form of mental Novocaine, anaesthetizing that storage compartment in the brain which houses all the emotional baggage you haul around with you. The lack of wind heightened this state of suspended animation, urging me to forget the life that I led beyond this river, beyond this country; to think only of the Nile.

And so, I climbed out of the sleeping bag, freshened my mouth with toothpaste and mineral water, tidied up the mattress which had become my designated bedsit, and reassumed my place on the deck. We sat dead in the water, going nowhere. A small motorized fishing boat passed us by; the fishermen dragging nets behind their craft and using a large stick to smack the surface of the water in an attempt, I presumed, to render the fish senseless. They shouted greetings of *Ael Salamae* as they left us behind; a salutation that was immediately taken up by a group of young girls who had gathered on the west bank of the river. Seizing upon me as a possible source of quick revenue, they rushed down to the shore and held up their rag dolls for sale. 'One pound, one pound', they shouted, but when they realized I wasn't a buyer, they dropped the price to fifty piasters. Across the river, the concrete-slabbed luxury hotels blanched in the sunlight.

But soon, we left these tourist enclaves behind, as a light breeze finally got us sailing. We remained close to the west bank, frequently ploughing through an aquatic field of reeds. Mahmoud negotiated our way out of this congestion through the deft application of his wooden pole and, for a kilometre, we coasted at a slugglishly steady rate. Then Gabar beached us near a small hamlet and disembarked, giving me a quick wave of farewell as he walked off into freshly ploughed countryside. Tayeb said he would rejoin us further up river tomorrow with fresh supplies. I asked Tayeb how Gabar would know where to find us in twenty-four hours time.

'He knows where we are by the wind. If good wind comes, we make Isna tomorrow. If no wind comes, he finds us before Isna.'

That seemed logical enough. Consulting my map I discovered that the town of Isna was around 45 km upriver—a formidable distance to cover in a day given the present windless conditions. A modest gale would have been most welcomed, but judging by the cloudless, porcelain blue sky, that was about as likely as a freak snowfall. We pushed off again, drifted another quarter of a kilometre, watched the slightly billowing sail turn into a flat, lifeless sheet, and then decided that emergency measures were required. Tayeb waded to the shore and, taking hold of a rope attached to the bow, he pulled us along while Mahmoud and I stood on the stern and used the increasingly handy wooden poles to propel us through another shallow patch of reeds. This bit of manual labour had the desired effect, as we soon cleared this obstacle course and were rewarded for our efforts with a zephyr that sent us tacking towards the east bank. En route, Mahmoud turned on the radio and Tayeb and he sat absorbed in one of the many soap operas that dominate the Egyptian airwaves during the daytime. I couldn't follow the story, though I gathered it was somewhat histrionic in content, as it featured a shoot-out, an actress screaming *Doktor! Doktor!*, the arrival of detectives, and a musical score that relied heavily on the use of melodramatic crescendos. After a deep-voiced announcer came on, inviting us to tune in next week for a further instalment of this ongoing saga, there was a news broadcast. The first item, naturally enough, concerned President Mubarak, and I asked Tayeb whether he looked favourably upon his president. Suddenly, Mahmoud began to speak. After nearly a day of silence, a barrage of Arabic poured out of him. It was animated and frequently hot-headed rant, the gist of which was that he was not one of Mr Mubarak's greatest fans.

'Mubarak bad, Sadat good', Tayeb said and then pointed to a small pile of foodstuffs which Mahmoud had laid out in preparation for lunch. 'You see that bread. One piaster under Sadat; three piasters under Mubarak. That tin of tomatoes. Ten piasters before, twenty-five piasters now. Mubarak, he causes this. Mubarak no good.'

Tayeb's straightforward assessment of Mubarak's economic policy was a forceful reminder that the vast uneducated majority in Egypt judged the regime in Cairo not by its foreign policies or by the rhetoric of its official media. Only one factor shaped their opinion of those who governed them: the price of food. They did not care who controlled the destiny of the country, as long as the costs of basic provisions were kept down. And when I asked Tayeb if he would welcome an Islamic fundamentalist takeover of Egypt, his answer was chillingly direct: 'If they make bread cheaper, I like them.'

Mahmoud shared his opinion. Holding aloft the tin of tomato paste, he complained bitterly again that Mubarak had almost doubled its price since coming to power. He also complained that he couldn't get the bloody tin opened with the only kitchen knife he had at his disposal, so I brought out my Swiss Army knife and showed him the can opener. This brought a momentary smile to his face, and with a nod of thanks, he settled down to prepare a lunch of aubergines and potatoes. Our political discussion had come to an end; it was back to the business of a river journey.

We drifted through a reassuringly habitable landscape— groves of palms, acres of sugar cane, unbroken fields worked by oxen. It was an extended green belt; a narrow strip of arable land hemmed in by sand and bare sullen cliffs. Along its banks, communal activities were taking place: men seeding the land, women baptizing the family laundry in Nile water. A floating hotel—the Sphinx II—plowed by with a full compliment of passengers on its sundeck. Someone pointed to the women standing thigh-deep in the river and there was a rush to the railings. Seen from the lowly perspective of the *Al Aslam*, it looked like a firing squad had assembled, as Nikons and Fujicas and Polaroids were trained on the women who ignored this attention and kept their heads bowed. The photo opportunity ended, the passengers returned to the poolside, the women continued washing their clothes.

Further on, the river divided, becoming a two-lane thorough-fare. The Sphinx II disappeared down the main drag; we opted for the secondary route and docked on the small finger of land that bisected the Nile. The sun was at optimum strength, forcing me to change into a pair of swimming trunks. Mahmoud served up lunch and Tayeb gave me the midday weather forecast: 'No wind, no go.'

Ninety minutes frittered away until a low-key breeze began to ruffle our sail and we ventured further upstream to where the river merged again into one main channel. A barge, its engines completely opened up, cruised down the middle of the river at an enviable clip. Tayeb stood on the stern and began shouting to its pilot in the hope that he might give us a tow. Mahmoud and I joined him, desperately waving and crying out for recognition, like men stranded in the bush who see a search plane overhead. But it was to no avail. The barge rolled on, ignorant of our existence. We seesawed in its wake and were about to settle down to another extended sojurn in the doldrums when, suddenly, there was a jolt. After picking myself off the deck, I saw that we had been in a head-on collision with a small dock that jutted out into the water. As collisions go, it was minor league; a bit of chipped paint work on the bow, a momentary case of the shakes for the three of us. But Mahmoud was outraged and immediately accused Tayeb of dangerous driving and taking his eyes off course and embarrassing him in front of a *hawagah*. Tayeb, who translated this exchange for me later on, countered that Mahmoud was just as much to blame, as he too had been distracted by the barge and hadn't been paying attention to the river. I decided that it was best not to referee this dispute and waited until a Mexican stand-off developed before pointing out that a modest wind was now blowing and it would be a pity not to take advantage of it. Mahmoud, still fuming, picked up a pole and disengaged us from the dock. Tayeb took up the captain's position in the stern—a point that did not go unnoticed by Mahmoud—and the *Al Aslam* continued its slow voyage south.

Three in the afternoon is the time when the sun over Egypt begins to reduce its voltage and starts a gradual slide into night. Lying on my mattress, I put my journal aside for the moment and surrendered to lethargy in the form of a nap. When I awoke, we were beached on a dirt bank next to three rusted barges. Above the bank was a small town; the town of Armant. Already, our arrival had drawn a crowd of schoolkids, who huddled around the *Al Aslam* shouting 'What's your name?' and 'Hello, hello' non-stop. They insisted that I take their photograph and several of them wanted to show me how they swam, and stripped off their school uniforms and dove into the Nile. It was the stuff of Victorian travel chronicles: the 'white explorer' rolls into a riverside settlement and the 'simple natives' become performing seals for his entertainment. But I found nothing entertaining about this display of unsynchronized swimming, and I prayed for a bit of wind to get us out of here. But even if there had been a breeze, we wouldn't have left Armant, as Tayeb said that he had family here and was planning to visit them this evening. So, we sat on the *Al Aslam* and tried to ignore the gang of adolescents who kept beseeching me for ballpoint pens, chocolate, and *baksheesh*. Eventually, a severe looking gentleman, dressed in a crisp *galabiya* and carrying a walking stick, came scurrying down the side of the river bank. At the sight of this authoritarian figure, the kids scattered, especially as he had his stick raised and seemed eager to use it. Having dispersed the mob, he approached me.

'I am policeman for Armant', he said. 'I am sorry for this.'

'Doesn't matter', I said. 'They're just schoolboys.'

'They are little bastards', he said and smiled, showing me a perfect set of steel dentures.

Sunset brought with it the moon and a night patrol of rats. Three of them appeared in shadowy silhouette on the river bank, looking formidable. As they ventured down to the water's edge—following the scent of a pot of *ful* being cooked on top of our camping stove—Mahmoud immediately pulled in the gang-plank. This was a wise move, as two more rats showed up to join the party. Tayeb reached over the side of the *Al Aslam*, picked up a convenient rock and hurled it into their midst. They got the message and took flight, only to return several minutes later while we were eating a dinner of *ful* and macaroni, washed down with tea. Their presence was not conducive to al fresco dining, and we bolted our food and washed up with extreme haste.

After tea, a little girl came down to the river bank and shouted to Tayeb.

'That's my cousin', he said to me. 'She say my wife want to see me.'

'Your wife?'

'My wife, she live in Armant. You want to meet her?'

We walked up into the darkened village. Armant appeared to be closed down for the night. It was a one-industry town, relying on a large sugar factory to keep itself financially buoyant. Tayeb's uncle, however, didn't work in the factory; he ran a small shop that dealt exclusively in Cleopatra cigarettes. We shook hands after being introduced, and he told Tayeb to bring me upstairs to the family living quarters. We entered a hallway with a mud floor. Rabbits and pigeons roamed this corridor, using it as an indoor exercise yard. A pair of chickens had berthed themselves on the stairs, forcing us to step over them as we walked up into a room that was furnished with a large double bed, a wooden bench, and a make-shift table on which sat a large television. Two boys were asleep on the concrete floor, and four girls in dressing gowns were sitting near them, wrapping sunflower seeds in cones of newspaper. The girls stood up and Tayeb pointed to one of them who looked about his age and said, 'This Safa. She my wife.'

'You're married at eleven?', I said.

'No, no', Tayeb said. 'This becomes my wife maybe ten years. It is all arranged.' He turned and said something to her, and she obediently went off. 'I tell her to get you tea.' Another of the sisters motioned for me to sit on the wooden bench and handed me a cone of sunflower seeds. 'This Wafa', Tayeb said. 'She my brother Adel's wife. They marry maybe five years.'

The felucca mafia was certainly a family affair. Life among this clan followed a strict blueprint. If you were a male, you became a boatman. You started working the river at a young age, graduating from deckhand to cook to captain of your own vessel. Before you reached puberty, your father would already have chosen a wife for you from among his many nieces. Your geographic horizons would never stretch farther than the Nile. You would never marry outside the extended family, you would never choose a profession other than that which was chosen for you. Everything was pre-ordained and uniform—like the river itself.

For the women of this tribe, the pattern of their lives was even more rigorously pre-determined. Childhood and school were simply staging posts on the road to marriage and motherhood. It was a no-option social contract which every Egyptian woman —bar the educated minority in the cities—unknowingly signed at birth. Safa would marry Tayeb. Wafa would marry Adel. They would breed and their children would repeat the process. The ancestral blueprint would be followed; the social architecture of the family would remain standardized and never be altered.

Safa returned to the room carrying a tray of tea and sweets. 'She is good wife, yes?', Tayeb asked me. I smiled. Wafa sat next to me and said she was learning English in school and asked me to write down my name in her exercise book. I obliged, and then wrote out a Dick-and-Jane style exercise for her to copy, saying it out loud as I scribbled: *'My name is Safa. My country is Egypt. My town is called Armant. I have a Mommy and Daddy and three sisters and two brothers. We live in a . . .'*

'Room', she said, cutting me off. 'We all live here. This room.'

Six kids and two parents in one room.

Wafa's mother came in, interrupting this impromptu English lesson. I guessed that she couldn't have been more than thirty, but six births had added at least a decade to her face, and she was now heavily pregnant again. Tayeb said that she ran a street stall—sunflower seeds being her principal commodity—and as she sat down to tear up more strips of newspaper and fashion them into cones, she told Safa to turn on the television.

The picture tube flickered into life and the family fell silent as this week's episode of *Falcon Crest* brought them into a world of Porsches and Rolls Royces and deeply tanned actors speaking deeply tanned dialogue. The screen cast a glow on the weakly lit room, bathing it in the synthetic colours of western affluence. Mother and her brood stared up at the screen, transfixed. They seemed lost in its garish imagery—in its version of a fantastical society totally removed from their own—and hardly noticed when I excused myself to return to the boat. I wasn't in the mood for cruel ironies that night, and watching a New World fairy tale in a room which housed a family of eight struck me as an example of cross-cultural confusion I could live without. So, I walked down to the river bank and reboarded the *Al Aslam*. Mahmoud was already asleep, wrapped up in the spare sail and blanket that served as his bedclothes. The radio was on and Om Kalsoum was bawling into the night. I undressed, slid into the sleeping bag and lay there listening to the Egyptian Edith Piaf sing of the man who jilted her, while another platoon of rats held a track meet on the river bank. I was still awake when Tayeb returned.

'Why you no like *Falcon Crest*?', he said.

* * * * *

I slept fitfully—the mosquitoes seizing upon me as likely prey and performing a marching dance on my face. Sitting up, I noticed that Tayeb and Mahmoud had protected themselves from such attacks by covering their heads with sails, so I dug out a towel and mummified myself from the neck up. Somehow, the dreaded flying squad managed to penetrate my defence system, and I stirred again at five, smoked a cigarette, and considered the nocturnal light. There was a reasonable breeze blowing, the water slapping against the sides of the felucca with metronomic regularity, and the Nile was a jet-black canvas marked by an occasional brushstroke of moonlight. Staring into that undulating void eventually had the desired effect and I surrendered to the mosquitoes and sleep.

Three hours later, I woke to discover that we had abandoned Armant and were floundering somewhere upstream. Tayeb handed me a glass of tea and repeated the previous day's weather forecast: 'No wind.' The late night promise of a gusty day had failed to materialize, making me wonder if Allah was on a daytime dosage of tranquilizers which only wore off after sunset.

'No wind today, no Isna today', Tayeb said. Indeed, after three days on the river, Isna had become our geographic Holy Grail. Had Chekhov's Three Sisters been cut adrift in a felucca, no doubt they would have started referring to that major Nile town as 'Moscow'. Like all seemingly unobtainable destinations, the mere mention of its name conjured up a certain mystique. According to my Baedeker's, Isna was nothing more than a pleasant district capital featuring a Ptolemaic temple in which 'the ram-headed local deity' was once worshipped. But sitting in a becalmed vessel, I chose to picture it as a place of bright lights and cosmopolitan buzz; an end to our static existence on a windless Nile.

But, for the moment, it remained beyond our reach. Mahmoud didn't seem to care. He had the radio tuned to a station playing a solid hour of hits by the late and much-lamented Lebanese crooner, Farid el-Atrash, and was singing along with him. If we reached Isna tomorrow, fine; if not, *maaleesh*. I envied his ambivalence to time, but doubted very much if I could exist in his world. So often in the West we fool ourselves into believing that a return to a more elemental existence is a cure-all for our overmortgaged lives. We dream of tropical atolls, backwoodsy hideaways, the Magic Mountain. We crave after the supposed *simplicity* of Mahmoud, and look upon his meanderings up and down the river with something approaching jealousy. But when we envisage ourselves living in his 'natural state', we super-impose our own social context onto his surroundings. His mud house becomes our architect-planned ethnic dwelling; his bed-roll, a futon or a stripped pine bed. We filter out all that is bleak and grubby, and imagine a state of nature that is pleasing to the eye. In short, we become tourists in his world, wanting what we assume to be his uncomplicated, free-flowing existence, but with all the creature comforts we have come to expect from living in a so-called developed nation. And as I climbed out of my sleeping bag to begin another day of idleness, I realized just how much of a causal trespasser I was among the Nile boatmen. For a few days, their domain was inviting, but I knew that I could only drift so far with them before my own sense of time finally caught up with me.

A wind finally caught up with us and Tayeb, in control of the tiller, sent us tacking across to the east bank. It was a short glide and we docked next to a water buffalo, snout high in the Nile. Tayeb, following the buffalo's example, stripped off his *galabiya* and dove into the river, encouraging me to do the same. It was tempting—especially since three days without bathing had turned me into a no-go zone—but I had read reports prior to my journey in which the Nile was described as an effluent penicillin culture and best avoided by delicate *hawagahs*. To Tayeb, the river had always been his bathtub; to me, it was a bacteriological health hazard. Once again, I was reminded of my interloper status within this community. Had I been a 'true man of the river', I would have dived in. Instead, I remained the timid, cautious and very rank foreigner.

Tayeb climbed back into the boat, slipped on his *galabiya* without drying off and then disapppeared off into the wooded river bank. When he returned ten minutes later, Gabar was with him, carrying a bag of fresh supplies. He greated me with a quick nod, took his place in the stern, and guided us back into the Nile's central channel. Another floating hotel went by, its back-wind enabling us to briefly overcome the downriver current. Mahmoud kept singing along with Farid el-Atrash, Tayeb borrowed paper from me and drew line drawings of the *Al Aslam*, Gabar fixed his gaze on an unflappably blue sky, and I tried to work on my journal. We all had our methods of killing time, of blocking out this spell in the doldrums. But I eventually found that the cooking sun drained away my will to be industrious, and

I sank gently into a stupor, focusing what little attention I had left on the passing landscape.

You have to look closely to notice the Nile's visual variations. Considered broadly, it's a scenic film loop: the same groves of palms, the same open fields, the same patches of encroaching desert. On closer inspection, however, the terrain yields up interesting subtleties. A ploughed field, promising abundant crops, lies opposite a dense wood. Look west and you're in an agrarian idyll; look east and it's the jungly, forbidden bush. At times, the river banks become the walls of a narrow, seemingly endless tunnel. But just when claustrophobia is about to set in, the walls drop away and your peripheral vision is restored to you as the landscape is dramatically enlarged. And then there are more open fields, more groves of palms, more carpets of sand, and you find yourself being as lulled by the river's repetitive imagery as by its ebb and flow. The mental Novocaine has dulled you completely. You just want to drift.

And drift we did, our progress measured in yards rather than kilometres. At one pount, we found ourselves opposite the main Luxor-Aswan road. A steady flow of traffic headed south and I momentarily thought how easy it would be to bail out at this point. I could ask Gabar to steer us across to the east bank, pay him off, walk up to that road and hitch a lift to Aswan. By nightfall, I could be standing under a shower, drinking a beer, using a proper toilet rather than the bushes, sleeping in a bed with clean, cool sheets. But looking at that serpentine channel of water which stretched out in front of us, I knew that I wanted to follow it for a few more days; to see this journey out to some sort of logical conclusion.

Mahmoud spun the dial on the radio, and Farid el-Atrash was replaced by Hank Williams. The Voice of America was broadcasting a documentary on the Grand Old Opry—the Royal Opera House of country and western music—and Mahmoud tried to hum along to 'Your Cheatin' Heart' as the *Al Aslam* staggered on to another small island of land that divided the river. Tayeb indulged in a bit of childish clowning: he stood on the bow, puffed his cheeks, and began to blow on the sail. Gabar was not amused, especially as it did no good.

Snookered by the lack of wind we ate lunch opposite an industrial plant which was dumping some foul substance into the river. It was one of the few signs of heavy industry along the Nile, and the sight of that milky brown waste cascading towards us strengthened my resolve to avoid all physical contact with the water. It also strengthened Gabar's resolve to get us a little further upstream, so he ordered the now-standard emergency procedure—Tayeb pulling us along from the shore with a rope, while Mahmoud and I did a double-act with the wooden poles. It was futile, sweaty work and though we managed to escape out of that steady flow of industrial left-overs, the *Al Aslam* soon found itself in another snag. The overhanging branches of a tree grabbed our mast in a stranglehold and threatened to carve a most unwanted airvent in our lateen sail. Mahmoud immediately went into gladiatorial battle with the tree, fighting off its limbs with his wooden pole, and once we were disengaged, Gabar decided to call it a day. The sail was pulled up, the anchor dropped, the deck tidied. Stalemate on the Nile. No natural force to propel us forward, no chance of making Isna by morning. And nothing to do but wait for the arrival of evening. I took off my wristwatch and buried it in my bag. Time had been temporarily made redundant.

When night came, Gabar pulled out the oil lamp and rigged it up with a new wick he had bought during his day off the river. I worked by its subdued flame, papering over the large gaps in my journal. Mahmoud bunked down early after serving us another dinner of fried aubergines, and I repossessed the radio long enough to catch a news report on the BBC World Service. The main story of the hour was that, in the aftermath of the Egyptair hijacking, Libya had accused the Egyptians of trying to use the incident as an excuse for declaring war on Tripoli. This seemed highly improbable, but the announcer did mention that 100,000 Egyptian troops had gathered near the Libyan border, that all roads west of Mersa Matruth had been closed to non-military personnel, and that Cairo's air defence system was on full alert. Terrific, I thought. The grand finale of my journey would be trying to fly out of a city under the threat of dive bombers. Still, I doubted very much if this current spate of tension between the two countries would amount to anything more than a mutual exercise in muscle flexing, soon to be abandoned once the repercussions of the carnage at Malta died down. And anyway, listening to this report over 700 km away from the capital gave it an air of unreality; a sense that this minor contretemps was taking place in a land far removed from this one. The Nile was insular and parochial, and therefore comforting. Gabar didn't want to hear about Libyan-Egyptian tensions, and shrugged off

Tayeb's translation of the news bulletin. What does it matter?, he appeared to be saying. It is not my world, it will never by my world, so why worry about such things? Turn off the news. Turn on Om Kalsoum.

Perhaps Gabar was right. Why sit on a darkened river and consider the volatility of two combative nations? So I surrendered the radio to him and listened while he wandered through the airwaves until Madame Kalsoum was coming through loud and clear. He sat on the stern, smiling that wistful smile of someone hearing songs from his youth. In the distance, I heard the sounds of oars breaking water, and then saw the faint outline of a small rowboat gliding towards us. Two fishermen, dressed in heavy black *galabiyas*, pulled up to our stern. They whispered greetings and then sat silently for the next twenty minutes listening to the Nightingale of the Nile. When the programme ended, they bid us a hushed farewell and slipped back into the darkness. As I turned down the oil lamp and climbed into my sleeping bag, I looked back at Gabar. He was still sitting in the stern. And he was still smiling.

* * * * *

Wind! A cold black wind on a cold black morning. It fluttered our tightly furled sail and turned the Nile into a restless sea, white-capped and choppy. The sun had yet to make an appearance, but Gabar wasn't waiting until our route ahead was clearly lit. Scrambling out of his bedclothes, he barked a series of commands, and Mahmoud and Tayeb were quickly on their feet, hoisting the anchor, hoisting the sail. And then we were off, keeling to the starboard side as we tacked to the middle of the darkened waterway.

The lateen sail grabbed the wind, sending the *Al Aslam* upriver at an accelerated clip. The opposing current was no longer an obstacle; we were overcoming it, thumbing our noses at it, taking revenge for the days in which it defeated our progress. Gabar's attention was totally focused—this was the first chance he'd had to show off his skills as a captain, and he navigated us through the swell with aplomb, flying us low over a river which had stopped being a docile child and was now throwing a full-scale temper tantrum. Tayeb looked at me and smiled. 'Good wind', he said.

The Nile opened up, transforming itself into an expressway without speed limits. We stayed in the middle lane, Gabar letting the sail out to maximize our acceleration. Isna—only twelve km in front of us—was suddenly becoming a realizable goal.

'This wind, we go Isna three hours', Tayeb said. 'This wind, Aswan in two-three days.'

For the next hour, the momentum was with us and we cut an optimistic swathe through the water, stacking up kilometres, racing against the current. But then, with the sun at full wattage, we turned a bend which brought us out of the wind pocket and into an area of maddening tranquility. Allah had applied the brakes. We were going no further. And the romance of the river had come to an end.

* * * * *

We arrived in Isna next morning; a niggardly breeze finally inching us forward after a twenty hour siesta in the doldrums. It was now Saturday; the day I had planned to be in Aswan. As Gabar docked us on a sandbank just outside of the town, I did some quick calculations. Four and a half days on the Nile had brought us 60 km upriver, and there was still 140 km left to cover. If we got lucky with the wind, we might make Aswan in thirty-six hours. If Allah remained under sedation, we wouldn't be seeing it for a week.

I looked up at the sky: solid blue without a hint of cloudy intimidation. I looked up at our sail: dormant, apathetic, down for the count. I reached into my bag and checked the date of my air ticket home: it was eight days away. And then I caught sight of the sandstone barrage that spans the Nile at Isna and quickly decided: that's the finish line for my river journey.

So I asked Gabar, through Tayeb, whether he would mind if I abandoned ship here. He shrugged his shoulders. And when I tried to apologize for my premature departure, he silenced me with one word: *maaleesh*.

Money exchanged hands, goodbyes were said, I walked the gangplank and stepped on to dry land. As quickie divorces go, it had been neat and painless. Hiking up the river bank, I reached a road and turned back to give the *Al Aslam* a final valedictory salute. But it had gone. Back down the river. Back home. Back to the world of *maaleesh*.

As I walked into Isna, a strong wind began to blow. It didn't let up for the next three days.

Chapter Seven
Sunstroke

THE NUBIAN WORE a Rolling Stones tee-shirt and concealed his eyes behind a pair of reflector sunglasses. He was the first mirror I had seen in four days and the image which appeared in his looking-glass goggles was that of a jungly *hawagah* in urgent need of an après-Nile shower and shave. I approached him at an awkward moment. He was standing on the platform of the railway station at Isna, using a toothpick to perform a bit of elementary root canal work on an inside molar. And when I asked him if he knew when the next train to Aswan was leaving, he responded by spitting a large gob of blood at my feet and said, 'The next train is all third class. Real shit train. You should take the bus.'

'How long does the bus take to reach Aswan?', I said.

Another gob of blood landed near the tips of my brogues. 'Depends', the Nubian said. 'The drivers, they are fucking crazy, so maybe you get there in two-three hours. It all depends how fucking crazy the drivers are.'

I left the Nubian to his dental work and wandered over to a small group of cafes that served as the Isna bus depot. A group of veiled women with heavy bundles had parked themselves in the middle of the road, much to the annoyance of a policeman who was trying to move them on. He barked orders at them, but they remained oblivious to his commands and didn't budge until a lorry transporting around two dozen live chickens came barrelling down this dirt-paved thoroughfare. Judging from the speed at which the lorry was travelling, the man behind the wheel had evidently been trained in the 'Move or You Die' school of driving, and the women scattered. Perhaps the Nubian was right—all drivers in Isna were 'fucking crazy'.

In the wake of the lorry came an air-conditioned tour bus with tinted windows. It idled momentarily, and taking a chance, I ran over to it and asked the Egyptian tour leader if it was heading to Aswan. The tour leader—a haggard man in his early thirties who looked as if he hadn't slept for the past week—confirmed that Aswan was its final destination, but seemed hesitant about taking me on as a piece of excess baggage.

'The tourists, they are Swiss', he said, 'They may object to somebody travelling for free.'

In an attempt to make myself seem more respectable, I told the tour leader to inform his passengers that I was a foreign correspondent urgently trying to reach Aswan to file copy. The tour leader shot me a conspiratorial smile—as if to say, 'You expect me to buy that story?'—but then turned back to his Swiss charges and pleaded my case in fluent French. He must have been a skillful advocate because when a vote was taken to see if I would be accorded a free ride, I won by a two-to-one majority.

However, there was a catch. As a freeloader, it was demanded that I be segregated from the rest of the passengers, so the tour leader told me to enter the bus by the rear door and find a place in the extreme back seat. This party of Swiss tourists had evidently spent some time in Alabama during the 1950s. But being in no position to demand equal rights, I accepted my second class status and moved to the back of the bus.

A sharp cold front of air-conditioning chilled me as I flopped into a vinyl seat and watched Isna vanish behind a swirling curtain of dust and exhaust fumes. Seen through the tinted back windscreen of the tour bus, the effect was like watching a freshly developed photograph recede into blackness. The darkroom had been flooded with light and Isna had again become a grainy negative in my mind; the stuff of memory. I regretted leaving it so quickly, remembering that on the Nile it had been the destination which I had craved. And though I could have been easily taken in by its appeal as a staging post—a place whose fly-blown cafes and shabby bus depot gave it the texture of a border town—ten weeks spent meandering through Egypt's geography had finally begun to dull my appetite for loitering. I no longer wanted to be a notebook-carrying nomad, zigzagging in and out of a landscape dense with incongruities. Now, after weeks of relying on happenstance to propel me forward, of accumulating fragmentary pieces of the complex jigsaw puzzle that is modern Egypt, I needed to run out of road; to find some sort of terminus that would force me to halt and look back over my shoulder at the territory I had covered.

I also needed to be liberated from this tour bus as quickly as possible. The coach was filled with a collection of stern-looking tax consultants and their wives from Genévè et Lausanne, all of whom seemed to have a similar taste in wind-breakers. And having talked my way onto this moveable Swiss canton, I now found myself cast in the role of the *gastarbeiter*, risking deportation if I stepped out of line. My grubby appearance probably had something to do with this. It evidently offended their national obsession with hygiene and deodorants, and I was eyed with distaste by several matronly types. I sensed that they looked upon me as a westerner who had let the side down by falling into the same unwashed state as many of the *fellahin* working the fields along our route south. Had conversation been possible, I would have happily explained to anyone interested that my seediness was due to being out of contact with running water for the past few days. But conversation was impossible; something I discovered when I tried to speak to a gentleman reloading a battery of Nikons several rows away from me.

'Savez-vous où l'autobus arrive à Aswan?', I said, trying to reactivate my schoolboy French. I received a curt *'Non'* in reply and the man turned away. So I walked to the front of the bus and asked the tour leader where the coach would be stopping in Aswan. He didn't get a chance to answer me, as he was interrupted by a woman in the front row. She pointed a menacing finger in my direction and snapped, 'Vous me bloquez la vue!'

'Comment?', I said.

'Faire un photo c'est impossible quand vous êtes là', she said, getting somewhat overheated. I looked out the window. We were travelling through an industrial desert; a landscape of power plants and small pre-fabricated factories. Unless you happened to be a photographer on assignment for *Manufacturing Today*, it was a scenic vista of little interest. But that was beside the point as far as my friend in the front seat was concerned. Rather, the subtext of her rant was utterly clear: she had paid for this journey, I hadn't, and she was damned if some scrounger was going to block her view.

'Dites-lui de s'asseoir', she barked at the tour leader. Her order needed no translation. I returned to the back of the bus and took a vow of silence for the rest of the journey.

My three hours with this congenial group was a grim insight into a package tour Egypt. As we pushed south, there were shouts from the coach party for the driver to halt any time a cluster of camels was seen in the distance. Cameras would then be pressed against the tinted window, followed by a muted volley of clicking shutters as yet another visual souvenir of the desert was imprinted on to Kodachrome. An hour out of Aswan, there was the obligatory stop at an archeological monument— the Temple of Horus in the town of Edfu. Here, more shutters whirled and clicked as the group was led on a short inspection of this old Ptolemaic ruin and were then encouraged to shop in the site's souvenir bazaar. One stallholder made a real killing when two citizens of Genévè et Lausanne transformed themselves into Francois et Marcel of Arabia. To the accompaniment of hearty communal laughter from the group (not to mention more detonating camera shutters), Francois et Marcel were kitted out in white *galabiyas* and white headscarves, and then posed for photographs with the merchant. The merchant himself eschewed 'native garb' in favour of jeans and a sweatshirt; an intriguing role reversal which turned what should have been a jokey holiday snap into a sly piece of cultural commentary. The West and Egypt had traded places for a moment, trying on each other's vestments. For the Swiss tourists, dressing up in traditional Egyptian raiments was a costume party prank; a chance to play the clown. For the merchant, however, wearing jeans and a sweatshirt was a cultural statement; an indication that, at least in matters of dress, his sensibility had come under American influence. But whereas Francois et Marcel would divest themselves of their exotic get-up as soon as they reboarded the tour bus, I doubted very much if the merchant would swap his Levis for a *galabiya*. He could wear the casual attire of the West without causing comment, while the European could only don Egypt's informal robes in the spirit of masquerade.

After this impromptu photo call, the group dutifully heeded the command of the tour leader and climbed back aboard the bus. I resumed my place in the back seat and watched Swiss democracy in action again as a vote was taken as to whether the coach should now proceed directly to Aswan or stop en route at yet another ancient left-over, the Temple at Kom Ombo (where, during the Ptolemaic era, the priests of the god Horus cornered the faith healing market). The group seemed in favour of the detour until the tour leader explained that they were behind schedule and would have to sacrifice lunch in Aswan in order to see the temple. This news brought about an immediate reversal of public opinion, especially when one particularly vociferous anti-Kom Ombo lobbyist in the group pointed out that lunch in Aswan had been included in the price of the package. This argument seemed to decide the matter: Kom Ombo's famed temple of healing lost out to chicken-and-chips by unanimous consent.

Using my copy of Baedeker's *Egypt 1929* as a makeshift pillow, I tried to nap during the final leg of the bus journey. But sleep was impossible, due to the decision of one Swiss woman to lead the assembled company in a sing-song. You have never lived, I decided, until you've travelled along the Nile banks of Upper Egypt listening to a Swiss coach party work their way through 'Frère Jacques' and 'Do the Hokey-Pokey'. It was like being in a Francophone Butlins, surrounded by a group of camp counsellors. And after sixty minutes of this choral bonhomie, the sight of Aswan's breeze-block outskirts was immensely cheering.

I had expected my return to urban life to be marked by the usual trumpet voluntary of car horns which I had come to associate with metropolitan Egypt. But Aswan on the Saturday afternoon was a model of decorum and restraint. No jellified traffic, no human swirl spilling out into the street. And as the tour bus sped along the Corniche, I found myself wondering if we had taken a wrong turn somewhere and had ended up on the Cote d'Azur. On first inspection, there was something vaguely haute Mediterranean about this riverfront city. Everything about the place said 'new money'—its yacht club strip of hotels jettying out into the Nile; its tree-lined waterfront promenade; the box-like geometry of its tourist cafe restaurants. This was, I sensed, Chemise Lacoste territory; a resort attempting to be Cannes without the high gloss. Could geography be playing games with me? After all, I had begun this journey in the company of that sad, displaced European called Alexandria. Now, however, at the end of my travels, I seemed to have stumbled upon another European; a south of France playboy displaying his *dolce vita* lifestyle for all to see. It was as if I had come full circle, leaving the ancien regime of Alexandria in search of a modern Arab state and then—after thousands of kilometers on the road—popping up again in a new-fangled version of what I had fled months earlier. Alexandria was a vision of the cosmopolitan past in Egypt. Could Aswan be a vision of what it hopes to be its cosmopolitan future?

Certainly, the Cataract Hotel appeared to be an embodiment of these two visions. It was located around a kilometer beyond Aswan's Corniche and, like a member of the ascendancy, it had sequestered itself away from the community up a long discreet avenue. At the end of this drive was a sprawling Victorian mansion in reddish brown hues; an art deco sign displaying the hotel's name above its doorway. Behind this venerable establishment, however, was a high rise block which belonged in a Romanian holiday resort on the Black Sea coast. This was the New Cataract; the hotel in which my Swiss companions would be billeted. I watched them file off the bus, stare up at this stark monolith, and then sneak envious glances at the old hotel. Their disappointment was acute. The romantic myth of colonial Egypt stood before them, but they were being denied it. Instead, they would remain impounded in the functional realities of the contemporary package tour.

The clerk behind the reception desk in the Old Cataract sized me up carefully and decided he didn't like what he saw. He stated the price of a single room in a challenging tone of voice, as if to imply that I obviously couldn't afford it. The appearance of my Visa card, however, brought about an immediate personality change, as his supercilious manner gave way to click-of-the-heels servility. Plastic money, I decided, buys you the most spurious form of respect.

The Old Cataract still retains all its delusions of Edwardian grandeur. Marble floors, intricate lattice woodwork, vaulted ceilings, and a terrace with cane tables and chairs which is worked by waiters in starched white livery. But its greatest attribute by far is the overt theatricality of its setting, as it overlooks the most grandiose stretch of the Nile imaginable. My room had a small balcony which commanded a front-row view of this scenic backdrop—an extravagant bend in the river, along which feluccas coasted by the ancient ruins of Elephantine Island; their lateen sails catching the full midday burn of the sun. Had I been searching for the archetypal image of 'timeless Egypt', this vista would have won hands down. For here was the myth of the country in all its picture postcard perfection; the eternal tableau of light and water and ancient spectacle. And, for a moment, this vision of the fabled past blotted out any hints of Egypt's present-day realities. That is, until somebody reclining by the hotel's pool switched on a ghetto blaster and the sound of ABBA singing 'Money, Money, Money' became a late twentieth century clarion call, wafting out over the Nile.

* * * * *

Later that day—after standing under a shower for the better part of an hour and fleecing my face of five days worth of beard—I left the hotel and set off on a little inspection tour of Aswan. As I strolled along the Corniche—passing a tourist restaurant whose menu advertised such delicacies as 'Toasted Meats', 'Softwater', and 'A Piece of Sweat'—I remembered an Egyptian friend telling me that what he liked most about Aswan was its tidiness. 'It is very clean', he said, summing up an opinion frequently voiced throughout the country. In a nation whose civic temperament veered towards the haphazard and the slovenly, Aswan was always held up as the one Egyptian city which could easily win the Good Housekeeping Seal of Approval. It was easy to see why. Like Luxor, it had a tourist-based economy, but with little in the way of big league Pharaonic memorabilia on show, it had to rely on its riverfront appeal to pull in the crowds. 'On account of its charming situation and its equable and dry climate', wrote Karl Baedeker in his guidebook, 'Aswan is in great favour as a health resort.' And indeed, had you come to the city during that era, you would have found yourself in a pleasant back-water, in which the Cataract was the main watering hole in town. On the other hand, had you been hanging around Aswan during the years 1567 to 1320 BC, you would have found yourself in a boom town which lay on the northern border of Nubia. At the time, Nubia ('Gold' in the ancient Egyptian lexicon) was the commodities market of the Pharaonic world, rich in precious metals, ivory, wood and incense, as well as being the principal recruiting ground for slaves. And as Aswan was the major clearing house through which all this booty passed into Egypt, it enjoyed an extended period of economic upswing, during which it was considered one of the premier cities of the Egyptian empire. But when the empire came asunder after 1100 BC and Nubia regained its independence from Egypt, Aswan's fortunes went into a tailspin. And though this ancient trade centre—the Pharaoh's version of Hong Kong—regained some of its pre-eminence during the Middle Ages when the forces of the Caliph Omar took control of the country, it was the dream of harnessing the power of the Nile that eventually led to the development of Aswan as a major urban centre.

The Nile has always been a temperamental waterway, and one upon which the entire survival of the country has depended. In fact, in the ancient Egyptian calendar the autumn was known as 'Inundation', for this was the season when the annual flooding of the river took place. And being a desert nation, the level at which the floodwaters rose was a matter of great national concern. Which is why the Ram God Khan was one of the most hallowed and dreaded of all ancient deities, because he was the gent who decided whether the flood was going to be of the high or low variety. If it was a high flood, this meant good times ahead, as the waters (which first rose in Upper Egypt and then migrated to the north of the country) provided the necessary irrigation to produce a bountiful harvest. If, however, the floodwaters were low, the ancient Egyptians had a 'Brother, Can You Spare A Dime?' situation on their hands; a period of famine and general economic bad news.

Of course, while doing their best to keep the Ram God Khan happy, the engineers of the era were also working out ways of controlling the floods by means other than the chancy and gruesome business of offering up ritualistic sacrifices. A system of water gauges, known as Nilometers, were installed in Upper Egypt to determine exactly when the waters would rise and how high the flood would be, thus giving the agrarian community advance warning of whether to expect a waterlogged or parched year. Later on, around 600 BC, the occasional canal made its appearance on the landscape, and though further advances in irrigation techniques continued through the ensuing two and a half millenia, the fact remained that the agricultural prosperity of Egypt was still reliant upon an annual high flood. And the Ram God Khan had a reputation for not always delivering the goods.

A dam was the only logical way to guarantee that the country was irrigated on a regular and chance-free basis, as well as to ensure that there would be a constant water-supply even during periods when the level of the Nile was feeble. And in 1902, the British opened the first Aswan Dam at a sight just below the ancient island of Philae. Though it was quite a tourist attraction at the time, being one of the grandest engineering feats on the planet, and though it did significantly increase the amount of arable land in Egypt, it required frequent modifications and had to be heightened on two occasions during its first thirty years of operation. More importantly, the first Aswan Dam did not totally control the Nile's schizophrenic personality, with the result that the country continued to watch the annual floodwaters rise with the trepidation of a gambler in desperate need of a winner.

It was Nasser who decided to find a permanent solution to this headache. Shortly after taking power, he commissioned a team of German engineers to draw up plans for a new dam to be located 7 km upriver from the original barrage. But this was not simply going to be an updated version of the 1902 structure. Rather, this was going to be a High Dam of spectacular proportions. A dam that would generate phenomenal amounts of hydro-electricity. A dam that would end the nation's dependence on high flood-waters. A dam that would bring immense prosperity to Egypt, as it would make even vaster tracts of land arable. In short, a dam that would transcend mere technological achievement and enter the realm of contemporary metaphor, informing the world that Egypt had arrived as a modern state.

Like the Pharaohs before him, Nasser thought big. Unlike the Pharaohs, however, Nasser didn't have the necessary cash to underwrite such a monumental construction project. Outside finance for the High Dam would therefore have to be found, and thus began a search for financial backers; a search which ultimately ended up sparking off a major international crisis. The Americans were approached first and, in December 1955, agreed to put up a no-strings loan of $56 million. Shortly thereafter, the British rowed in with an additional $14 million, and then the World Bank followed suit in January 1956, signing a tentative agreement with the Egyptian government to provide a $200 million load towards the project. Then the diplomatic gamesmanship began. Nasser objected to the World Bank's demand that, in exchange for fronting the Egyptians a hefty chunk of change, they would be allowed to oversee the country's balance sheets. The World Bank, for its part, would not budge on this pre-requisite for the loan, and negotiations between the two parties began to break down. Meanwhile, London and Washington began to express distrust of Nasser. When General Glubb—the commander of the Arab Legion in Jordan—was sacked, the British smelled Egyptian collusion in the affair, while the Americans took umbrage at Nasser's flirtations with the Soviet Union and his decision to establish diplomatic relations with the People's Republic of China. The upshot of all these misgivings was the abrupt announcement by the Americans in July 1956 that they were rescinding their loan offer. The domino effect came into play, as the British pulled out of the deal twenty-four hours later, followed quickly by a World Bank statement declaring that they too were abandoning the High Dam project.

Nasser didn't take long to react to this joint Anglo-American exercise in belittlement, and his retaliatory action was something of an international *coup de theatre*. On July 26th, the Egyptian president proclaimed that the Suez Canal had been nationalized. And by October of that year, Egypt was at war against the combined forces of Britain, France and Israel.

The Suez War was one of those curious confrontations where the winner claimed victory without having achieved success on the battlefield. Militarily, Egypt didn't have a chance against three such formidable opponents, and if it hadn't been for the pressure brought to bear on the tripartite forces by the super-powers and the United Nations, Nasser most certainly would have gone down to defeat. As it turned out, he came out of the conflict as the undisputed champion of the Arab world, and turned to the Soviets for economic aid. And though relations between Moscow and Cairo were often fraught—especially as Nasser, the head of a Muslim state, refused to toe the godless Marxist-Leninist line—the Soviets nonetheless finally provided the bankroll required to build his great technological dream. But perhaps one of the supreme ironies of contemporary Egyptian history is that Nasser didn't live to attend the High Dam's official opening. For he succumbed to a heart attack only three months before the new barrage—on which he had staked so much of his country's reputation—finally became operational in January 1971.

However, as I made my way down Aswan's Corniche, it struck me that Nasser's premature death wasn't the only irony to be found in the history of the High Dam. After all, the construction of the dam had transformed Aswan, turning a small waterside town into a burgeoning metropolis. Yet while the dam itself was, at one time, a symbol of the West's rejection of Nasser, the modern city which had developed 12 km downriver of this contemporary monument had become yet another testament to Sadat's *rapprochement* with the free-market economies of Europe and America. As in Luxor, there was the usual strip of five-star hotels lining the Nile, but Aswan had gone one step further than its sister city to the north and—with the exception of the Old Cataract—had obliterated any hint of the past. Crossing the main thoroughfare, I cut up a side street and found myself in the city's souk: a concrete arcade of shops. The gaudy vigour of Egyptian market life had no place in Aswan, for here the mercantilism was antiseptic and severe. Even the shopkeepers and touts who lined this geometric arrangement of backstreets seemed to reflect the cooly subdued milieu of this streamlined bazaar. Whereas in Luxor, hucksters indulged in fast-talking operatics when confronting a *hawagah* who had ventured into the souk, Aswan's merchants adopted a tone of exaggerated *politesse*. Their sales pitch was one of old world courtliness—a slight bow, a whispered 'Please you will see my shop', and a demure smile when you declined the offer. Luxor may have been the manic American out to make a quick buck, but Aswan was definitely the discreet Swiss banker.

And yet, for all its low-key urbanity, it was difficult to warm to this hard angular cityscape. I spent several hours wandering its thoroughfares and eventually found the repetitive imagery of its buff-coloured buildings stultifying. But it was precisely this sterility which found favour among so many Egyptians. To them, Aswan was their urban showpiece—the proof that they too could create clinical cosmopolitanism on the Nile.

However, once you peered behind this reinforced concrete veneer, all the other less worldly aspects of contemporary Egypt became apparent. In the train station, where I stopped to book a ticket for the overnight sleeper to Cairo in two days' time, the forecourt was being used as a makeshift dormitory by the homeless. Back alleyways yielded up predictable scenes of marginal living in the most basic of dwellings, and just opposite the Corniche's strip of riverfront hotels, men sat in cafes, spinning out the day with endless games of *towla* (backgammon). I stopped at one of these establishments—the Continental Cafe—and soon found myself ensconced in a marathon *towla* session with a Nubian gentleman in his sixties. He was evidently a habitué of the Continental, and something of a shark when it came to *towla*. Like a clever pool hustler, this gent hung around the café looking for easy dupes like me to sucker into a few games of high-speed backgammon. Money wasn't his object, though. Rather, as long as I was willing to supply him with non-stop glasses of tea, he was content to play with such a rank amateur. And as we whittled away the hours huddled over the board and the dice, I began to learn a thing or two about the finer points of *towla*. To win at the game you mustn't try to impress your opponent with displays of bravado. Instead, you must realize that during the course of play you will often find yourself trapped in a corner from which there is no apparent escape. Given time, however, you will eventually find a way out of this cul-de-sac and back into the contest. It is, in short, a game that not only tests your abilities as a tactician, but also your stamina and patience. Aggressive playing will not decide the game in your favour. Adopting an attitude of *maaleesh*, on the other hand, might just give you the competitive edge. And for this reason, *towla* is the one board game that best reflects the Egyptian state-of-mind today. For though the country currently finds itself cornered—snookered by its economic woes and its status as a dependent nation—it still shrugs its shoulders in the face of its monumental obstacles and says *maaleesh*, in the belief that, somehow, everything will work out in the end. And if it doesn't, it will throw the dice again and hope that, this time, luck is in its favour.

After losing ten straight games of *towla*, I settled the tea bill and walked back along the Corniche, admiring the soft-focus silhouette of Aswan by dusk. The half-light tempered the town's graph-paper crispness, giving it a sort of 'Nubia by Sunset' holiday brochure aura. And when I reached the Old Cataract, I loitered momentarily on the terrace to watch as the cinemascope sweep of the Nile faded to black. Drunk on such over-the-top visual romanticism, I staggered into the hotel's nightclub and discovered that the floorshow was in progress. It was a pot-pourri of 'indiginous culture' built around a 'Salute to Nubia' theme, and featured a display of native drumming, a display of native war dances, and a selection of native hits crooned by a dude with thinning hair, a pencil-thin moustache and a shiny double-breasted suit. He looked like he had just graduated from morticians' school and sang in an extended monotone. The audience for this divertissement was a party of Swedish tourists and a table of glassy-eyed Japanese businessmen. I watched as the native dancers—their faces streaked with the Nubian equivalent of warpaint—did a choreographed number with spears and shields. I watched as the native dancers led a conga-line of Swedes and Japanese around the nightclub. I watched as the crooner worked his way through an interminable medley of Nubian favourites. I watched as a member of the Japanese party passed out and ended up using a plate of half-eaten chips as a pillow. And taking a cue from him, I left the nightclub, returned to my room and collapsed into the first proper bed I had seen in days.

* * * * *

It was Mark who told me the story of Kamil and the French woman.

Mark was an American tour guide based in Luxor. We met over coffee and a few games of *towla* at the Continental Cafe. He was a lanky ex-lumberjack in his thirties who, three years earlier, had given up his job working for a paper company in the forest of northern Maine and had been watching his passport fill up with foreign visas ever since. By his own definition he was something of an itinerant; a guy who lived out of a duffle bag and dropped into a country long enough to earn enough cash to move on. 'I'm a professional odd-jobber by trade', he said, and reeled off his curriculum vitae: tending bar in a beach resort in Costa Rica; part-time fisherman in Belize; English teacher in Tangier and Malaga; night watchman in London. 'I kind of like to move around', Mark said. He also explained that while working illeg-ally in London ('I only had a six month tourist visa and I kept expecting British immigration to nail my ass'), he met a fellow American who ran a travel agency which specialized in Adven-ture Holidays. And the gent was looking for a native English speaker to bring groups of adventure-minded tourists up and down the Nile. And Mark—who was tired of doing the midnight-to-dawn security guard shift in an office block in Vauxhall—convinced his compatriot that he was the man for the job. 'So the guy decided to give me a shot', Mark said, 'and sent me down to Luxor a year ago to find a felucca man who was willing to work exclusively for us. And that's how I met Kamil.'

Kamil was a thirty-year-old boatman from the West Bank of Thebes who had just taken charge of his family's felucca. And Mark said that he was utterly delighted by the exclusive deal that the London travel agency offered him, especially as it meant that he had an assured income during the height of a depressed tourist season. More importantly, the constant work enabled Kamil to flee Luxor on a regular basis. And Kamil wanted to be away from home as much as possible because (as he confided to Mark) his domestic situation was a disaster.

It seems that Kamil had been married for four years to a second cousin who was ten years his junior. It had been an arranged marriage and they'd wed when his wife was only sixteen. When she was seventeen, a local doctor diagnosed her as being sterile; a diagnosis which immediately sent her into a deep depression because—according to the strict social blueprint of the felucca mafia—a married woman's primary role is to have children. And therefore, a barren woman is one whose purpose in life has been taken away from her. Unable to cope with her grief—with what she saw to be the collapse of her world—Kamil's wife became so withdrawn that she refused to sleep with him anymore. At first, Kamil believed that this was simply a phase she was going through; that time would eventually bring about the destruction of the *cordon sanitaire* she had erected in their bed. But rather than ending her depression, time only seemed to deepen it, and the *cordon sanitaire* remained in place. Three years after the discovery that she was infertile, Kamil's wife still remained an advocate of chastity within marriage, with the result that Kamil used the river more and more as an escape hatch; a way of temporarily absconding from a marriage that sounded very much like Strindberg-on-the-Nile.

And while ferrying Mark's 'Egyptian Explorers' between Luxor and Aswan, Kamil made a discovery: he loved being in the company of *hawagahs*. They introduced him to a social order that was previously alien to him—a place where marriages weren't arranged and where your family did not automatically choose your calling in life. They came from lands which he considered exotic: Britain, France, America. They were well-travelled and bragged amongst themselves about the number of countries they had visited. They talked about their houses or apartments and how they were hoping to buy bigger houses or apartments. They came equipped with flashy accessories: Japanese cameras, Swiss watches, 'personal stereos'. And—most surprising of all—they didn't adhere to traditional sexual roles. Many of the women on the felucca tours were single. They were free to travel alone. They told Kamil that they lived away from their families and were more concerned with their careers than with getting married and having children. And even if they did eventually decide to marry, this didn't automatically mean that they would give up their jobs and become obedient wives.

Of course, it wasn't as if this was Kamil's first encounter with the apparent affluence and liberal mores of the West. After all, the shops in Luxor were filled with booty from Europe and Japan. The television brought images of technicolour lifestyles in America. And growing up in a felucca family meant that, from an early age, he had come into contact with tourists and could even speak a passable English. But, perhaps, it was his doomed marriage that gradually forced Kamil into comparing his own lot with those of the *hawagahs* on his boat. Whereas before (as he told Mark) he did not question the fact that he would spend his life on the West Bank of Thebes, now he saw that his was a tightly constrained existence. All that he had accepted in the past—his arranged marriage, his work as a boatman, the two-roomed dwelling that he would live in until he died—now seemed like a prison in which he was condemned to remain forever. He had none of the apparent freedoms enjoyed by his western clientele. He possessed none of their luxuries. And he realized that, as long as he remained in Luxor, he never would. But how could he—a felucca man who could barely read or write—ever find a way out of his circumstances?

Dominique was his one great hope. She was a Parisian in her late thirties; an art teacher in a lycee who came to Egypt in early September to float up the Nile on one of Mark's escorted felucca holidays. 'A true arty-farty type', was how Mark described her. 'Totally flakey and not exactly playing with a full deck. And really into the whole idea of "experiencing" Egypt. She kept going on about how she wanted a real native insight into the country; how she wanted to "touch the Egyptian soul" and all that kind of crap. And I think that's why she decided to have a little number with Kamil—because that was her way of going ethnic for a week.'

Within a day of setting sail from Luxor on Kamil's felucca, it became obvious to Mark and the five other adventurous tourists on the expedition that Dominique had designs on their captain. Ignoring the others, she made the stern her domain and set about chatting up Kamil. This proved to be a difficult task, as English was the only common language that the pair had between them and neither of them spoke it with anything approaching fluency. Still, language didn't really matter in this instance for, by nightfall, Dominique had made her intentions very clear. As the rest of the passengers bunked down in sleeping bags on the deck of the felucca, Dominique picked up a mattress and a blanket and led Kamil into the woods beyond where they were docked. They were next seen again at daybreak, and as they reboarded the boat Dominique gave her fellow passengers a look of triumphant scorn. Mark said, 'It was as if she was telling us, "I don't give a shit about what you think I'm doing. Just don't interfere".' Kamil, for his part, avoided looking at anyone and, climbing back into the stern, set sail again up the Nile.

For the next four days, the felucca became a divided community, with Mark and the five tourists keeping to themselves on the main deck, while Dominique and Kamil turned the stern into a makeshift *niche d'amour*. And except for meal-times—when Kamil would become the chef—the two groups tactfully avoided each other, especially since Kamil and Dominique didn't seem to mind indulging in public displays of affection.

'I couldn't get over it', Mark said. 'I mean, here was Kamil—who I always thought of as a shy kind of a guy—acting like he was a high school kid who'd just learned how to neck. The two of them couldn't keep their hands off each other, which sort of got embarrassing for the rest of us, to the point where we were all relieved when they disappeared into the woods at night. Not that I begrudged the guy a good time, especially since I knew all about that iceberg of a wife he had back in Luxor. It's just that I kept thinking: she's treating all this as some sort of a weird holiday romance and he's not. I mean, for her, screwing an illiterate boatman—a guy with five steel teeth, for Christ's sake—was probably the best souvenir she could have had of Egypt. A real great story to tell all her pals back on the Rive Gauche. But I knew that Kamil was in this for keeps. You should've seen the way he looked at her. I've never seen somebody so smitten. But could you blame him? I mean, a woman coming on to you like a ten ton truck isn't exactly the sort of thing that's in a felucca man's realm of experience. So naturally the poor bastard thought, "This is it. This is the real thing." And Dominique was so carried away by the whole idea of having a 'romance on the Nile' that I don't think she realized the damage she was doing. When we finally got to Aswan and she had to head back home, she should have told Kamil that the party was over. But instead, there was this big teary-eyed scene at the railroad station before she got on the train for Cairo. And you should've heard what she told him: "I love you . . . I can't stand the thought of leaving you . . . we must find a way of being together." And Kamil believed every word of it.'

Not only did Kamil believe Dominique's declaration of love; he was also convinced that it was only a matter of time before she gave him the word to join her in Paris. And so, while pining for her in the weeks that followed her departure from Egypt, he remained optimistic that he would soon be leaving the West Bank of Thebes for good and beginning a new life in France.

It took almost three weeks for the letter to arrive from Paris; an agonizing wait during which Kamil became obsessed with the daily comings-and-goings of his local postman. Worst yet, when he finally did receive Dominique's communique, Mark was away in Cairo for several days. And being unable to read (and also refusing to trust anyone he knew who could read with his secret), he spent an anguished seventy-two hours awaiting a translation of all those indecipherable words which criss-crossed the two pages of her letter.

Kamil was at the railway station in Luxor when Mark arrived on the overnight train from Cairo, and immediately dragged his American friend off to a cafe. 'You should have seen the state of that letter when he handed it over to me', Mark said. 'It looked like he'd been clutching it for three straight days and hadn't let go of it once. And when I started reading it, I felt like getting back on the train to Cairo because I didn't want to have to break the news to him.'

The letter—written in careful English—went like this:

> *My darling:*
> It was all a wonderful dream. I will never forget you, my 'homme du Nil'; my Egyptian 'amoureux'. The days and nights that we had together will stay with me forever, and you will always hold a special place in my heart. But you must realize, my darling, that it could never work between us; that try as we might, our worlds are so different that we could never build a life together. And I could never think of you being any-where but on that beautiful river. How could I take you away from such beauty? It would be wrong of me to make such a demand. And so, I must be brave and say goodbye to you, though I cry as I write this . . .

As kiss-off letters go, it was heavy on the slush. And though Mark tried his best to gently explain to Kamil that he was being given the push, the boatman refused to believe him. Instead, like a barrister desperately searching for evidence in a case already lost, he focused in on certain key phrases—*You will always hold a special place in my heart . . . I cry as I write this*—citing them as proof that she still loved him. Rejected lovers often play this torturous game. They refuse to accept the obvious and instead ransack their dismissal notice for some small hint that they are still wanted. Kamil too succumbed to this form of self-delusion. The more times he had Mark re-read Dominique's letter to him, the more he became convinced that she *did* want him to join her in Paris, but was simply afraid that he couldn't bear to leave his 'beautiful river.'

'The guy simply wouldn't listen to reason', Mark said. 'And it kind of put me in an impossible situation because I realized that if I came right out and said, "Look, she's politely telling you to fuck off", it still wouldn't have gotten through to him. As far as he was concerned, she was his one and only chance to make a new life for himself, so naturally he couldn't accept the fact that she was slamming the door on his dream. He had to keep on hoping that there was going to be a happy ending to this fantasy of his because that's all he had to hold on to. And therefore, when he asked me to be his scribe—to write Dominique a letter on his behalf—I couldn't refuse him. Even though I knew it would do no good.'

The letter which Mark ghosted on Kamil's behalf was a marriage proposal and a plea. 'He told me to tell Dominique', Mark said, 'that he wanted her as his wife and would do anything to be with her. "I'll leave my family", he said. "I'll leave my country. I'll learn French. I'll find work in Paris. I'll do whatever you ask. Just please, *please* say that you want me to join you".'

But Dominique never said anything, for she chose not to reply to Kamil's letter. Nor did she choose to reply to the second letter which he had his scribe write—a letter in which he begged her for some reaction to his marriage proposal. Months went by, but Kamil refused to give up hope. 'Tomorrow I will hear from her', he kept telling Mark. For his part, Mark began to notice that a pair of dark crescent moons had found a permanent home beneath Kamil's eyes, and that he was becoming sullen and uncommunicative when dealing with the tourists he still ferried up and down the river. 'It got to the point where I started getting complaints from some of the passengers on our expeditions',

Mark said. 'They'd take me aside and say, "Why won't he talk to us? Why does he look at us with such hatred?" I finally had to tell Kamil that his attitude wasn't particularly good for business, and that he should forget about Dominique because it was obvious she was never going to write to him again. And that's when Kamil handed in his notice and said that he didn't want to work for us any more.'

'I tried my best to talk him out of quitting—especially since I felt kind of terrible about what had happened to him—but he wouldn't change his mind. That was six weeks ago and I haven't seen him since, though one of the local boatmen I know said that Kamil was picking up some work here and there, but was turning down any jobs involving tourists. In fact, he told this guy that he would never let a *hawagah* on his boat again.'

How you gonna keep 'em down on the farm after they've seen Paree? Was that the moral of this story? But Kamil never got to see Paree. Rather, he had only glimpsed the idea of Paree through Dominique. And she, in turn, had only glimpsed the idea of Egypt through him. They had both been seduced by each other's veneers; by the allure of the alien. And yet, while Dominique's world had remained intact after this *amour sur le Nil*, Kamil's had come apart. Had Dominique assumed the role of the colonialist— imposing herself on a native culture, reaping what she could from it, and then writing it off after it had served it purpose? And had Kamil been cast in the role of 'the exploited peasant'—the simple *fellah* who had been taken in by the tantalizing eau de toilette of the West, only to be then put in his place when he wanted to wear it himself? Or had they simply succumbed to an ailment common to all hot spots? An ailment called sunstroke.

Sunstroke. How is it caused? By an excessive encounter with the heat of the sun. What are its physical manifestations? Light-headedness, bewilderment, a blurring of vision, followed by acute prostration and collapse. When you're sunstruck, you act foolishly. Having exposed yourself willingly to a climate that is foreign to your temperament, you're overwhelmed by it and pay the price. And when you eventually recover from your indulgence, you vow never to expose yourself to such an alien climate again.

Kamil had made that vow. And judging by her silence in the face of his marriage proposal, so had Dominique. They had both given in to the spirit of sunstroke, and out of their temporary bedazzlement had come misunderstanding, embitterment, distrust. It was, in a way, an inevitable outcome because sunstroke deadens your critical judgement. While under its dangerous spell you see only what you want to see and ignore all the warning signs of impending infirmity. If you're strong—if you have the resources to fall back on—the sickness is only temporary. But if you possess a weaker disposition, its effects are more long-term.

When Sadat ended Egypt's client relationship with the Soviet Union and moved into the American camp, he too was afflicted with sunstroke. Smitten with all things western—his suits were Saville Row, his pipe tobacco Dunhill, he bragged about the number of American movies he had watched, and he even had Frank Sinatra sing in front of the Sphinx—his Open Door policy was similar to Kamil's brief affair with Dominique; a deluded romance, based on the notion of breaking away from your own identity by falling in love with the possibilities of another culture. And, for a while, the romance worked—especially if you happened to be a member of the mercantile classes who made a killing during the first heady years of *infitah*. The Americans themselves were also sunstruck with Sadat during this period. After the Camp David treaty, they put him on the covers of *Time* and *Newsweek*. Henry Kissinger proclaimed him to be 'the greatest statesman since Bismark.' He was the man of peace. The Nobel Prize laureate. The hero.

Such intoxicating times! Such blind infatuation! No wonder Sadat eventually paid for this *amour fou* with his life. All the predictable side effects of sunstroke had shrouded his vision, to the point where he could no longer see the jeopardy in which he had placed himself and his country. He was like a divorcé who had remarried a wealthy woman, and then began to dispense some of her largesse to his favourite sons, while ignoring the rest of his brood. And eventually, some of his children began to object to their stepmother's values, believing that they were destroying the traditional bonds of the family. So they offered their father a choice—her or us. But, by this point, Daddy was so besotted with—and economically dependent upon—his wealthy patroness that he refused to give her up. And his decision so infuriated the most conservative of his sons that they saw no alternative but to destroy him.

Sunstroke: exposing yourself to an alien climate can be dangerous to your health. And weren't the threats that Egypt now faced—the rising tide of Islamic fundamentalism, the forebidding spectre of economic collapse—all symptoms of this ailment?

In fact, wasn't the entire history of the country since the 1952 revolution one long chronicle of sunstroke? A local businessman I met on one of my last days in Aswan summed it up very neatly. As we shared a pot of tea on the terrace of the Hotel Cataract, he pointed to that absurdly mythic bend in the river and said:

'I see a future for my country, but only if we begin to change so many attitudes. I look at those men who sit in cafes ten-twelve hours a day. They drink the tea, they smoke the hookah, they play *towla*, and they have no ambition beyond this. But this is a great problem in Egypt. Nasser guaranteed everybody a job— like a father to his children. It is this paternalism in Egypt that causes so many problems. A father, he will look after his children until he dies. He will raise them, feed them, choose their work for them, choose the person they will marry. In the West, the children leave home at a certain age. But in Egypt, the children remain children for many years.

'And why do they remain children? Because our country has never found its own way. We have been pushed this way and that way. We have tried socialism under Nasser, capitalism under Sadat. But we have never decided which way is right for Egypt. We have always let others show us their way, but we have never allowed ourselves to stand alone.'

Standing alone. Finding its own way. Ending its dependency on others. Could Egypt achieve such an independent status? Or would it always remain the child in need of fostering? Certainly, the realities of geo-politics—and of Egypt's position as a so-called developing nation—had meant that over the past three decades it had been involved in separate holiday romances with the world's two great powers. Each of them had courted Egypt because of her strategic importance and her leadership role in the Arab world. And Egypt, in turn, had readily accepted their favours out of the belief that their largesse would enable the country to remake itself anew. Like Kamil and Dominique, the superpowers and Egypt fell in love with what they could get out of each other. But Egypt—the weaker party in both relationships —inevitably came down with the more long-term dose of sunstroke. Adopting a variation on the Soviet model, it had created a mammoth state bureaucracy and system of subsidies which had impeded all economic development. Adopting a variation on the American model, it had created a consumerist culture which had not only accentuated the gaps between rich and poor, but had also led to the resurgence of militant Muslim groups opposed to the imposition of heretical foreign mores. And the end result of each of these infatuations was a future charged with uncertainty. Indeed, the patient's prognosis was a troubling one, for the after-effects of Egypt's sunstroke had left the nation severely debilitated and struggling to redefine its identity.

And meanwhile, somewhere on the Nile between Luxor and Aswan, Kamil was also struggling to redefine his identify by rejecting all things foreign. Like his country, his illusions had been smashed, and he too was starting to understand the importance of standing alone.

* * * * *

On my last morning in Aswan, I hired a taxi to take me to the High Dam. The driver was a fast-talking operator named Sallah who spoke with the rapidity of an auctioneer trying to make a quick sale. Only in Sallah's case, what he was trying to sell me was a guided tour of every monument that lay between the Cataract Hotel and Lake Nasser.

'You want to see tomb of Aga Khan?', he said.

'Just the Dam', I said.

'No want to see Philae Temple?'

'Just the Dam, please.'

'I show you monastery of St. Simeon . . .'

'No thanks.'

'You no want to see monastery, no want to see Philae Temple. What you want to see?'

'Just the Dam.'

'But you miss all monuments. All tourists want monuments.'

'I'm not one of them.'

'You very strange tourist.'

I couldn't argue that point, but still had to spend several more minutes convincing Sallah that I wasn't really interested in taking in any of Aswan's archeological curiosities. And when I told him that I hadn't visited a single temple, pyramid or ancient excavation during the past two-and-a-half months he looked at me dubiously and said, 'What you been doing all that time in Egypt?'

'Just looking around', I said.

'You very strange tourist.'

We set off in his Skoda and soon found ourselves traversing a desert landscape dotted with telephone and electrical poles. After a few kilometres we reached the Old High Dam which now looked like an oversized example of Edwardian bric-a-brac. Below this, the Nile had petered out into a mere stream, curving around a twisted series of rocks in a shallow basin.

'It goes to Cairo', Sallah said, pointing to the river. Then again, with Sallah, everything went somewhere as 'It goes to . . .' was the verbal form he used to explain the geography south of Aswan. After leaving the Dam and heading further into parched open country, we passed a cluster of ugly concrete structures about a mile off the road.

'What are those buildings?', I said.

'It goes to university for Aswan', he said.

'And is the airport nearby?'

'It goes five kilometres from here.'

A little further on, we came to a set of gates, announcing our arrival at the Aswan High Dam. After paying a small entrance fee, Sallah parked the Skoda in front of a rather totalitarian monument consisting of five towering white concrete pillars crowned by a white concrete circle. A reflecting pool of water surrounded the structure, emphasizing its overblown self-importance. Sallah cocked a finger in its direction and said, 'It goes to Lotus Flower Monument.'

In ancient Egypt, the lotus flower was a beloved species of flora, and one which inspired Pharaonic architects to design a popular decorative pillar known as the Lotus Column. But as I approached this recent attempt at Pharaonic giganticism, it wasn't the marble floor emblazoned with the lotus flower that first caught my eye. Rather, it was a huge slab positioned between two of the columns, on which had been carved a Koranic inscription flanked by the seals of Egypt and the USSR. A highly realistic bas-relief of Sadat had been sculpted next to a more mythic fresco of Nasser, leading me to suspect that Sadat's face had been a last minute appendage to the monument, executed with great haste in the wake of Nasser's death. And though the Koranic symbols for water, agriculture, knowledge, and the sun adorned the other columns, it was those two chiselled faces that dominated the monument. A monument in praise of kingship. A monument in praise of superpower patronage. A monument in praise of a dream. A dream of a new Egypt. A sunstruck dream from which the country was only now emerging.

I left the concrete flower and Sallah drove us on to the dam itself.

A dual carriageway bisected its two walls and, leaving the car, I stood on its southern flank and looked out at Lake Nasser. Where there had been desert now there was water, for the lake had come into existence when the Dam was completed; a 500 km pond which had permanently submerged much of northern Nubia. Had I been game, I could have found a steamer heading south to the Sudanese border town of Wadi Halfa, passing the famed colossi of Abu Simbel along the way. But I knew that I wanted to go no further; that this was the place where I would finally halt. So I spent some time gazing at Nasser's lake. The water shimmered, the Temple of Kalabshah was dappled by the sun, and the landscape beyond was an unbroken, untouched series of low-lying hills stretching into perpetuity. Then I crossed the dual carriageway and looked north to the hydroelectric plant, the new houses, the power cables, the Nile. The contrast was striking. South—the mythic Egypt. North—the brave new Egyptian world. South to Africa. North to Europe. Standing there on the great Egyptian technological dream, I sensed that I was precariously balanced between two worlds which met at this juncture. Caught between its many self-images, Egypt's dilemmas seemed to find symbolic expression in its monumental dam. For here the myth and reality fused—the river begetting power and life; the lake the promise of land eternal.

My journey was over. I had touched bottom. From now on, the remaining days would be a slow progression northwards. And Sallah wanted to hasten my departure in that direction. Pointing up the Nile, he said:

'The taxi, it goes back home. You go home?'

'Yes', I said. 'I go home.'